Chesapeake Bay in the Civil War

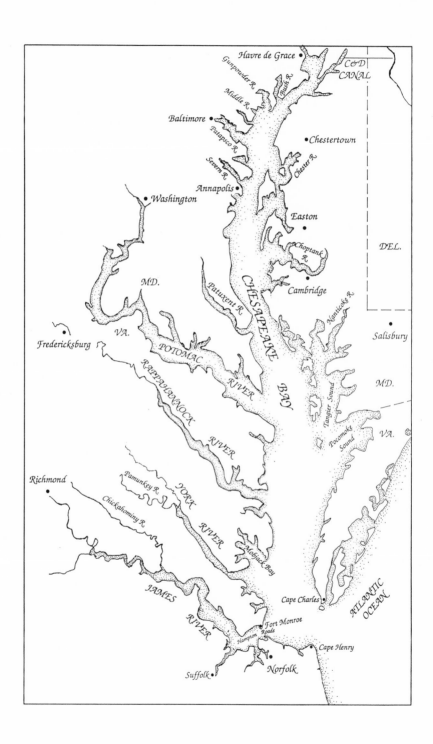

Chesapeake Bay in the Civil War

By Eric Mills

TIDEWATER PUBLISHERS

Centreville, Maryland

Library of Congress Cataloging-in-Publication Data

Mills, Eric
     Chesapeake Bay in the Civil War / by Eric Mills. — 1st ed.
        p.   cm.
     Includes bibliographical references (p.) and index.
     ISBN 0-87033-479-4 (hc)
     1. Chesapeake Bay Region (Md. and Va.)—History. 2. Maryland––History—Civil War, 1861-1865. 3. Virginia—History—Civil War, 1861-1865. I. Title.
F187.C5M55 1995
975.5'1803—dc20   95-49361
                                                    CIP

Manufactured in the United States of America
First edition, 1996; second printing, 1996

To
James H. Mills, who took a grateful
youngster to Civil War sites

CONTENTS

Preface

FOR THOSE OF us fascinated by the Civil War as well as by the lore and history of the Chesapeake Bay, there has been a gap where the two great fields of interest meet. In the nation's defining clash, obviously the Chesapeake saw its share of excitement. It had to by virtue of its location. As Rear Admiral John D. Hayes, USN (Ret.) pointed out in the November 1961 issue of U.S. Naval Institute *Proceedings*, the Chesapeake Bay and the Shenandoah Valley were the principal geographic factors framing the Eastern theater of war. The Chesapeake and its riverine fingers linked the Union and Confederate capitals; control of key points, such as Fort Monroe, along this water system was crucial in dictating the flow of the fortunes of war. The Bay was an all-important crossroads at an all-important moment in history.

I sought the story of the Bay during the war. Information was piecemeal. There have been a number of books on Maryland in the war, on Hampton Roads, the *Monitor-Virginia* duel, the Peninsula Campaign, and other salient aspects. But nowhere could I find a volume that specifically set its sights on the Chesapeake country as the geographic focus for a Civil War study. I delved deeper. The more I looked the more I realized that it was a story that wanted telling. For much transpired here.

Even after the fall of the Virginia Eastern Shore in 1861, the fall of Norfolk in 1862, and increased Federal patrols up countless creeks and coves, the Bay remained a nexus of strange action and a hotbed of movement both North and South. It was among the most exciting periods in the long and colorful history of the Chesapeake. These waters rarely, if ever, were livelier before or since.

It is a story of gunboats, smugglers, privateers, and the movement of mighty armies, of Lincoln on a deck and Jeff Davis at a fortress wall, of cavaliers and street-brawlers, ironclads and wild piracy, political prisoners and prison-camp hell, shoreline artillery and tidewater guerrillas, blockade-running oystermen and the unsung sailors of the Potomac Flotilla. This is their story, the story of the Chesapeake Bay in the Civil War.

As I wrote this book, I acquired many causes for gratitude. Special thanks are due to

- Curator of Manuscripts Jennifer Bryan, Assistant Curator of Manuscripts Jessica Pigza, and Manuscripts Assistant Robert W. Schoeberlein of the Maryland Historical Society; additional gratitude is extended toward Mr. Schoeberlein, who specializes in Baltimore civilian issues related to the war, for pointing me toward the Wardwell Reminiscences and other helpful papers;

- Reference Assistant John E. White of the Southern Historical Collection at the University of North Carolina at Chapel Hill for his expedience in availing me of the John Taylor Wood Diary and for the permission to quote therefrom;

- Special Collections Librarian Alice Creighton and Manuscripts Librarian Mary Rose Catalfamo of the United States Naval Academy Special Collections branch for assistance with archival images;

- the helpful staffs of the U.S. Naval Academy's Nimitz Library, the National Archives, the Maryland State Law Library, and the Virginia State Library;

- Chris Tyree for his photographic talent in culling images from the past;

- Richard Polk and Sally Covey for their cartographic advice and assistance;

- my former colleagues at the Chesapeake Bay Maritime Museum for their encouragement, with especial thanks to Curator Pete Lesher for access to the CBMM *Harper's Weekly* collection;

- the Brandts for their Richmond hospitality;

- my parents, parents-in-law, and other family members for their constant and multifaceted support;

- above all, my wife Harriet, whose love is coupled with saintly patience;

- and lastly, to those who lived here through trouble, and who saw war spill down into the Bay country.

Chesapeake Bay in the Civil War

CHAPTER 1

"That foul assassin's den!"

ON JANUARY 9, 1861—the same Wednesday that Mississippi quit the United States—thirty U.S. Marines came up from the Washington Navy Yard and garrisoned Fort McHenry at Baltimore, Maryland.

The city sprawling below the fort's guns was seething with Southern sentiment and was so infamous for violent politics that it had the nickname "Mobtown." The marines carried weapons and rations and rode up by rail. Three U.S. Army artillery companies, speeding east from Fort Leavenworth, would get here by the twelfth. For now, First Lieutenant Andrew J. Hays and his marines manned the batteries and kept an eye on the hotbed nearby.

It was a rowdy, volatile maritime city, the biggest city on the Chesapeake, a Southern city, really, but on the regional edge, and with a diverse enough populace that it had a split personality in 1861. This was the city whose passion for thuggish street-gang political warfare was renowned and denounced far and wide. The home of political clubs like the Plug Uglies, the Rough Skins, the Blood Tubs, the Black Snakes, the Red Necks, the Ranters, the Stay Lates, the Bloody Eights, the Butt Enders, the Hard Times. They raided one another's meetings, they fought on election days with rocks and cudgels and guns, they turned polling places into deadly battlegrounds. Street violence as a form of political expression was a Baltimore tradition.

Yet it was a city that, despite its brawling political reputation, was a popular place to hold national party conventions. In the fateful election year of 1860, Baltimore had played host to not one, but two Democratic

A view of Fort McHenry, Baltimore.
Harper's Weekly, Chesapeake Bay Maritime Museum Collection;
subsequent *Harper's* images also are courtesy Chesapeake
Bay Maritime Museum

National Conventions; the great party had gone schismatic into Northern and Southern factions. And the Constitutional Union Party, a short-lived gallimaufry of former Whigs and head-in-the-sand Know-Nothings, had held its first and only national convention in Baltimore in 1860.

It was a city with slavery, the northernmost Dixie metropolis. But it was situated in Maryland amid the largest population of free blacks in North America; by 1860 the Old Line State's total of 84,000 free blacks was closing in on the declining number of slaves—87,000. In Baltimore, the number of slaves had dropped from 6,000 to 2,000 since 1830; in those same three decades the number of free blacks had risen to more than 25,000. They were sailors, stevedores, blacksmiths, barbers, bricklayers, oystermen, and carriage-drivers. They had their own banks, churches, neighborhoods, and fraternal orders.

It was a city of Southern social webs, where young society belles flaunted rebel black-and-white cockades and wore secessionist ribbons on fancy dresses. But Baltimore had a swelling immigrant population, mainly German and Irish, largely leaning northward in the monumental issues dividing the country. The Germans in particular were aggressively antislavery, and their German-language newspapers were some of Maryland's original abolitionist publications. And despite its Southernness, Baltimore had given birth to the fourth abolitionist organization in the United States—the sixth such organization in the world—back in 1788.

It was a city whose big-business interests—the growing railroad lines, the thriving shipping lines—wanted to straddle the fence as America's decades-old divisiveness came to a head. Their ties to the South were profitable and atavistic, but their ties to the North and West were lucrative and growing and not something to cast off.

It was a city that, geographically and politically, lay right along the faultline of a nation about to be ripped in two.

That it was strategically vital was obvious. The largest rail center near Washington City, Mobtown stood between the national capital and the rest of the loyal Union. Maryland surrounded Washington on three sides, and as slave states began seceding en masse, this northernmost slave state had large, loud factions who clamored to secede as well. And on a cold day Lieutenant Hays and his men gazed over the guns of Fort McHenry, home of "The Star-Spangled Banner," overlooking the entrance to the contentious city's harbor crowded with side-wheel steamers and gaff-rigged schooners unloading and loading their passengers and cargoes and steaming and sailing out of the harbor, past the mouth of the Patapsco, into Chesapeake Bay.

The Bay: two hundred miles of inland sea winding from its mother river, the Susquehanna, down through Maryland and Virginia to Capes Henry and Charles and the Atlantic beyond. The history of the republic lay at anchor on the inland sea: the first English settlement in the New World, the first shipload of Africans in chains, the British surrender at Yorktown. In the coming fight in 1861, the Bay was of immeasurable worth, an ultimate determinant of outcome, for whichever side could control her. Up the Chesapeake's second-largest tributary, the Potomac, lay the U.S. capital. Up the Chesapeake's third-largest tributary, the James, lay Richmond, soon to be the Confederate capital. Who dominated the Chesapeake water highway dictated which direction the war would flow.

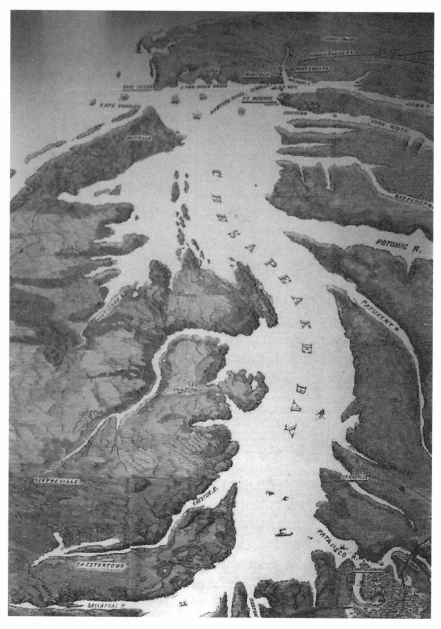

CHESAPEAKE BAY.
Harper's Weekly

In the Maryland and Virginia tidewater a plantation society existed on two centuries of tradition, tobacco, and slave labor. The rich legacy of great homes and a charmed life among meandering picture-book water settings had as its antithetical by-product a rich legacy of slave anger. From Nat Turner below the James to Harriet Tubman and Frederick Douglass on the Eastern Shore of Maryland, the anger manifested itself in different famous figures in different forms, from armed insurrection to organized escapes to eloquent outspokenness.

Slavery as an economic institution was on the wane by the mid-1800s, at least in Maryland. But perhaps the desire to perpetuate slavery went beyond economics. The social hierarchy was at risk from the rising presence of free blacks. Back-to-Africa movements routinely fizzled. The old order was threatened.

Washington was preparing for a new president and preparing for the worst. Surrounded by slaveholding states, endangered from within by its own proslavery elements, the city was in the wrong location at the wrong moment to be as sparsely guarded as it was. Trouble was expected at the upcoming inauguration. The Washington Navy Yard, the city's main arsenal, was rumored to be an attack target. If a mob got to the arms and ammunition stores, they could stop the inauguration. The yard commandant, a tough naval patriarch, issued January orders: "This yard shall not be surrendered . . . and in the event of an attack I shall require all officers and others under my command to defend it to the last extremity, and should we be overpowered by numbers the armory and magazine must be blown up."

He had a hawklike face and an aristocratic bearing, determination unmistakable in the set of his mouth and the look in his eyes. In his sixties, a walking legend of the Old Navy, he was a commanding presence, one easy to look up to. In his younger days he had been considered one of the strongest men in the navy, and he was characterized by physical courage and iron will. During his forty-seven-year naval career he had served in the Mediterranean, chased pirates in the Caribbean, helped suppress the illegal slave trade, fought in the Mexican War, and as flagship captain on Commodore Perry's 1853 Japan expedition, had been the first American to set foot on Japanese soil. Closer to home, Franklin Buchanan had

COMMANDER FRANKLIN BUCHANAN.
U.S. Naval Academy Archives

co-founded and served as first superintendent of the U. S. Naval Academy.

Baltimore-born, grandson of a Declaration Signer, Buchanan had become part of Eastern Shore society in 1835 when he married Anne Catherine Lloyd. The Lloyds were the apex of the gentry in Talbot County, Maryland, and near their famed ancestral home, "Wye House," the Buchanans had their own distinguished Miles River residence, "The Rest." Franklin Buchanan owned slaves and had no love for the politics of the Republicans coming to power. He carried out his duties, nonetheless, seeing to the security of the Washington Navy Yard and preparing to defend it, bracing for the arrival of the man from the prairie whose ascension had caused a fuss.

Abraham Lincoln and a detective and a heavily armed friend left the carriage in the shadows and sneaked onto a train car in a West Philadelphia railway station. It was 10:50 P.M., Friday, February 22, and the president-elect was en route to his inauguration. But he had to get through Baltimore first.

Since leaving Springfield, Illinois, Lincoln had zigzagged across five states on a rushed itinerary of personal appearances, speeches, handshakes, and assurances to a nervous public. Now, before reaching Washington, he had to traverse a Southern city for the first time on the trip.

Rumors flew of a plot to stop him. They came in many versions: Lincoln was going to be shanghaied south on a boat waiting in Baltimore Harbor and held hostage. Three thousand Baltimore hoodlums were going to stop his entourage by staging a riot, then consummate the event with a broad-daylight assassination. And so on.

But it was Baltimore, and that lent the lurid stories a more fearful feasibility. After all, the city had made no official gestures for reception of Lincoln and his retinue—such silence itself was a slap in the face. Lincoln had received a paltry 3 percent of the vote in Mobtown.

He wasn't one to cower before a rumor. He and his wife and sons were due to make an appearance before the citizens of Baltimore. That was the plan, and he intended to stick to it. But in Philadelphia Lincoln was approached by detective Allan Pinkerton, who brimmed with dire forecasts. The railroad had hired the detective to investigate any potential problem. Pinkerton had gone to Baltimore with a team of operatives and set up shop on South Street under the alias of John H. Hutchinson, a Southern stockbroker. He and his agents haunted the saloons, hotel lobbies, boardinghouses, and billiard parlors of Baltimore, worming their ways into underground societies such as the National Volunteers and the Palmetto Guards. The more he dug, the more Pinkerton envisioned a vast, evil scenario with elaborate ingredients: a Bel Air militia group; the collusionist Baltimore Police Department; a charismatic ringleader named Cypriano Ferrandini, whose barbershop was in the basement of Barnum's Hotel, that most noted of secessionist watering holes; eight men with daggers at Calvert Street Station. Pinkerton urged Lincoln to alter his travel plans.

As further warnings came by telegraph and courier from such reliable sources as Winfield Scott and William Seward in Washington, and when Baltimore had still failed to send a delegation to Pennsylvania the next day, Lincoln yielded. He would travel through the hostile zone unannounced, in secret, at night, and ahead of schedule.

He was accompanied by Ward Hill Lamon, burly frontier friend and bodyguard. They met Pinkerton at the station. The arrangements had been made, the telegraph lines were cut, and Abraham Lincoln slipped through darkness toward destiny.

The Republican had won last November's election with less than two million popular votes, not a majority, but the largest chunk in the four-way race. The two Democrats, John Breckinridge and Stephen Douglas, nominated at the separate Baltimore conventions, canceled each other out, paving the way for the rail-splitter's win. John Bell, the Constitutional Union candidate, also nominated in Baltimore, didn't fare well most places, but he'd done better than Douglas and Lincoln in Maryland. Lincoln, running on a platform opposing slavery expansion into the territories, of course didn't carry a single Southern state.

South Carolina withdrew from the Union in December 1860 and, by the time of Lincoln's nocturnal railroad skulk, had been followed by six slaveholding sister states. As Lincoln boarded that train it had been two weeks to the day since the renegade states had adopted their own constitution. And it had been four days since Jefferson Davis had been inaugurated provisional president of the Confederate States of America.

Upon boarding the sleeping car, Lincoln had quickly concealed himself behind berth curtains. When the conductor came, Pinkerton handed over the unseen "sick man's" ticket. Every now and then Lincoln told a joke, but kept his voice low. Pinkerton had agents stationed along the route, and he would go to the platform to see their signals. The train reached Baltimore at 3:30 A.M. A Pinkerton operative boarded, whispering "All was right." The car was uncoupled from the train and horse-drawn through Baltimore to Camden Station by the harbor. Built by the Baltimore & Ohio Railroad in the early 1850s and taking up three city blocks, Camden was one of the largest railroad stations in America and among the largest in the world. The president-elect and company waited, tense, Lamon armed to the teeth and ready for anything, the silence broken only by an Irishman's boozy shouts. Finally the car was coupled to another train. As they pulled out from the Camden yards and left Baltimore behind them, "the apprehensions of the President-elect and his friends diminished," recalled Lamon, "with each welcome revolution of the wheels."

The next day, the train that was supposed to be carrying Lincoln left Harrisburg and arrived in Baltimore at 12:30 P.M. A raucous crowd, estimated at fifteen thousand, had flocked to Calvert Street Station and spilled into surrounding streets. Some yelled obscenities, surrounding the stopping train and poking their shouting heads into the windows of the cars carrying Mrs. Lincoln and the rest. It took half an hour to get the presidential party onto carriages. The dawning realization that Abraham Lincoln wasn't on the train didn't do much to please the crowd. The rowdiness followed the carriages on their stops downtown. The party boarded the Washington train and chugged away from the foul-mouthed horde at 3 P.M.

Pinkerton's plot theory was never proven. To Lincoln, the incident was an embarrassment, an ignominious beginning. Editorial cartoonists had fun. Southerners reveled in the evidence of cowardice. Lincoln's supporters had trouble defending the nature of his arrival. Lincoln regretted it, and Mobtown resented it. On Monday, March 4, inauguration day, Republicans had poured into Washington from far and wide to cheer their man on. Hotels were packed, and tired travelers slept in lobbies. Republican well-wishers weren't the only visitors. Throughout the weekend, gangs of Baltimore toughs had been arriving for the occasion, not to hail the new chief, but to get inebriated and show their contempt with war-whoops and obstreperous antics.

Federal forts and installations all along the Southern coastline had been seized by the rebels. The new president appointed Gideon Welles, a Connecticut man, secretary of the Navy. His first order of business was to bring the boats home. In March 1861 the U.S. Navy had forty-two vessels in commission. Most were serving in foreign stations. Secretary Welles ordered the recall of all but three. *Pocahontas* and *Cumberland* were among the first to return, ordered to Chesapeake Bay and arriving on March 12 and 23, respectively, heaving to off an important piece of federal property called Fort Monroe.

It also was called the "Gibraltar of the Chesapeake," this heptagonal bastion, with thirty-five-foot granite walls surrounded by a moat, perched on a seventy-acre piece of Virginia connected to the Old Point Comfort mainland by a long, narrow strip of beach. Fort Monroe stared out on the lower Chesapeake Bay and commanded its waterways, controlled the confluence of the Nansemond, Elizabeth, and James Rivers where they all merged and met the Chesapeake at the strategically vital deep-water channel and harbor of Hampton Roads.

Fortifications of one form or another had existed hereabouts, off and on, since the early Colonial period. The Fort Monroe of 1861 had been born in the wake of British depredations in the War of 1812, which drove home the need for a coastal defense system. Construction began in 1819. By the 1830s Fort Monroe stood as the strongest point in the emerging chain of coast defenses. It was the U.S. Army's artillery-training head-quarters as well as an imposing defensive bastion. In 1831 a U.S. Army Corps of Engineers second lieutenant named Robert E. Lee came to Fort Monroe, assigned to the ongoing construction of fortifications. He lived and built here until 1834. His wife was with him. George Washington Custis Lee, their first son, was born in Fort Monroe.

Another battery sat out in the middle of the channel on Rip Rap Shoal. The Rip Raps and the fort together constituted a heavy-gun gauntlet. Across Hampton Roads, on the jagged semicircle between the Elizabeth River and the Bay, was Norfolk, the major city of the lower Chesapeake, a shipbuilding center, the southern terminus of Baltimore steam lines, and a busy port. Across the Elizabeth was a giant navy yard that the United States could ill afford to lose if Virginia ended up seceding after all.

Here, a dozen miles below Fort Monroe, enclosed within a high brick wall on the Elizabeth's left bank, was the Norfolk, or Gosport, Navy Yard, one of the three largest and busiest naval yards in the country.

BIRD'S-EYE VIEW OF HAMPTON ROADS, WITH FORT MONROE
IN THE RIGHT FOREGROUND.
Harper's Weekly

THE ENTRANCE TO FORT MONROE.
National Archives

Here was a sprawled complex of machine shops, foundries, warehouses, docks, and workers' quarters. Massive amounts of provisions, naval stores, machinery, tools, and ammunition were stockpiled at the yard, along with about two thousand pieces of heavy artillery.

An expensive, state-of-the-art granite dry dock, capable of servicing the largest ships afloat, augmented the yard, and there were a dozen navy vessels anchored or beached in varying degrees of needed repair.

There was the gargantuan, old 120-gun ship-of-the-line *Pennsylvania*, now in use as a receiving ship. There were five large sailing ships laid up in ordinary: the 50-gun frigates *Columbia*, *Raritan*, and *United States*; and the 74-gunners *Columbus* and *Delaware*. Another 74-gun frigate, *New York*, was out of the water. There were two 28-gun sloops of war, *Germantown* and *Plymouth*, and the four-gun brig *Dolphin*, all of them ready for sea.

And now, there was the recently arrived *Cumberland*, mighty flagship of the Home Squadron, back from the Gulf with a three-hundred-man crew and enough firepower in her heavy battery to keep troublemakers on both sides of the river from getting out of hand.

And there was *Merrimack*, the navy's pride, flagship of the Pacific Fleet, a powerful forty-gun steam frigate laid up for machinery repairs. A modern ship, she was more important than all the rest at the yard. She had circled the world and won universal praise. Her estimated value, when fully outfitted for sea, was $1.2 million.

The total estimated value of the Norfolk Navy Yard and its property was $9,780,000. It was a naval treasure trove in hostile territory. Many, if not most, of those who worked here, including a large part of the officer staff, were proudly Southern and just waiting for the word that Virginia had seceded.

But Virginia hadn't seceded yet, and Lincoln was wary that any show of force would tip the scales the wrong way. The Virginia state convention had been in session since February, and the prevailing Washington thought was to act cautiously and deferentially. Any show of doubt in Virginia's loyalty, such as forces arriving with great sabre-rattling to protect the Norfolk Navy Yard, might drive the state out of the Union. So Welles sent *Cumberland* there to keep an eye on things,

THE NORFOLK NAVY YARD.
Harper's Weekly

ordered an extra 250 men to the lower Bay, and alerted the aging yard
commandant, Captain C. S. McCauley, to avoid any threatening gestures.

The waiting game ended. USS *Pawnee*, a ten-gun steam sloop, weighed
anchor at Hampton Roads on April 10 and left the Chesapeake. Her
mission was to join two ships en route from New York and proceed
south along the coast to relieve some soldiers holed up at Fort Sumter.

The Confederate cannonfire began on Friday, April 12, 1861. The soldiers still flying the Stars and Stripes over the fort in Charleston, South
Carolina, surrendered after thirty-four hours. *Pawnee* and the other
vessels, held up by a storm, were too late. On Monday, April 15, the day
after the Union garrison evacuated Sumter and the Confederates occupied the fort, Lincoln issued his call for seventy-five thousand militia to
serve for three months, to crush the nascent rebellion.

Virginia no longer wavered. Its ordinance of secession was passed
on April 17, and the Old Dominion announced its intention to adopt the
constitution of the provisional government of the new Confederate
States of America. The lower Chesapeake was now a war zone.

On the eve of Sumter, Welles had sent Commander James Alden and Chief Engineer Benjamin Isherwood from Baltimore down to Norfolk to hasten the repairs on *Merrimack* and get her out of there, fast. Welles considered Commodore McCauley at the navy yard to be "feeble and incompetent for the crisis." McCauley—sixty-eight years old, slow, tipping a bottle, and flanked by Southern officers feeding him false advice—had said it would take a month to ready *Merrimack*; Isherwood had a week. He put around-the-clock mechanic crews to work.

The day before Virginia announced secession, Welles had written Flag Officer Garrett J. Pendergrast, commander of *Cumberland*, to postpone departure for Vera Cruz and help prepare for a massive withdrawal of ships and stores from the navy yard. On the seventeenth, the day Virginia announced it was quitting the United States, Norfolk rebels went out in the channel and sank three lightships, obstructions to bottle in the vessels at the navy yard. Lieutenant Thomas O. Selfridge offered to take the brig *Dolphin* down to Sewells Point to prevent more such mischief. McCauley said no.

The next day, Chief Engineer Isherwood reported that he had *Merrimack* ready to move. McCauley said no.

Welles dispatched orders to Captain Hiram Paulding, now in command of *Pawnee*, which was back in the Chesapeake after Sumter, to make for Norfolk and take command. "On no account should the arms and munitions be permitted to fall into the hands of the insurrectionists, or those who would wrest them from the custody of the government; and should it finally become necessary, you will, in order to prevent that result, destroy the property."

Washington, surrounded and scantily guarded, expected aggression. Militia campfires could be seen on Arlington Heights across the Potomac River. The city was ill-prepared to repel an invasion. Those who could, fled.

In the North, there was a great arousal of patriotism. From state to state, militia groups mustered to answer the call. The capital was threatened, and its rescue was the rallying cry. But, like Lincoln before his inauguration, the volunteers had to get through Baltimore first.

On April 18, the day that the U.S. Armory at Harpers Ferry was abandoned and burned, and that Robert E. Lee turned down the offer to command the Union forces, four companies of the Twenty-fifth Pennsylvania Volunteers boarded a train in Harrisburg and headed for Washington. They soon reached Baltimore, where the day before, a massive secession rally had been held. Four days earlier, the barque *Fanny Crenshaw* had flown the palmetto flag of rebellion from her mizzen topmast, nearly sparking a waterfront riot. Now, on April 18, bold miscreants had raised the secessionist flag on Federal Hill, taunting the troops at Fort McHenry.

The train pulled into Bolton Station and the Pennsylvania volunteers disembarked. A crowd had gathered, hurling nasty language and hooting. The regiment marched, flanked by Baltimore police, through the city to Camden Station. Jeering citizens threw bricks and chunks of pavement. Nickolas Biddle, a black orderly attached to Company A of the Twenty-fifth Pennsylvania, became the first man injured by hostile action in the war as the flying stone cracked his head. The bruised, insulted Pennsylvanians passed through the Mobtown gauntlet and boarded the train waiting at Camden Station. They had the honor later that day of being the first troops to arrive in Washington after Lincoln's beckoning. Two U.S. Artillery companies traveling with the Pennsylvania volunteers remained in Baltimore to buttress the Fort McHenry defenses.

Friday, April 19, was the anniversary of the Battle of Lexington and Concord, and seven hundred sons of Massachusetts were marking the occasion by hastening south to defend the capital. The Sixth Massachusetts, based in Lowell, had been quick to respond to Lincoln's call. Just three days after receipt of orders, the regiment was marching proudly through New York City, to great cheering and fanfare. The following morning, the nineteenth, they were in Philadelphia, preparing to pass through Baltimore. Word got to their commander, Colonel Edward F. Jones, that a Baltimore welcoming party, rather opposite the one in New York, awaited.

As the train rolled out of Philadelphia Colonel Jones ordered ammunition distributed and weapons loaded, and he worked his way through the train cars, personally issuing his instructions to the crowded rows of fresh-faced recruits. "You will undoubtedly be insulted, abused, and perhaps assaulted, to which you must pay no attention whatever, but march with your face square to the front and pay no attention to the mob, even if they throw stones, bricks, or other missiles; but if you are fired upon and any one of you is hit, your officers will order you to fire. Do not fire into promiscuous crowds, but select any man whom you may see aiming at you, and be sure you drop him."

They got to Baltimore about 10:30 A.M. At the President Street Station they were loaded onto horse-drawn train cars that pulled them along Pratt Street, westward past the waterfront, to the locomotive waiting at Camden Station. As the cars moved along Pratt, the mob grew in size and surliness, heaving bottles and bricks and jeers. The cars carrying the first seven companies made it through. The rest did not.

Richard D. Fisher watched from the window of his counting-house on the second floor of 54 South Gay Street. "I saw an acquaintance of mine seize the bridle of a horse attached to a sand-cart and dump the sand on the railroad track. This set the example. Gentlemen merchants, Irish draymen and Negro laborers tumultuously joined in dragging across the track anchors, chains and other obstructions, rendering the further transit of cars impracticable."

The blocked driver unhitched his horse team, rigged them up to the rear of the car, and headed back toward President Street Station. Now every car behind him had to do the same, the logjam on the tracks growing as horses were hastily unhooked and brought about. All the while, the mob was getting bigger, meaner, and louder.

Four companies, 220 men, were back where they started. Captain Albert S. Follansbee, in charge of the separated and stranded men, ordered them off the cars and into marching formation. They set out on foot to cut their way across town through a mob that had swelled to what looked like thousands. Panic was setting in, and the men marched on the double-quick now. It spurred the mob to see the soldiers running like that. The crowd screamed, yanked paving stones out of the street-bed, hurled them at the soldiers, and threw bricks and bottles and anything else they could get their hands on, too. As the soldiers crossed

THE SIXTH MASSACHUSETTS FIGHTS ITS WAY THROUGH
THE BALTIMORE MOB, APRIL 19, 1861.
Harper's Weekly

the Jones Falls bridge, which was undergoing repairs and strewn with lumber and tools, some stumbled. And shots rang.

Two soldiers dropped, wounded by the nonstop projectile barrage. Another soldier dropped, shot dead. And as the mob howled and cheered for Jefferson Davis and secession, the Massachusetts men struggled along Pratt Street, stopping now, aiming muskets, firing a volley into the throng, taking a few attackers down. The mob waved the rebel flag and shouted and replied with pistol-fire now, as well as rocks and bricks.

Then they were all met by a small middle-aged man brandishing his umbrella and calling for calm. Mayor George W. Brown had been overseeing the action at Camden Station, where Marshal George P. Kane had set up a police cordon between the soldiers already there and the quickly gathering crowd. When Mayor Brown heard of the riot raging on Pratt, he told Marshal Kane to bring some men and follow him. Top hat and umbrella firmly in hand, the mayor charged, running half a mile to where the soldiers were fighting through the mob.

"They were firing wildly, sometimes backward, over their shoulders," the mayor recounted. "So rapid was the march that they could not stop to take aim . . . . The uproar was furious. I ran at once to the head of the column, some persons in the crowd shouting, 'Here comes the mayor.'" Brown shook hands with Captain Follansbee and marched alongside. "My presence for a short time had some effect, but very soon the attack was renewed with greater violence. The mob grew bolder. Stones flew thick and fast. Rioters rushed at the soldiers and attempted to snatch their muskets, and at least on two occasions succeeded. With one of these muskets a soldier was killed. Men fell on both sides . . . . The soldiers fired at will. There was no firing by platoons, and I heard no order given to fire . . . . It was impossible for the troops to discriminate between the rioters and the by-standers, but the latter seemed to suffer most."

Marshal Kane showed up with police between Light and Charles Streets. They threw themselves between the rear troops and the pursuing mob. The lawmen drew their revolvers, and the marshal hollered, "Keep back, men, or I shoot!"

"The mob," said the mayor, "recoiled like water from a rock." By 1 P.M. troop trains were pulling out of the Camden yards.

Robert W. Davis, Irish-born and Virginia-wed, a prosperous and well-liked merchant, was standing with friends on an elevation near the Redley Street distillery, watching the departing trains. Some said he shook his fist, others that he threw something. A musket barked from a train window, and Davis was dead.

Richard Fisher, who had watched the riot escalate at the corner of Pratt and Gay, wrote, "I well remember that, standing beside me, was a Spanish sea-captain, whose vessel was then in port to my consignment, and who said to me in Spanish, 'You seem much agitated; this is nothing; we frequently have these things in Spain.'

And I replied, 'In Spain, this may mean nothing; in America, it means Civil War.' "

On the anniversary of the day when Massachusetts militiamen became the first to die in the Revolution, four Massachusetts militiamen—Luther Ladd, Sumner Needham, Charles Taylor, and Addison Whitney—be-

THE WAR'S FIRST DEATH BY HOSTILE FIRE:
LUTHER C. LADD OF THE SIXTH MASSACHUSETTS,
KILLED IN BALTIMORE.
Harper's Weekly

came the first to die by hostile fire in the new war. Thirty-six others were wounded in the Baltimore riot. Twelve Baltimoreans were killed, an unknown number wounded. Across the North, "Through Baltimore or over it!" became the indignant cry. And in Boston they were singing a song damning Baltimore as "that hold of pirates—that foul assassin's den!"

On the afternoon of the Baltimore riot a mass rally was held in Monument Square. Mayor Brown and Governor Thomas Hicks were among the speakers, pleading for calm. Hicks, an Eastern Shoreman, intoned, "I am a Marylander, I love my state, and I love the union, but I will suffer my right arm to be torn from my body before I will raise it to strike a sister state."

Armed units from outlying counties were pouring into the city. Rebel flags and Maryland flags waved, and the U.S. flag was hardly anywhere to be seen. Word spread that Baltimoreans were going to attack Fort McHenry. A junior officer at the fort threatened to fire on the Washington Monument, standing tall on the city skyline. He was warned that if he did so, "there will be nothing left of you but your brass buttons to tell who you were."

The mayor and governor rattled off communiqués to President Lincoln. "A collision between the citizens and the Northern troops has taken place in Baltimore, and the excitement is fearful. Send no more troops here." And, "The people are exasperated to the highest degree by the passage of troops, and the citizens are universally decided in the opinion that no more troops should be ordered to come . . . . Under these circumstances, it is my solemn duty to inform you that it is not possible for more soldiers to pass through Baltimore unless they fight their way at every step."

The mayor and the governor did not hear back from Lincoln that evening. Maryland militiamen and Baltimore policemen sped north of the city and burned bridges. Northern troops could no longer enter Baltimore by rail. Washington was cut off from the North.

Originally, it had just been called the Naval School. It had opened in 1845. Fort Severn, which housed it, had been built in 1808 and was located on Windmill Point, where the Severn River met Annapolis Harbor. Fort Severn was surrounded by a high wall, which, it was said, had made it a desirable location for the school, not so much for keeping anyone out, but for keeping high-spirited young blades in.

The school was the brainchild of Navy Secretary George Bancroft, who had appointed Commander Franklin Buchanan to his site-selection committee and then had made him superintendent. The Mexican War interrupted Buchanan's stint at the school's helm, but he returned afterward, and his recommendations for improvements had much to do with shaping the school, which became known as the Naval Academy in 1850.

ANNAPOLIS, WITH USS *CONSTITUTION* IN THE FOREGROUND.
Harper's Weekly

In 1861 the academy was headed by Captain George S. Blake. Under the guidance of Lieutenant George Rodgers, midshipmen learned the ropes on as famous a training vessel as a young American could ask for—"Old Ironsides" herself, the USS *Constitution*. The great symbol of American naval might, she was the venerable fighting frigate celebrated in foc'sle songs and schoolboy texts.

Throughout the winter of 1860–61, as states seceded, academy boys from those states bade goodbye to their friends in Annapolis and turned to the South. Earlier in the year, when an honor man of the graduating class resigned to follow his home state of Alabama, all of his classmates had paraded him past the officers' houses to the gate, singing him a sad farewell song. When Commandant C. R. P. Rodgers looked out his doorway and angrily asked what all the rule-breaking ruckus was about, and they told him, he gave them permission to carry on.

"War, that terrible calamity, is upon us, and worst of all among ourselves," a Naval Academy instructor wrote in his diary after news of Sumter. The instructor, John Taylor Wood—grandson of President Zachary Taylor and nephew of Jefferson Davis—had served in the navy since 1847. His varied tours of duty had included one as gunnery officer on

NAVAL ACADEMY MIDDIES LEARN THE ROPES ABOARD "OLD IRONSIDES."
Harper's Weekly

the flagship of the Mediterranean squadron. His academy instructor-
ship, a position he had lobbied heavily for, was just two months old
when war broke out. Maryland was a fitting residence for Wood; it
reflected his own troubling dualism. His father, Major Robert Crooke
Wood, an army surgeon and staunch Union man, was a Rhode Islander.
John Taylor Wood's mother, Anne Mackall Taylor, eldest daughter of
"Old Rough and Ready," was from Louisiana. And as people started
taking sides around him, the teacher of gunnery, seamanship, and naval
tactics at the academy told his diary, "I feel perfectly miserable, belonging neither to the North or South . . . ."

Annapolis was even more solidly Southern in its sentiments than
Baltimore, and the day after the Pratt Street riot, the threat of Maryland
secessionists to the Naval Academy seemed imminent. If the state ended
up seceding—and it looked like it might—Confederate sympathizers
would be bound to try to take the strategically situated campus, and to
capture the USS *Constitution*. To commandeer Old Ironsides would be
both a tactical and a highly symbolic coup. On April 20 Navy Secretary

Welles wired Academy Superintendent Blake: "Defend the *Constitution* at all hazards. If this cannot be done, destroy her."

Late that night, a steamer hove to off Annapolis. The academy officers braced for an attack from Baltimore rebels down to seize the naval grounds. General quarters was sounded on *Constitution* anchored in the Severn. Her four 32-pounders were run out at the stern. As gunnery crews manned battle stations, George Rodgers hailed the steamer.

She was the ferryboat *Maryland*, down from the head of the Bay with Brigadier General Benjamin F. Butler and 724 tightly crowded men of the Eighth Massachusetts Volunteers.

Cut off by land route from the North, Washington had only one hope: Chesapeake Bay. And as Ben Butler's steamboat full of troops put in at Annapolis, it began to look like Washington might have a chance.

Butler's regiment had reached Philadelphia by the nineteenth as word of the Baltimore trouble spread and the railroad lines were being destroyed. Thwarted, stymied, Butler was given good advice by Captain Samuel F. DuPont of the Philadelphia Navy Yard: Since the overland way was no longer tenable, they should take to the Bay. The rebels may have destroyed the rails, but they didn't control the Chesapeake yet.

S. M. Felton, president of the Philadelphia, Wilmington and Baltimore Railroad, offered the use of *Maryland*, which served as ferry transport for train travelers crossing the Susquehanna. Butler brought the Eighth Massachusetts down to Perryville, Maryland, at the mouth of the Susquehanna, arriving on the evening of the twentieth. They squeezed aboard the steamer and headed down the Chesapeake, reaching Annapolis by midnight.

Baltimore had been avoided, and Washington lay ahead. But before they could get to the capital the Eighth Massachusetts men had gandy-dancer work to do. The surrounding countryside's rebellious Marylanders had trashed the railroad track, ripping it useless all the way to Annapolis Junction. But once it was fixed, it was a short shot to the capital, and there would be no Baltimores to pass through.

Now that the troops were here, it was clear that Annapolis wanted garrisoning as well. And Old Ironsides needed a tow out to the deeper offshore Bay, away from riverside rebels.

THE SOLDIERS OF THE EIGHTH
MASSACHUSETTS ON THE FERRY
STEAMER *MARYLAND* ARRIVE
ALONGSIDE *CONSTITUTION* AT ANNAPOLIS.
Nimitz Library, U.S. Naval Academy

A teary-eyed Captain Blake supposedly said to General Butler, "Thank God! Thank God! Won't you save the *Constitution*?"

The general, thinking Blake was referring to the document, not the ship, said, "Yes, that is just what I am here for."

The old frigate was aground at her moorings. Without even disembarking his overcrowded men after their journey, Butler put *Maryland* to work, pulling *Constitution* out of harm's way into the Bay.

Another Massachusetts volunteer outfit also appeared on the Chesapeake the Saturday that Butler bypassed Baltimore. The Fourth Massachusetts shipped down the Atlantic, sailed up through the Virginia Capes, and put in at Fort Monroe. Captain Hiram Paulding on *Pawnee* took on the newly arrived troops. There was work to do about twelve miles south.

Chief Engineer Isherwood had done in four days what Commodore McCauley of the Norfolk Navy Yard had said would take a month. *Merrimack* was ready to steam up and ship out. In the days since the secession announcement, Virginia militia units had been building up strength around the naval yard. Time was wasting; there was no reason to mollify Virginia sentiments anymore. *Merrimack* was fueled up, stoked, crewed, and set to make her break. And still, McCauley said no. He said to wait.

An exasperated Isherwood suspected the curmudgeon of drunkenness. Drunken or sober, McCauley was making a costly procrastination.

The rebels' channel obstructions at Sewells Point weren't enough to keep the navy vessels from getting through. *Pawnee* steamed past the sunken hulks and headed up the Elizabeth. With the Fourth Massachusetts, Paulding had enough troops to hold the navy yard until a bigger force could be brought down. The ships could be saved. Except for one problem: They had all been scuttled.

McCauley had hung fire, waited far too long, and then, when there actually was still hope, had panicked and ordered the ships destroyed on the twentieth. *Pawnee* arrived two hours too late.

Paulding's plan had been to spread the ships out along the river from Norfolk to the channel, then hold the position until more vessels and reinforcements arrived. The plan had to be scuttled like the ships in the yard. With *Pawnee*, *Cumberland*, and 250 Massachusetts volunteers, there was still a chance of holding the yard. But Paulding opted to complete what McCauley had started. Demolition parties raced, running powder fuses into workshops, storehouses, and shiphouses, loading combustibles into the sinking ships, setting explosives on the dry dock. McCauley had already ordered the yard's big guns spiked. It was only a temporary debilitator; with a few hours' work the guns would be able to speak again. So Paulding had his men go at the artillery with sledge hammers, to smash the trunnions and truly decommission the guns. It didn't work, and after an hour of futile banging they gave up.

By 2 A.M. the yard was ready to ignite. But now Commodore McCauley, his sobbing son announced on the quay, refused to abandon his post. Commander Alden managed to convince the old veteran that to stay would be suicide. They got him aboard. *Pawnee* hooked her hawsers into *Cumberland* and departed with the big ship in tow.

Two small boats were left behind for the firing parties' escape. At 4:20 A.M. a signal rocket shot up from *Pawnee's* deck and cut a bright spitting arc across the darkness. Fuses were lit, sinking ships were torched, and the Norfolk Navy Yard became a blistering, booming Hades of sky-high flames and exploding ammunition. It turned the black sky daylight-bright, and miles away they heard the noise.

There was the great *Merrimack*, which Isherwood had done so much to save, her proud masts now like toothpicks in the engulfing blaze as she burned to the waterline. There was the giant four-decker *Pennsylvania*, the largest American ship-of-the-line, her unmanned guns roaring a final spectral salute as she burned. The torching teams got to their boats and escaped through the burning tableau—all of them except John Rodgers and his men, in charge of blowing up the dry dock (which hadn't blown up). This group was now separated from the water by towering walls of flame.

Norfolk rebels were pouring into the yard. Rodgers and company brassed it out at the front gate, walked right past the enemy, and were downriver before the rebels could catch them.

Colossal though the blaze had been, the damage to the facility was largely superficial. The South reaped huge benefits from the Norfolk Navy Yard, acquired in the opening days of the Civil War without a fight. The heavy artillery they rescued unscathed from the yard would rain death upon the Yankees again and again, from shore batteries along the Potomac and on down through the South. The factories, foundries, and massive supplies of the yard would be of inestimable value to the Confederate cause. The huge dry dock was undamaged. And as for the scuttled, smoking ships, some of them, including *Merrimack*, were salvageable.

It was around noon on that same Sunday, April 21, that the steamer *Boston* sighted Cape Charles, adjusted her course, and entered the Chesa-

USS *PENNSYLVANIA* GOES UP IN FLAMES DURING THE BURNING
OF THE NORFOLK NAVY YARD.
Harper's Weekly

peake. She passed within hailing distance of a trading schooner at the mouth of the Bay. The schooner captain informed the men on the steamer's crowded deck that the Norfolk Navy Yard had been burned and that the secessionists were moving on Hampton Roads.

Colonel Marshall Lefferts stood aboard *Boston* and took in the bad news. The dashing Lefferts was commander of the famed New York Seventh Regiment, the toast not only of Manhattan but of the nation. Its rolls traditionally filled with well-heeled, well-connected, prominent businessmen, the Seventh was held up as the ideal volunteer militia unit in America. Its members exuded patriotism, honor, élan, and just enough gentlemen's-club exclusivity to give them a touch of glamour. Some might consider them dandies, but the soldiers of the Seventh would prove time and again, as they had on this cramped, overloaded old coastal steamer, that when there were no truffles to be had, they could eat sea biscuits as well as the next man.

THE NEW YORK SEVENTH REGIMENT EN ROUTE TO
ANNAPOLIS ABOARD THE STEAMER *BOSTON*.
Harper's Weekly

Two long days ago they had paraded down Broadway one thousand strong. It had seemed as if the whole city was out to cheer them on, Stars-and-Stripes bunting hanging from every building and Old Glory waving from every window and in every woman's and child's hand along the grand thoroughfare. Lincoln had issued the call. The Seventh was off to rescue the capital. But, like Ben Butler's boys, they got as far as Philadelphia when they ran into difficulty.

While Butler had opted for an upper Chesapeake route to Annapolis, Lefferts had chosen to travel the roundabout course, coming up through the capes and the lower Bay. The long way offered two choices: to steam right up the Potomac to the capital, or to make for Annapolis if the Potomac proved too perilous.

With the schooner captain's news of rebel hell breaking loose, the Potomac, with its long, hostile Virginia shore, was sounding less tenable. If the overburdened, awkward-maneuvering *Boston* got in a scrape with a shore battery or a rebel boat, the men of the Seventh would be trapped like rats. When they passed the mouth of the Potomac at 9 P.M. the dispatch boat they'd telegraphed ahead for was nowhere to be seen. (Washington never got the telegram—the lines had been cut.) So it was on to Annapolis.

A thick fog enveloped *Boston* as she approached the town in the predawn hours of April 22. Lefferts and his men found *Constitution* at anchor offshore and the steamer *Maryland* stuck on a mud bank. The latter had run aground after towing *Constitution* out, and Butler's weary men were still crammed on board, now stranded. While the one steamer helped free the other, Lefferts got filled in: how the mayor of Annapolis and governor of Maryland both were vehemently protesting the landing of troops here, how the surrounding fields and forests were crawling with secessionists.

Butler and Lefferts worked together in the next crucial days. Now on hostile ground, Butler, the ranking officer, argued that he had authority over the Seventh. Lefferts countered that one state's militia didn't have to answer to another state's commander. Butler clashed with Lefferts, and Butler would rub others the wrong way in the war. A lawyer by profession, Butler was shrewd, sometimes brilliant. But he was fated to earn a litany of nicknames in the coming conflict. They ranged from the merely cruel—"Old Cockeye"—to the suggestive—"Teaspoon," "Spoons" (references to thievery)—to the worst, which stuck the most—"the Beast."

His manner wasn't softened by his appearance. Unruly hair cascaded down the sides of his shiny, protruding dome. His off-kilter eyes were hooded by pendulous folds of skin. The sagging, frowning countenance was exaggerated by a drooping mustache. In both appearance and personality Ben Butler stood out, and he stood in contrast to the gentlemanly Lefferts. But the task that fell to both of them was nothing short of rescuing the U.S. capital. The New York Seventh and the Massachusetts Eighth had both avoided Baltimore. They still had a gauntlet to run.

Governor Hicks ordered the legislature to convene at Frederick instead of Annapolis. The state capital was turning into a military zone, for one thing. For another, though Hicks was a 100-proof Dixie Dorchester Countian, he nonetheless remained at heart a Union man. Removed from the secessionist nest of Annapolis, cooler heads might prevail in

LEFT, COLONEL MARSHALL LEFFERTS OF THE NEW YORK SEVENTH
REGIMENT. *RIGHT,* THE LAWYER AS SOLDIER: BY MAY 1861 BENJAMIN
F. BUTLER WENT FROM BEING BRIGADIER GENERAL IN COMMAND
OF THE EIGHTH MASSACHUSETTS TO MAJOR GENERAL IN
COMMAND OF U. S. FORCES AROUND FORT MONROE.

National Archives

the crucial legislative session that began on April 22. Maryland had to
decide whether it was going to secede.

It looked like it was going to. One commander thought it inevitable
and based one of the big decisions of his life on the secession certainty.
On April 22 Franklin Buchanan resigned from the U.S. Navy.

Eighteen days earlier, President Lincoln had attended the wedding
of Buchanan's daughter Nannie. The April 3 ceremony had taken place
at the Washington Navy Yard. Lincoln tried to shake hands with another
Buchanan daughter, fifteen-year-old Elizabeth. She refused the president's hand. He called her a "little rebel." She softened up somewhat as
he charmed her with his warmth and wit and gave her bonbons.

That was all a world away. It was war now, and maybe Franklin
Buchanan's devotion to Maryland was heightened by his disdain for the
Republicans and disgust at the tramp of soldiers' boots upon his native

state and across his old Naval Academy grounds. Whatever weighed on him in those heady April days, it was enough to make him cast away a forty-seven-year naval career. He took the resignation to the Navy Department and handed it over in person. The next day, at noon, he gave a farewell address to the men of the Washington Navy Yard. Reported the *National Intelligencer*:

> The parting scene was very impressive and affecting. The late commandant briefly addressed the men, counseling them to be loyal to the Government whilst in its service, expressing the unfeigned regret which he experienced in severing the ties which had existed between them . . . .
> During the delivery of this address tears coursed freely down the bronzed cheeks of the patriotic workmen, and at its close three hearty cheers were given for the retiring commandant. No wonder indeed that there should have been such a heartfelt manifestation of feeling by these honest sons of toil in bidding adieu to Captain Buchanan, for he was truly their friend and their counselor. He had watched over their interests no less faithfully than he had guarded those of the Government. His administration of the Yard has rarely, if ever, been equalled, certainly never excelled; and we can truly affirm that a more patriotic heart never throbbed in the breast of an American officer. While in his keeping, the American flag would have been upheld even at the cost of the last drop of his blood; and we have heard him declare that it should never be hauled down while he or one man under his command was left to defend it.

Somehow, for him, the flag didn't stand for the same things anymore. Buchanan went home to the Eastern Shore.

"It is difficult, if not impossible, to keep up with the terrible whirl of events which are breaking over us," John Taylor Wood wrote in his diary on April 19. Two days earlier he had taken the evening train from Annapolis to Washington to have a long discussion with his mother and father about the crisis. "He is for the Union unconditionally," Wood said of his father. "I wish sometimes I could feel so."

Wood's brother Robert Jr. had already gone over to the Confederacy. Uncle Jefferson Davis had made him an adjutant general on Braxton Bragg's staff. John Taylor Wood wrote on April 20, "My sympathies for the South are becoming more and more enlisted. I must soon quit."

The arrival of the first troop steamer off Annapolis and the sense of being invaded led John Taylor Wood to write on April 21, the day he resigned from the U.S. Navy, "My blood is boiling over with indignation . . . ."

On April 24 USS *Cumberland*, fresh from her escape out of the Norfolk Navy Yard, captured a tug and schooner in Hampton Roads. They were smuggling arms and ammunition to the South. It was only the beginning.

That same day, the USS *Constitution*, with the Naval Academy midshipmen still faithful to the Union, departed Annapolis under tow of USS *R. R. Cuyler* and accompanied by the steamer *Harriet Lane*. The academy that Franklin Buchanan had molded was moving to Newport, Rhode Island, for the duration of the conflict.

Earlier that day the members of the Class of 1861, Northern boys and Southerners not yet departed, gathered together, smoked a peace pipe, and took an oath of undying friendship. The drum sounded final formation. They all fell in. C. R. P. Rodgers had the band play "Hail, Columbia" and "The Star-Spangled Banner." He addressed the student body with an impassioned plea to all of them, Northerners and Southerners, to stand by Old Glory. When he was finished, he said that anyone who wished to fall out could do so.

The Southern boys and some border-state boys stepped out from the line. Northern and Southern friends shook hands, hugged, wept. The Southern boys walked on out through the front gate of the academy. The Northern boys were taken by tug to Old Ironsides.

And the *Constitution* left the Chesapeake Bay.

CHAPTER 2

A flying flotilla is born

THE NAVY WAS leaving, the army taking its place. The New York and Massachusetts soldiers occupied the Naval Academy grounds in time to bid Godspeed to the middies. Late on the night of April 23, 1861, the steamer *Baltic* and other transports entered Annapolis Harbor. The Sixth, Twelfth, and Seventy-first New York regiments had arrived. The influx of troops to and through Annapolis had begun and would continue.

Theodore Winthrop of the New York Seventh was a well-traveled young author covering the march to Washington for the *Atlantic Monthly*. "Has anybody seen Annapolis?" he wrote. "It is a picturesque old place, sleepy enough, and astonished to find itself wide-awaked by a war and obliged to take responsibility and share for good and ill in the movement of its time."

The Massachusetts Eighth set about repairing the railroad track and the sabotaged engine. The regiment boasted a number of adroit Yankee mechanics. Private Charles Homans of Company E looked over the disabled engine—and found his own name scratched on it. "The old rattletrap was an old friend," wrote Winthrop. "Charles Homans had had a share in building it. The machine and the man said 'How d'y'do?' at once." Homans and his fellow mechanics in the ranks got the locomotive working again, and Homans got to be the engineer. Two miles of track were repaired by the time the New York Seventh formed up and began marching out of Annapolis on the morning of April 24.

THE NEW YORK SEVENTH PAUSES TO REST ON THE MARCH
TO ANNAPOLIS JUNCTION.
Harper's Weekly

They garnered no cheers from the Annapolis crowd, said Winthrop. "Although we deem ourselves a fine-looking set, although our belts are blanched with pipe-clay and our rifles shine sharp in the sun, yet the townspeople stare at us in a dismal silence." They pushed ahead, Massachusetts men repairing tracks, New Yorkers marching and providing protection for the rail gangs. When troops tired in the unseasonable heat they hopped for a spell on the wheezing makeshift train. The New Yorkers' howitzer was menacingly mounted on a platform car at the front of the train, but they met no opposition. Progress was held up at the Millersville bridge, which took hours to make crossable again. The track destruction became more thorough as Annapolis Junction drew nearer, and the Seventh had to heft crowbars alongside the Eighth to keep things moving along. They marched through the night and early on the twenty-fifth, straggled out from swampy woods into a wheat field just a mile or so from the junction. From here on, the track was intact. A

THE EIGHTH MASSACHUSETTS REPAIRS THE RAILROAD,
REOPENING THE ROUTE FROM ANNAPOLIS TO WASHINGTON.
Harper's Weekly

STEAMERS TRANSPORT NEW JERSEY TROOPS ACROSS CHESAPEAKE BAY,
ON THE WAY TO WASHINGTON VIA ANNAPOLIS, MAY 1861.
Frank Leslie's Illustrated Newspaper

train from Washington had come for them. They were relieved to see it, and not just for the sake of sore feet. "Until we actually saw the train awaiting us, and the Washington companies, who had come down to escort us, drawn up, we did not know whether our Uncle Sam was still a resident of the capital."

By noon on April 25 the New York Seventh—the first regiment to reach the capital since it had been cut off from the North—was marching before the White House. Colonel Lefferts shook hands with a widely smiling Abe Lincoln. The way had been found, the route opened up. Washington was no longer isolated, thanks to the Bay, to Annapolis, and to a repaired stretch of rails. Troops poured in. The Indianapolis militia came eight hundred miles by rail to Philadelphia; from there, it was by boat down the Bay. The Chesapeake & Delaware Canal emerged as a boon to timeliness. On May 5, departing from Trenton, New Jersey, fourteen propeller steamers carrying four regiments and four pieces of artillery made it to Annapolis in twenty-eight hours. Crowds lined the C&D Canal to cheer the floating parade. The *National Intelligencer* reported: "It is stated that the fourteen transports, with a strong convoy . . . made a splendid appearance, steaming in two lines down the Chesapeake."

Around the time that Virginia seceded, Levi White of Baltimore happened to be going to Richmond. A Baltimore engraver he knew asked White for a favor, since he was going to Richmond anyway. The engraver had made some Virginia military buttons; he wanted White to find out if there was a market for them in Richmond. White scouted around the city and talked to a clothesmaker and a sutler. He came back to Baltimore with good news for the engraver: The market was limitless.

"For many months after that I kept my friend the engraver busy making Virginia buttons," said White, "and I was also kept just as busy on my part getting these buttons to Richmond."

Soon, Levi White was smuggling more than buttons. On one of his Richmond runs he met Brigadier General Josiah Gorgas, CSA, chief of ordnance for the War Department. General Gorgas also asked White for a favor, since he was going back north anyway. The Confederacy needed musket caps. The Ordnance Department had started up a factory, but had no efflorate of potassium. The general asked Levi White to find five hundred pounds of potassium, if possible.

The potassium was not to be found in Baltimore, but "a good Southern friend in New York" found what White was looking for at a big drugstore there. White bought out the store's whole supply, two cases, or more than five hundred pounds. He had it shipped to Baltimore by way of the C&D, then delivered to a South Frederick Street merchant's warehouse. As soon as the potassium stash arrived, White had it loaded onto a boat and hauled across the harbor to Curtis Creek.

Detectives were trailing the suspicious shipment. The New York friend wired a warning to White. The detectives traced the potassium cases to South Frederick Street, "but as water leaves no trail they could trace them no farther," said White.

By the time the detectives searched the warehouse, "the potassium was 'boating' it to Arundel's shore. A vigorous search was made, but the detectives were baffled. In a few days the potassium was delivered to the Confederate States Ordnance Department, at Richmond, and with its aid began the musket cap industry of the Confederate States. But it was a close shave!"

Levi White would sail down and up the Chesapeake with great frequency for the next few years. General Gorgas was grateful for the potassium and had more requests for White, who noted that "from that time to the end of the war I was a special agent of the Confederate States Ordnance Department."

At the New York Navy Yard, steamers were being converted into gunboats, being readied for Chesapeake service. A pair of thirty-two-pounders now jutted from the side-wheeler *Thomas Freeborn*, while *Reliance* and *Resolute*, small, swift screw-steamers, got a twenty-four-pound howitzer apiece. The three boats were at the heart of a plan conceived by Commander James H. Ward, who at war's outbreak had foreseen the importance of well-patrolled water access to the capital. In April Ward had proposed to charter and equip "a flying flotilla . . . with a view to service in the Chesapeake and its tributaries; to interrupt the enemy's communications; assuredly keep open our own; drive from those waters every hostile bottom; threaten all the points of a shore line

COMMANDER JAMES H. WARD,
CREATOR OF THE POTOMAC FLOTILLA.
National Archives

accessible to such a force exceeding 1,000 miles in extent; protect loyal citizens; convoy, tow, transport troops or intelligence with dispatch; be generally useful; threaten at all points, and to attack at any desired or important one."

Welles approved; Ward got to work. He was active, energetic, in his fifties, a veteran of distant seas, a Connecticut Yankee career officer with thirty-eight years of service behind him. Formerly a professor at Annapolis, he was the author of well-regarded writings on gunnery, tactics, and the naval uses of steam. The press called Ward "one of the best educated men in the navy."

Ward had served on USS *Constitution* and he was in the Mediterranean Squadron, the African Squadron, and the Gulf Squadron. He spent his time on leave writing his treatises on tactics and once spent a year's leave at college. When the Civil War began, he had been at the navy yard in Brooklyn for a few years, on duty as commander of the receiving ship *North Carolina*.

Now, he took command of the recently purchased side-wheeler and put Lieutenant D. L. Braine in command of *Reliance* and Acting Master William Budd of the U.S. Coast Survey in command of *Resolute*. To the three steamers would be added three shallow-draft schooners. *Pawnee* and the screw-steamer *Anacostia* joined forces with them once they arrived. A humble armada, it would grow. And it would become known as the Potomac Flotilla.

While the Chesapeake's new gunboat navy got ready to steam south, Brigadier General Butler entered Baltimore and took Federal Hill. The Department of Annapolis, a new military command, was designated on April 27 and Butler made in charge. It encompassed the country for twenty miles on either side of the Annapolis-Washington rail route. Butler moved his headquarters to Relay House on May 4 and set his sights on Mobtown nine miles away. He sent a spy disguised as an organ grinder (complete with monkey) into the city and now professed information about a pending attack by a horde of Baltimore rowdies. On May 13, in pouring rain, Butler entered the city with more than a thousand men. The troops—which included the Baltimore-familiar Sixth Massachusetts—got off train cars and marched through wet streets to Federal Hill, the thunderstorm not deterring the onlookers. Butler issued a proclamation: Loyal citizens would be safe. Normal business could be conducted. No groups of armed men, except those loyal and official, could gather. No Confederate flags or emblems could be shown.

The city's Union faithful held a mass rally in East Baltimore on May 14. It was the same day that a schooner loaded with pikes and rifles was seized in the harbor. And on the northeast corner of Gay and Second Streets, soldiers cleaned out a warehouse full of muskets and munitions. It came to more than sixty wagonloads—nearly three thousand flintlock muskets and more than three thousand pikes. It was city property, but it was a volatile city. The troops took the stash to Fort McHenry, where they could keep an eye on it.

THE FIRST DIVISION OF PENNSYLVANIA VOLUNTEERS, UNDER MAJOR
GENERAL GEORGE CADWALADER (BUTLER'S REPLACEMENT), ARRIVES
AT BALTIMORE HARBOR, MAY 15, 1861.
Frank Leslie's Illustrated Newspaper

Meanwhile, the Maryland Assembly session at Frederick was breaking up. On May 14, on the train at Relay House, riding in company with Governor Hicks and several other prominent politicians, popular Baltimore inventor/tycoon Ross Winans was pulled from his chair and arrested on Butler's orders. Winans was an outspoken secessionist. "If such a man, worth $15,000,000, were hanged for treason, it would convince the people of Maryland, at least, that the expedition we were on was no picnic," explained Butler.

But the entire bloodless conquest of Baltimore had been done without orders, and General-in-chief Winfield Scott scolded Butler via telegram on May 14. By May 16 Butler was transferred to Fort Monroe. He later said that if he hadn't been pulled from Baltimore, he would have hanged Winans at Union Square.

Winans was thrown in Fort McHenry, taken to Annapolis, and then released. But Lincoln gave Butler a consolation prize while shuffling him off to Fort Monroe: The president promoted the lawyer to major general.

The new major general was heading down into busy waters. Throughout the lower Bay, U.S. naval vessels were probing into coves, patrolling up rivers, gauging rebel shore-battery firepower, trying to clamp down on a brisk and growing illicit commerce between shores, and learning that the enemy was crafty, elusive, and aware of every nook and cranny in the watery maze.

Among the rebels of the tidewater, organized resistance was encouraged, as in the May 9 proceedings of the Advisory Council of the State of Virginia, which urged that "prompt steps be taken to encourage the formation of home guards in all the counties bordering on the Chesapeake Bay and its navigable tributaries . . . ." Citizens should band together, said the council, "establishing convenient places of rendezvous; selecting, along the banks of the rivers, bays, and creeks, suitable posts for rifle-pits; erecting signal stations along the rivers, and establishing a system for giving warning of the enemy's approach . . . ."

The *Richmond Dispatch* joined in sounding the clarion call: "All over the State, particularly in the Tidewater and Potomac counties, there are a great many men who do not belong to companies . . . . They have not regulation weapons, but almost every man of them has a rifle, or a shot-gun, or a flint-lock musket, and one or more pistols of some kind. All these men should form neighborhood squads of from five to fifteen . . . . Such squads are to act as guerrillas, and if the enemy approaches their section of the country, hang upon his outskirts, fill the hollows, hide behind trees, in ditches, anywhere that they can best protect themselves and cut down the enemy . . . and every man they drop will be furnishing Virginia with at least another weapon."

"Washington was now a fortress," wrote the Seventh New York's Theodore Winthrop. "The capital was out of danger, and therefore of no further interest to anybody. The time had come for myself and my regiment to leave it by different ways." Two days after his regimental month's service was done, the young author accepted a position as staff officer with Benjamin Butler, whom he had come to admire as "the Grand Yankee of this little period of the war." Winthrop made for Old Point Comfort.

More troops and artillery were arriving at Fort Monroe. The fort total was up to nearly 2,200 men by mid-May and nearly 4,500 by the end of May. Ben Butler arrived at the fort and took over from Colonel Justin Dimick, who maintained command of the garrison regulars. The

THE MOAT AND SEAWARD FACE OF FORT MONROE.
Harper's Weekly

outpost began to expand beyond the fort. Butler sent the First Vermont and Second New York into camp on the mainland, at the other end of the bridge. It came to be called Camp Hamilton. From here, the troops began probing into nearby Hampton, prompting the rebels to pull out.

The main rebel camp was up the peninsula around Yorktown, a force of about 2,500 Confederates there commanded by Colonel John B. Magruder, the flamboyant "Prince John." The rebels may have withdrawn from Hampton, but they continued to ride down and scout about with regularity.

The Atlantic Blockading Squadron, fourteen vessels commanded by Flag Officer Silas Stringham at Hampton Roads, provided the U.S. naval presence. The Confederates, meanwhile, were erecting a powerful battery on Sewells Point, four miles from Monroe and guarding the entrance to the Elizabeth. An estimated three thousand to four thousand Confederate troops under Major General Benjamin Huger were amassed behind the Sewells Point guns, ready in case of an attack on Norfolk.

COLONEL JOHN B. MAGRUDER
COMMANDED THE REBEL FORCES IN
THE YORKTOWN VICINITY IN
THE WAR'S EARLY PHASE.
National Archives

MAJOR GENERAL BENJAMIN HUGER
COMMANDED THE CONFEDERATE
TROOPS DEFENDING NORFOLK.
National Archives

On May 27 the Federals gained good ground: Newport News. Aided by the navy, which provided the steamers *Quaker City*, *Monticello*, and *Harriet Lane* for transports, Butler landed a detachment of regulars and three volunteer regiments, some 2,500 men, at Newport News. They took the high ground, entrenched, put up a battery of four eight-inch Columbiads, and named the new outpost Camp Butler.

Butler's expansions beyond the fort walls would be of far-reaching value. But his most far-reaching, influential move of all was a clever bit of legalistic hocus-pocus he concocted on May 24. Three slaves laboring on the Sewells Point battery fled in a boat and escaped to Fort Monroe. A Confederate officer came under flag of truce, and Butler met him at the fort entrance. The Confederate, speaking on behalf of the slave owner, asked Butler to fulfill his Constitutional obligation under the Fugitive Slave Law and return the runaways.

Butler pointed out, "I am under no Constitutional obligations to a foreign country, which Virginia now claims to be . . . I shall hold these

Slaves make a mass exodus for the Union lines at Newport News
in the wake of Butler's famed "contraband" ruling.
Harper's Weekly

negroes as contraband of war, since they are engaged in the construction
of your battery and are claimed as your property. The question is simply
whether they shall be used for or against the Government of the United
States."

The Confederate left, befuddled and angry. Butler had him over a
barrel. If a Southerner was going to insist that a human being could be
considered property, then Butler could invoke basic law: "Property of
whatever nature, used or capable of being used for warlike purposes,
and especially when being so used, may be captured and held either on
sea or on shore as property contraband of war."

It was a spur-of-the-moment stroke of genius. Butler shrugged it off,
saying to a major on his staff, "At any rate, Haggerty, it is a good enough
reason to stop the rebels' mouths with, especially as I should have held
these negroes anyway."

The exodus began immediately, a flood of runaway slaves to Old
Point Comfort. Butler put them to work, kept a roster, and quickly had

COMMANDER JAMES H. WARD (IN STRAW HAT) SIGHTS A GUN ON THE
DECK OF THE POTOMAC FLOTILLA'S USS *THOMAS FREEBORN.*
Special Collections, Nimitz Library, U.S. Naval Academy

to appoint a Commissioner of Negro Affairs "to take this business off
my hands, for it was becoming onerous."

Butler's contraband ruling echoed across the war. "The truth is, as
a lawyer I was never very much proud of it," Butler claimed, "but as an
executive officer I was very much comforted with it as a means of doing
my duty." Theodore Winthrop's assessment of the "contraband of war"
phrase was more generous: "It was an epigram which freed the slaves."

Commander James H. Ward and his new gunboat navy left New York
on May 16 and put in at the Washington Navy Yard on the twentieth.
The Potomac Flotilla's career began with Ward cruising the river on
Thomas Freeborn and looking for trouble spots.

Hierarchically, the flotilla came under the command of the Atlantic
Blockading Squadron, but would operate with a fair degree of auton-
omy, mainly working the upper Bay while the Atlantic Blockading
Squadron mainly worked the lower. The Potomac Flotilla's territorial

range was flexible, though, as was its mission. In its first ten days in action, the flotilla provided gun support in the invasion of Alexandria on May 24, then had its initial big shootout with rebel shore guns. From May 29 to June 1, *Thomas Freeborn*, *Anacostia*, and *Resolute* blasted away at the Aquia Creek batteries, with *Pawnee* eventually joining the fray as well. "The sight was a solemn one," wrote the on-deck correspondent for the *New York Herald*, "but not devoid of a sort of terrible beauty. The smoke from the enemy's guns, the flight of the shells, occasionally bursting in mid air, leaving a beautiful wreath of smoke where the explosion took place, the ricochet of the shots, skimming along the surface of the glassy smooth river . . . ."

Commander Ward, the gunnery professor, didn't shy from putting theory into action. "The forward gun—served by Captain Ward himself . . . fired a few rounds more at the depot batteries, so as to render the destruction complete. When this had been done to the entire satisfaction of Captain Ward, he trained his forward gun to bear on the hill battery, and blazed away."

THE POTOMAC FLOTILLA GOES INTO ACTION, FIGHTING THE REBEL
BATTERIES AT AQUIA CREEK, MAY 29–JUNE 1, 1861.
Frank Leslie's Illustrated Newspaper

Ward offered his own view of the events: "Several shots came on board of us, causing the vessel to leak badly . . . . Fortunately I have again neither killed nor wounded to report, though the shot at times fell thick about us, testing the gallantry of my people, which I consider of standard proof for any emergency."

A blown-up Virginia pier, some silenced guns, other guns out of reach—such were the results of the lengthy cannonade. The shore batteries would continually prove to be an amorphous foe, returning, relocating. In his initial inspection cruise of the Potomac, Ward had noticed some particularly danger-inviting bends in the river, one of which was Mathias Point, where battery construction was probable and sniper fire definite. "Disaffected Marylanders, they say, go over that way to join the Virginia forces; also that supplies pass. . . ." Ward noted. "If I chance by Mathias Point by daylight shall give it a critical inspection and go so close as to tempt their fire . . . ."

Virginia Cavalry Captain W. H. Werth of the Chatham Greys rode south from Yorktown on June 7 to see what the Yankees were up to at Newport News. With him rode two fellow Chatham Greys, some officers, and twenty men of the Old Dominion Dragoons. They reached the James River, where an eight-man squad spotted them and made a dash for the Union line. Werth galloped, hoping to cut them off before they got inside and sounded the alarm. Close to the fortifications now, he turned along the river and advanced, and suddenly he stumbled on a Union wood-cutting detail, thirty-one men in all. "I was then entirely alone. I halted and hid myself in a thicket only twenty yards from the party." As he watched, the eight men showed up and the word was out.

"I at once saw that I must do quickly whatever I intended doing, so I reined my horse back, and walked him out into the clearing in plain view of the whole party, and not more than twenty paces from them, picked out the commissioned officer, and shot him dead in his tracks."

The soldiers panicked, shouted, and retreated. Captain Werth made a one-man cavalry charge. "I put the spurs to my horse and rode into them at full speed (giving at the same time a loud walla-walla war-whoop), and then delivered my second shot, which brought another man (a private) dead to the ground."

The rest of Werth's riders had regrouped, and he rode hard to join them. Together they galloped after the fleeing regiment, but two companies of reinforcements came forward and the rebels reined in. They needn't have, though. The reinforcements caught the panic of the ones running toward them, and they all hurried back behind the entrenchments, yelling, "Virginia horsemen!"

Uncomfortably close to the guns of Newport News, Werth and his men rode off. Among other things the cavalryman noted about the Yankees he chased was this: "Their uniform corresponded with mine—gray cloth with black trimming."

Magruder's rebels were building fortifications at Little Bethel, less than ten miles above Old Point Comfort and about the same distance from Newport News. They also were digging in a few miles north at Big Bethel, an old church hamlet along the northwest branch of Back River—not far up from where it snaked into the Chesapeake below Drum Island Flats. The low, rolling land here was marshy along the creek bank and densely wooded along the roadside, becoming open field before the Back River bridge.

From Little Bethel, the salient outpost, the rebels were in convenient position to send out small, harassing bands of cavalry to Newport News and Hampton. Ben Butler decided to attack. He put Brigadier General Ebenezer Pierce in command. The plan was to send up troops from both Old Point Comfort and Newport News, get some of them behind the rebels at Little Bethel, cutting off their retreat, and then hit them from the front. Pierce hoped to sandwich the rebels, take the position, destroy the works, and then advance to Big Bethel. On June 10 after midnight, the move was made. There was one potential problem: Coming from different directions, when the troops crossed paths, there was a chance they might mistake each other for the enemy. So they were given a watchword to shout: "Boston."

Through the early morning hours they marched, troops from New England and New York, seven regiments accompanied by a Second U.S. Artillery detachment led by First Lieutenant John T. Greble, twenty-seven, West Point, a Regular Army officer in the field amid volunteers. Coming from the Old Point direction, the first to cross Hampton Creek

THE FIGHT AT BIG BETHEL, JUNE 10, 1861.
Frank Leslie's Illustrated Newspaper

were Hiram Duryea's Fifth New York Zouaves in their billowing britches and tasseled turbans. The First Vermont led the way from Newport News. The Zouaves and Vermonters were well ahead of the rest. Then the shooting started from the wrong direction: behind them.

Colonel John Bendix saw men in gray on horseback and showered them with small arms and cannonfire. It was Pierce, his own general. Now New Yorkers were firing on New Yorkers, and the "Boston!" shout was useless. The Vermonters in the vanguard backtracked and entered the fight on Bendix's side. Forward squads finally recognized one another. Twenty were wounded and one killed in the mistaken-identity clash. The troops moved on. They found Little Bethel abandoned, burned it, and moved on toward Big Bethel, where the authentic enemy was waiting.

For days the rebels had been digging in. A gun battery had the bridge crossing covered. Across the river they had thrown up an advance battery. At 9 A.M. the Northerners came into view. All that was visible above the forest shadows on the road were their bayonets in long shining rows, bespeaking a sizable column coming. At 9:15 Major George

Randolph, commanding the rebel artillery behind the bridge, fired the cannon. The shot bounced and ricocheted into the advancing ranks.

Greble's artillerymen returned cannonfire while the soldiers fanned out on either side of the road. The rebel cannon were keeping the Union line from advancing. The Fifth New York got close to the bridge and was mowed down. There was a ford downriver, another place to cross instead of the fatal bridge. Three companies of Zouaves tried to move down there and get across. Captain Werth of the Virginia Greys got there first, set up a naval howitzer, and blasted the Zouaves back. An advance on the rebel right fell apart, but the Confederates began dropping back as their forward battery was captured by the Zouaves. When the First North Carolina rushed the Zouaves and retook the battery, the momentum shifted again.

General Butler was back at Fort Monroe, but his staff officer was here. Theodore Winthrop led a final spirited charge to roll up the Confederate left flank. The volunteers followed the author across the creek and cut loose with a wild cheer as they moved on the abandoned earthwork. Winthrop stood atop a rail fence and waved his sword, shouting for them to follow. He was shot through the heart.

The charge disintegrated with the death of Winthrop. Along the main road to the bridge, Union sharpshooters were keeping up a heavy fire from a house they'd occupied, while Greble's cannonfire continued loud dialogue with rebel artillery. Private Henry Wyatt of the First North Carolina Infantry volunteered to dash over and set fire to the house. He made it across, shot and shell flying around him. Thirty yards from the house, a musket ball drilled his forehead and he fell, the first Confederate battle death of the Civil War.

The rebel cannon continued blasting at the house, a shell smashed a window, and fire torched upward. As the house burned down, the Union soldiers retreated. Four Confederate cavalry companies chased after them, and it turned into a rout.

Lieutenant Greble had kept up his cannonfire throughout the day from the most exposed position in the Union line. He was hit by the next-to-last artillery blast fired by the rebels. A company of the Second New York volunteered to venture back and rescue the abandoned gun.

FIRST LIEUTENANT JOHN T. GREBLE,
HERO OF BIG BETHEL.
National Archives

They successfully retrieved the cannon, on top of which they carried the body of John T. Greble, the first U.S. Army officer to die in battle in the Civil War.

The rifled cannonball took off his head. His wife and two infant children had been with him at Fort Monroe until April. She transported the two little ones to her father-in-law's in Philadelphia when the war came. The *Philadelphia Inquirer* said:

> For a few days past she had been busy in preparing some little luxuries and comforts to dispatch to her husband by the hands of his father, who was about to make a social visit to Fort Monroe; and on Tuesday morning, while the brave young soldier was lying stark and stiff upon the battlefield, his wife was engaged in eager delight over the completion of the gift which she supposed was to bring such glad surprise to her husband; and the father actually departed with it by the noon train for the South, while the electric

wires over his head were charged with the fatal intelligence of the boy's untimely death.

The schooner *Christiana Keen* ran aground in the Potomac near Mathias Point on the night of June 15. About thirty or forty men rowed out from Upper Machodoc Creek and burned the schooner. According to the master, the men wore gray uniforms and felt hats.

The burning of *Christiana Keen* was found to be the work of a certain Dr. Hooe, an avid rebel civilian housing soldiers, running supplies, and causing trouble from his riverfront base. Troops here had been firing on passing Potomac Flotilla gunboats. It was just a matter of time before the rebels got artillery on Mathias Point. On June 24 *Resolute* came calling on the doctor.

He wasn't home. Some Virginia troopers were there, however, and they cleared out after *Resolute*'s bow gun started firing. Acting Master William Budd went ashore and burned the house down.

Next morning at five, a landing party off *Pawnee* beached at Mathias Point and inspected the area. *Pawnee* kept up a shelling to hold the rebels back. There were said to be some six hundred of them in the area, one hundred of those mounted troops, and according to what a black man told the sailors, some two hundred of them "kept on the beach constantly."

On June 26 Commander Ward came to direct the denuding of Mathias Point. His *Thomas Freeborn* began the morning with a barrage of shot, shell, and grape thrown at the woods before landing. Ward went in with a party from *Freeborn*, Lieutenant J. C. Chaplin with sailors from *Pawnee*. Chaplin's crew fanned out and found the rebel pickets, who fired and ran off. The sailors gave chase, firing. Then, over the top of the hill, came five hundred rebels charging down.

Chaplin's men retreated to the beach. Ward ordered them back on the landing boats and told them to wait offshore. He returned to *Freeborn* and bombarded the woods again.

Soon Chaplin's men were able to go back to the beach. On the piney strip of the point's extremity, they labored to build a sandbag breastwork. By late afternoon they'd completed it, a modest but well-positioned Union foothold on Mathias Point. From *Freeborn*, Ward hailed,

"All hands on board!" Chaplin's men concealed their handiwork beneath branches and sticks and made ready to leave. Musket fire erupted.

The party ran to the boats, shot flying around them. Chaplin stayed on shore, exposed, making certain all his men got aboard. The last man couldn't swim to the boat with his musket, so Chaplin hoisted him on his shoulders and helped him out to the boat, unscathed save for a fresh hole through the top of his cap.

The musketry hail kept up, pelting the escaping boats. A flagstaff was shot. With blood pouring from the wound in his thigh, John Williams grabbed the falling, shot-riddled flag and waved it high, holding it up until alongside the *Freeborn*.

Commander Ward charged down to the forecastle deck. He ordered the thirty-two-pounder loaded with round shot. He sighted the gun and made ready to order "Fire!" A musket ball pierced his abdomen.

He turned to Harry Churchill, the boatswain's mate, and said, "Churchill, I am killed."

The commander fell. While Churchill held him with one arm, with the other he yanked the string, and the bow gun was fired.

Lieutenant Lee took charge now and barked, "Slip the cable and start her." The vessel moved out of range of the musketry. *Pawnee* was ordered alongside, and from her came Dr. J. A. Moore, the surgeon, onto *Freeborn*. With him was Frederick Ward, the fallen commander's son.

Dr. Moore declared the wound mortal, and within the hour Commander Ward was dead. His son was by him as he died. A witness said, "The most profound grief pervaded the whole of the officers and crew of the *Freeborn*." James H. Ward, creator of the Potomac Flotilla, was the first U.S. Navy officer to die in the Civil War.

When George N. Hollins of Baltimore was fourteen years old, Commodore Oliver Hazard Perry visited his home. The man of the hour after the Battle of Lake Erie was in Baltimore being entertained by many, including Hollins's parents. Young Hollins was in awe as he was summoned into the room and allowed to meet the hero. Commodore Perry looked approvingly at the lad and said he would make a "first-rate" midshipman. The boy's mother cried and the boy went to sea.

During the War of 1812 he served under Decatur and was a prisoner of war in Bermuda. He fought in the Barbary war of 1814–15 and took part in the capture of an Algerian ship and the freeing of Christian slaves. A sword was given the young man in honor of his gallantry. The navy was his life now. He became a lieutenant in 1829, commander in 1841, and captain in 1855.

In May 1861 Captain Hollins was commanding the USS *Susquehanna* at Naples when he received orders to proceed stateside. He did so, then resigned his commission in the first week of June. "Not until the 12th did I receive an answer," he recounted with disgust. "That was a 'dismissal' from the service of the old Government—that by a fellow who was splitting rails in the West while I had been serving my country."

Now, barely a fortnight later, Hollins docked a stolen steamboat at Coan River Landing, got hold of a Baltimore newspaper, and read it with alarm: Ward was dead. The flotilla boats had gone upriver, escorting the commander's corpse to funeral services at the capital.

It hurt the plan, a plan that had gone well so far with the aid of cutlasses, pistols, women's clothes, and calculated risks. Things had gone well so far. Now they would just have to improvise.

CHAPTER 3

The rebel shore

AFTER THE BLUNT and unceremonious finale to his forty-six-year naval career, George Hollins had headed south. He spent a few days in his hometown, his disgruntled feelings about the war situation made worse by the rolling-eye looks he was getting for freely voicing his opinions. There was one direction to go—farther south. On June 18 he left Baltimore on the steamboat *Mary Washington*.

She plied the Patuxent route. Disembarking at a Southern sympathizer's plantation, Hollins unveiled the plan he'd hatched: The steamer *St. Nicholas*, which ran from Baltimore to Washington, had been observed stopping alongside *Pawnee* of the Potomac Flotilla, "commanded by Yankee Ward, and which was a great annoyance to the boats on the Potomac." As a deliverer of supplies, *St. Nicholas* was able to get next to the flotilla vessel with routine ease and no suspicion. So why not, figured Hollins, gather a gang not averse to piratical endeavor, seize *St. Nicholas*, and then use her to capture the flotilla boat?

"I was told the plan could not be carried out, as there were so many Union men about," said Hollins. So he took his idea and kept moving south. He crossed the Potomac and, at one o'clock in the morning, showed up on the still-unburned doorstep of the helpful Dr. Hooe. "This gentleman was a perfect stranger to me, but he received me kindly, entertained me handsomely, he and his charming family so soon to be rendered houseless and homeless by the incendiary act of the vandal Captain Budd, of the United States gunboat, a name ever to be remembered, desecrated as the insulter of unprotected females, firing into barns

CAPTAIN GEORGE N. HOLLINS, CSN,
ONE OF THE RAIDERS RESPONSIBLE FOR
THE INFAMOUS *ST. NICHOLAS* INCIDENT.
Special Collections, Nimitz Library,
U.S. Naval Academy

and houses, and everything but what might have been expected of an officer and a gentleman."

Dr. Hooe chartered a buggy and escorted Hollins to Fredericksburg. There Hollins caught the train for Richmond. He went to Navy Secretary Stephen R. Mallory's office and was instantly granted a commission as captain in the Confederate States Navy.

Captain Hollins, CSN, took his *St. Nicholas* plan all the way to Governor John Letcher, who enthusiastically approved. He gave Hollins a draft for one thousand dollars to help make the thing happen. Then, the governor said, there was somebody he'd like him to meet.

He was another Marylander, Richard Thomas, scion of St. Marys County society and erstwhile West Point nongraduate who had gone off to fight pirates in China, fight with Garibaldi in Italy, and then returned in time for the war at home. During his Italian adventure he had adopted "Zarvona" as his nom de guerre, and now he went by Richard

Thomas Zarvona. In St. Marys, Colonel Richard Thomas Zarvona formed Zarvona's Maryland Zouaves, a rebel outfit decked in wild red uniforms. A reckless twenty-one-year old with a shaved head, Colonel Zarvona was a good man to have as an ally when trying something crazy and bold.

Hollins and Zarvona headed north, and on the way, Hollins ran into his sons George Jr. and Fred. They were Richmond-bound, but now they joined their father's exploit. Crossing the Potomac, it was on to Point Lookout "in a pouring rain, a nasty, dirty night." The point, jutting into the Chesapeake at the mouth of the Potomac, was a steamboat stop. Hollins signed the thousand-dollar draft over to Zarvona, who caught a boat north, where he would purchase weapons and rally some men. When he returned on *St. Nicholas*, Hollins would join him on board.

When *St. Nicholas* departed Baltimore on June 28, her sixty-some passengers included sixteen men, boarding separately but all there for the same reason, because Zarvona had recruited them to help him take the ship. But as the steamer made her way out of Baltimore Harbor, there was no Zarvona. "What worried me a lot was I couldn't find the colonel or anyone who looked like him," commented George Watts, one of Zarvona's recruits. "I could see the future of the whole expedition, and also I could see myself behind bars in Fort McHenry, and the picture didn't look a bit good to me."

Among the passengers was a lady registered as Madame La Force, "a mighty pretty young woman, stylishly dressed, flirting outrageously with some of the young officers," described Watts. "She talked with a strong French accent and carried a fan which she used like a Spanish dancer. That young woman behaved so scandalously that all the other women on the boat were in a terrible state over it."

St. Nicholas reached Point Lookout, and George Hollins boarded. As the boat steamed upriver, Hollins gave the signal. The flirtatious French lady went to her cabin, took off her dress, and turned into Richard Thomas Zarvona, with cutlass, pistol, and wild red Zouave trousers. The conspirators gathered in the cabin, and Madame La Force's three large trunks, laden with the finest French hats for the ladies of Washington, were opened and their contents divided among the men. One trunk was full of cutlasses, another carried carbine rifles, the third, Colt

A ROMANTIC NINETEENTH-CENTURY DEPICTION
OF THE *ST. NICHOLAS* CAPTURE.
Nimitz Library, U.S. Naval Academy

revolvers. The men burst forth from the French lady's cabin and took over the ship. Brandishing a brace of pistols, Hollins charged into the wheelhouse and told the captain to surrender.

The raiders quickly took over the ship. They forced the passengers and crew belowdecks, secured the hatches, and doused all the lights. Now *St. Nicholas* changed course, dashing across to the Coan River, on the Virginia side near the Bay. There was one more stop to make before attacking the flotilla gunboat. It was half past three in the morning as the stolen steamboat docked at Coan River Landing—the rendezvous point, where Confederate soldiers and sailors were to come aboard to help in the capture of *Pawnee*.

An hour passed. The passengers, mostly Southerners, were well treated. One of them declared, "Throughout the whole night not a single act of rudeness was perpetrated, all the passengers being treated with the greatest civility. The ladies were told by the commander that they were in the hands of southern gentlemen, and would be treated as his own sisters."

Indeed, noted Captain Hollins, "Although it was Sunday the ladies amused themselves by making Confederate flags out of the Yankee flags I had captured."

The reinforcements arrived—sailors from CSS *Patrick Henry* and soldiers of the First Tennessee Infantry. "They were well armed with rifles and bowie knives, and were anxious to meet the federal troops to test the accuracy of their rifles and the virture of their steel," recounted a passenger. "They had marched twenty miles the night before through the mud and rain, and were 'spiling' for a fight." Disappointment was waiting for them; there were no Federal troops on the river to fight after all.

As Captain Hollins looked at a Baltimore newspaper now, he discovered that *Pawnee*, along with the rest of the flotilla, had gone up to Washington City for the funeral of Commander Ward, killed two days earlier at Mathias Point.

It was time to improvise. Hollins declared his changed plan: "Finding there was no chance of capturing the *Pawnee*, and deeming it unsafe to remain where I was in a steamer without guns, I resolved to go up to Fredericksburg, and immediately ran out into the Chesapeake Bay." First, the passengers were allowed to leave. Then the rogue steamer rounded Smiths Point and headed down the Bay.

Up ahead the crew of *St. Nicholas* sighted "a fine brig," ripe for the capture. *St. Nicholas* ran alongside, and Captain Hollins and crew quickly stormed her and took her. She was *Monticello*, bound from Rio for Baltimore with a load of coffee. The brig's crew were taken prisoner, and a lieutenant placed upon her to sail her to Fredericksburg. Hollins allowed the captain and his wife to stay aboard the brig, "as I did not wish to terrify the lady or render her uncomfortable." Laden with fresh Brazilian bean, the brig constituted a choice prize. "The coffee, a full cargo, was a great treat to our 'boys in gray,' who were already beginning to endure some of the many privations that made them in later days 'truly an army of martyrs,'" said Hollins.

Barely an hour passed when *St. Nicholas* came upon another plum for the plucking: the schooner *Mary Pierce*, out of Boston with a load of ice for Washington. The rebels overtook her, manned her, and sent her on to Fredericksburg. "The ice just got there in time, for the wounded and sick in the hospitals were suffering from the want of it," Hollins said. "And the Yankee captain of the schooner attended the sale, and seeing the fine prices paid for the ice he came to me and proposed that he should go to Boston, get another vessel loaded with ice, bring her down and let me know precisely when to meet him that I might capture him, take the vessel to Fredericksburg, sell the ice and divide the proceeds. Would anyone but a Yankee have been guilty of such rascality?"

A third prize lay in store for the rebel corsairs: the coal-laden schooner *Margaret*, bound from Baltimore to Boston. Her cargo, too, was an answer to a prayer. She was, said Hollins, "a most fortunate prize, as I was on my last bucket of coal in the *St. Nicholas*. I filled up as I went along . . . ."

With *Margaret* in tow, *St. Nicholas* entered the Rappahannock and steamed up to Fredericksburg, where Hollins, Zarvona, and crew were welcomed as heroes. *St. Nicholas* was soon converted to a Confederate gunboat. Hollins was promoted to commodore. Zarvona was made a colonel of the Virginia volunteer forces and brought his Zouaves with him. Their derring-do on the Chesapeake Bay was celebrated through the South. In Richmond the swashbuckling Zarvona was treated as the man of the hour. In Baltimore a new broadsheet ballad celebrated the exploits of "The French Lady." Commodore George Hollins was assigned to New Orleans after a brief James River stint. But Colonel Zarvona, his partner in plundering, wasn't finished with the Chesapeake yet.

It was around three in the morning on June 27 that soldiers went to Marshal George P. Kane's house, roused him out of bed, arrested him,

GENERAL NATHANIEL BANKS. HE
ARRESTED THE BALTIMORE POLICE
COMMISSIONERS AND APPOINTED
A PROVOST MARSHAL.
National Archives

and threw him in Fort McHenry. Baltimore's chief of police was suspected of aiding the city's armed and organized rebel resistance, and his arrest was the first in a sweep that had the entire Board of Police Commissioners tossed behind bars.

General Nathaniel Banks, military commander in Baltimore since June, carried out the arrests, but the orders came down from Winfield Scott. Once Kane was behind bars, Banks issued a proclamation to the people of Baltimore. "Unlawful combinations of men" were stashing arms, smuggling supplies southward, and attempting to foment rebellion on the home front, declared the general. Marshal Kane was "not only believed to be cognizant of these facts," but "by direction and indirection both witness and protector to the transactions and the parties therein." Therefore, "the Government cannot regard him otherwise than as the head of an armed force hostile to its authority and acting in concert with its avowed enemies." Banks beefed up the presence of Federal troops in the city, and in the predawn darkness of July 1, four more men were arrested from their homes and incarcerated at McHenry. Charles Howard, William Gatchell, Charles Hinks, and John Davis—the police board—retaliated cannily, suspending from duty the entire city police force, which obeyed its jailed commissioners. Police barracks citywide were abandoned, achieving the desired result of leaving the citizenry in fear of anarchy.

But there were Union troops about in ever greater numbers, and to specifically replace the ousted police, General Banks appointed a provost marshal. He was wisely picked. Colonel John R. Kenly was a respected Baltimore native and a society man. A prosperous lawyer and a patriot, Kenly had been a local hero of the Mexican War. In the current conflict, he had been instrumental in recruiting Union men for military service in the First Maryland Regiment, and now he recruited some four hundred of the faithful to serve as Baltimore's police pro tem.

FEDERALS OCCUPY THE BALTIMORE POLICE HEADQUARTERS,
WHICH "RESEMBLED A CONCEALED ARSENAL," JULY 1861.
Frank Leslie's Illustrated Newspaper

The abandoned police headquarters "resembled a concealed arsenal," reported General Banks. "Large quantities of arms and ammunition were found secreted in such places and with such skill as to forbid the thought of their being held for just or lawful purposes." Eight cannon and 332 muskets, rifles, and pistols, and bountiful ammunition made up the ordnance stash commandeered by the provost marshal.

As more troops tramped into the city, the general insisted he was not imposing martial law, and he noted with pride that since denuding Baltimore of its police authorities, the city was "more quiet and orderly than for any time for many months previous."

Except for Hinks, who was paroled for health problems, the police commissioners spent nearly a month in Fort McHenry before being shipped off to Boston's Fort Warren by way of New York's Fort Lafayette. Their imprisonment lasted for sixteen months. Their supporters joined them in indignation, and the case was loudly argued. At the end of July the House of Representatives issued a resolution requesting that the president state the specific grounds on which these men had been made prisoners. Lincoln replied that "it is judged to be incompatible with the public interest at this time to furnish the information . . . ."

Fort McHenry's guest list was growing. On the night of July 2 three companies of the Massachusetts Eighth Regiment boarded the steamer *Hugh Jenkins* and left Baltimore for the Eastern Shore. They crossed the Bay, docked about a mile up the Wye River, and marched to the farm of Ogle S. Tilghman, a captain of militia in Queen Anne's County. He was arrested for treason, his home searched for an arsenal of weapons. Two guns were found. Tilghman was asked where the weapons were hidden for his militia company. He wouldn't answer. The soldiers marched him down to the river and took him to Fort McHenry. A neighbor came along as a witness against Tilghman. Once Tilghman was jailed, his home was searched again, this time by a detachment from Annapolis. They found no militia cache; they did, however, find a few waterfowling guns.

The most beautiful secessionist in Baltimore exited that July, accompanied by her sister and brother and a shipment of military stores for the Maryland Confederate troops. Auburn-haired Hetty Cary, the city's reigning belle, was leaving the world of Federal occupation and fear of

HETTY CARY, CELEBRATED BALTIMORE BEAUTY
AND RINGLEADER OF THE TROUBLEMAKING
"MONUMENT STREET GIRLS."
Nimitz Library, U.S. Naval Academy

forced Fort McHenry visits behind. She, her sister Jennie, and brother
Wilson were bound for Richmond.

Hetty and her sister were core members of the notorious "Monument Street Girls," coquettish pro-Dixie, high-society troublemakers.
They flaunted the secessionist colors in defiance of the new laws, they

A Baltimore belle flaunts the rebel colors and
taunts the Federal occupation troops.
Harper's Weekly

teased the troops, they sang songs to the South. Hetty had entered the
realm of Baltimore legend that year when she brazenly waved a Confederate flag from the window of her Hamilton Terrace home while
Federal officers walked past. The appalled junior officers wanted to
arrest her. But the colonel looked up and declared, "No, she's beautiful
enough to do as she damned well pleases!"

James Ryder Randall, an expatriate Baltimorean, had penned an
angry, state-patriotic poem on the heels of April 19. But it was Hetty's
sister Jennie who, by adjusting the refrain and putting the words to the

college song "Lauriger Horatius," turned Randall's "Maryland, My Maryland" into something that could make homesick soldiers cry.

Their brother Wilson Miles would soon distinguish himself in the Confederate army, eventually serving on the headquarters staff of Robert E. Lee, right up to the bitter end. And the Cary sisters, with their Virginia cousin Constance Cary Harrison, would soon be the undisputed triumvirate of Southern beauty in the Confederate capital. On the night of July 3, 1861, Hetty, Jennie, and Wilson Miles Cary made their crossing, secreting themselves through Southern Maryland and smuggling the supplies across the river.

While Southern agitators headed south or were herded to McHenry, the pro-Union element in Baltimore honored the Fourth of July and redressed the wrongs of April 19 by presenting a beautiful silk flag to the Sixth Massachusetts Regiment, still stationed out at Relay House. The April 19 bloodletting, that fresh stain on a city's already raucous reputation, still demanded remorse and retribution. A barber named Neale Green was enjoying holiday time on the beach at Fair Haven in Anne Arundel County. Green was suspected of having been a leading belligerent during the Baltimore riot. So Lieutenant Thomas Carmichael and John Horner—men representing Baltimore's new, pro-Union police force—now set out to bring the barber in.

With a detachment of policemen, they left port for dangerous waters seeming all the more dangerous in the wake of the *St. Nicholas* incident. "Piracy of the worst form," General Nathaniel Banks had called it. The waterfront buzzed with talk of the French Lady. Zarvona was expected to strike again, and soon. He and his crew were rumored to be at large on the Bay, in a pungy, seeking prey. Steamboat captains coming out of Baltimore were wary.

At Fair Haven, Carmichael and Horner got their barber. They arrested him and boarded the steamer *Mary Washington* to take him back to Baltimore. *Mary Washington* was the same steamer that had carried George Hollins south when he had left to join the Confederate Navy and had put forth the *St. Nicholas* plan. Now, coincidentally, *Mary Washington* had among her passengers Captain Kirwan, unseated skipper of the captured *St. Nicholas*, and two of his officers, released from Richmond and on their way back north.

Even more coincidentally, Zarvona himself and some of his men were also on board.

Kirwan and company recognized their *St. Nicholas* captors and told Carmichael, who instantly ordered the captain to dock her at Fort McHenry when arriving at Baltimore. Now a passenger stepped forward, demanding of Carmichael by what authority he had ordered the change of course. Carmichael replied that he represented the authority of Provost Marshal Kenly. The passenger drew a pistol. Women screamed. The passenger brandished the gun and threatened to throw Carmichael into the Bay. As women screamed and ran from the cabin, the lawmen drew their guns and aimed at the passenger. Under the disguise was Zarvona. His men gathered around him. Some of the male passengers surged forth to aid the police officers. Outnumbered and surrounded, the rebels were kept at bay until the steamer arrived at Fort McHenry. General Banks ordered an infantry company onto the vessel, and the rebels were arrested. All of them, that is, except Zarvona: He had disappeared.

The boat was searched for an hour and a half. They finally found him in the ladies' cabin, in a bureau. He was taken prisoner and held at the fort on piracy charges. Later, the piracy charges were dropped, and Zarvona was handed down an indictment from the U.S. District Court on a charge of treason. It changed his status from sea robber to political prisoner.

He eventually was transferred to Fort Lafayette. In April 1862 he nearly escaped, leaping off the sea-wall and swimming toward Long Island in a pounding storm. He was recaptured and remained a prisoner until 1863. After his release, Zarvona faded into obscurity. He was said to have turned up in Europe during the Franco-Prussian War.

Before Zarvona's capture, word had come from the Point Lookout dock that his next target was to be the Baltimore steamer *George Weems*. As she came downriver on her return run from Washington, Lieutenant L. B. Lowry of the Potomac Flotilla boarded her and warned her captain. There was a hostile reception on deck. "All steamers running from Baltimore should have a guard of United States soldiers on board," noted the lieutenant. "I observed sufficient from the manner and bearing of the passengers to satisfy me that all were enemies of our flag and the Union. The women did not hesitate to insult us by sneering remarks and cries of three cheers for Jeff. Davis."

Hollins and Zarvona and company were inspiring imitators, or at least fearful rumor of imitators. Secretary Welles received a memorandum "from a responsible source" warning of "a man of notoriously bad character named James C. Hurry, a resident of Baltimore." Hurry had laid plans to capture a steamboat on the Baltimore-Patuxent run; his men would board the boat either at Baltimore or at Millstone Landing on the Patuxent. "This Millstone Landing, or Point, is a position whence more smuggling of men and provisions is carried out than any other place in the Chesapeake waters," read the memorandum. "Small vessels are constantly plying between that position and the Rappahannock and Coan rivers."

Illicit trade flourished now, borne by too many smugglers in too many boats to control among myriad coves, creeks, and harbors of an inland sea where North met South. Dixie wanted for supplies, and there were plenty of Chesapeake men willing to load up their log canoes and run the gunboat gauntlet, whether for Southern patriotism or pecuniary profit.

"A pungy boat and schooner load with goods in Baltimore, clear for Deal's Island or Snow Hill, stop at Tangier beach inside the harbor, and wait for a suitable night, then run across the bay and enter the mouth of York River and discharge in Mobjack Bay, and at other times land in East River," a Baltimore citizen wrote Welles, describing one of the countless smuggling routes that were forming by the summer of 1861. An indigenous craft might turn out to be ideally suited for this new world of unlawful activity. You could fool a night watch the same way you fooled waterfowl. A guard sergeant on the Potomac said of the smugglers, "They use punts or low ducking boats, by which a person is enabled to pass within a short distance of a sentinel without being observed."

Captain Thomas T. Craven, appointed to replace the late Ward as Potomac Flotilla commander, was patrolling off the mouth of the Patuxent in mid-July when an oysterman gave him a tip: Two "suspicious" schooners were at anchor in the Nanticoke River on the Eastern Shore. He quickly crossed the Bay and steamed up the Nanticoke to about five miles above Vienna, and there they were: a pair of schooners laden with kettles, nails, and nearly one hundred tons of pig iron—Richmond-bound, according to the interrogated schooner crewman. One of the vessels had loaded in Philadelphia, the other in Baltimore. Craven seized them and had them taken to the Washington Navy Yard. He sent *Resolute* up the Eastern Shore's Wicomico River, where a schooner was reportedly loaded with ammunition for the rebels. He then detailed *Pawnee* to patrol the Bay from Smiths Point to the mouth of the Rappahannock, "where I am satisfied from information obtained while in Nanticoke, the greater part of the supplies furnished the rebels is conveyed from the eastern shore or Tangier Sound."

The schooner seizure had been instructive; it had shown Craven that the Eastern Shore was a smuggler's paradise. "Those points—Tangier and Pocomoke sounds—require a thorough examination, and as I can spare the vessels, a search will be made."

Not all Eastern Shore trickery was aimed westward across the Bay. Some illegal trafficking flowed straight south, across the state line. For such was the geographic/political uniqueness of the Eastern Shore. Its furthermost stretch—the long, jagged-edged strip that was the breaker between Chesapeake Bay and Atlantic Ocean—was of course nothing less than an isolated, remote piece of the Confederacy. The Eastern Shore of Virginia dangled out there by itself, flat, nondescript, narrow—but important in the potential threat it held by virtue of its location. It ended at Cape Charles at the mouth of the Bay. It offered back-door ingress to Maryland's eastern portion, as well as Delaware, and posed all sorts of potential for troublemaking in those quarters.

Unique maritime trickery arose around it. Winfield Scott in July received a letter from a concerned Eastern Shore citizen who had learned from the port collector at Snow Hill on Maryland's lower Eastern Shore "that provisions, ammunition, etc., are now carried to various parts of the eastern shore of Virginia by vessels owned by the rebels, who, by a fictitious sale of the vessel to citizens of Maryland, have their vessels licensed from this State."

Along with a fecund smuggling environment, the line where the Eastern Shores of Maryland and Virginia met was a natural crossing point for men as well as matériel. The letter to Scott warned that "there are 800 men drilling daily at Eastville, Northampton County, Va., and that enlistments are being made from Worcester County, Md., which borders upon Virginia. Not less than six young men left Snow Hill for that place during last week. . . . There is constant communication between the rebels there and secret traitors in this State, by which means information is carried to the western shore of Virginia by means of canoes across the Chesapeake. . . ."

The Union faithful among lower Eastern Shore Marylanders sensed an invasion looming. "It is feared by many here that there will be a movement from Eastville upward through this peninsula," Scott read in the letter. "It would find this part of the state entirely without protection, as the people in general are almost entirely destitute of arms, even had we the necessary organization; and the invaders would find a number of sympathizers in their route through these counties to render persons and property exceedingly unsafe."

If the rebs crossed the border and ascended the peninsula, they could expect the support of kindred spirits such as Humphrey Humphreys. A Salisbury man, Humphreys was "a colonel of militia and violent secessionist," who had a four-pounder field cannon stashed someplace and had been hankering to put it into action since getting his call to arms last April from Tench Tilghman in Talbot, and then being told to lie low once the Federal troops had taken control at Baltimore. Salisbury, the Delaware Railroad's southern terminus, was a hub of illegal trafficking by secessionists.

On July 23 an officer sensitive to the Eastern Shore situation took over at Baltimore. Major General John Adams Dix, a New Yorker, was in command of the Department of Maryland just a week when he began sounding the warning to the secretary of war. There were good Union men on the shore, organized and drilling, but they needed arming to do any good. "Governor Hicks thinks it important, and I concur with him. If I had the authority to arm eight or ten companies on the Eastern Shore of Maryland, I believe they could take care of themselves and do much to keep the secessionists in order."

The growing threat across the border alarmed Dix as well. "There is a camp of secessionists, variously estimated from one thousand to three thousand men, at Eastville, in Northampton, the lower county of the

MAJOR GENERAL JOHN A. DIX, THE DEPARTMENT
OF MARYLAND COMMANDER WHO SAW THE
IMPORTANCE OF QUELLING THE REBEL
ELEMENT ON THE EASTERN SHORE.
National Archives

Eastern Shore of Virginia. This is not in my department, but I would
suggest that three or four regiments should be sent there as soon as we
can spare them and break up this camp. The exhibition of such a force
and the destruction of the secession camp would have a salutary effect
throughout the Eastern Shore of Maryland and Virginia."

Potomac Flotilla patrols were likewise yielding late-July warnings.
Acting Master William Budd reconnoitered the lower Eastern Shore in
the USS *Resolute*, and the riverside got pretty hazardous. *Resolute* had

run up the Pocomoke and was on her way back down when she barely missed a greeting party of six hundred Virginia riflemen with a couple of fieldpieces rolled up from Horntown just for the occasion. But Budd caught wind of their approach and slipped downriver in the dead of night "below the point of danger. The insurgents came, but too late." Now safely out of there, with fresh intelligence and three captured reb-supplying vessels, Budd informed the secretary of the navy of the smugglers' pipeline running from Maryland down into Accomac County, Virginia, and from there across the Bay "in small schooners and large rowboats" by way of the Onancock, Pungoteague, and Cherrystone inlets, to the Rappahannock and the York.

Budd had learned that "a person named Wilson, proprietor of the Washington House at Princess Anne, Md., receives and harbors supplies and recruits. He forwards them by hacks and wagons to Newtown, Md. At the latter place H. Dryden, of the Union Hotel, forwards them to Virginia. Virginia hacks and wagons come and go to and from Newtown; the men and arms pass through daily."

Through phony licenses issued by the U. S. collector at Deal Island, Virginia owners registered as Maryland owners were loading up their vessels in Baltimore and running supplies to the rebels, Budd had ascertained. "In the river Wicomico, at Salisbury, a person named Parker is engaged in forwarding supplies obtained from Baltimore to Virginia." In addition to the zigzagging Bay route, the supplies were smuggled from up North to Chincoteague on the Atlantic coast, then overland across the Virginia Eastern Shore, where they were loaded onto Bay-crossing boats. "It is a matter of notoriety that articles of all kinds are constantly transmitted by way of Delaware and Maryland into eastern Virginia," Hiram Barney, custom-house collector in New York City, complained to Treasury Secretary Salmon P. Chase. From New York Harbor the coasters made their daily runs to the unguarded nooks and crannies of the Delaware shore, or directly to Virginia's Sinepuxent and Chincoteague bays.

It was all done with a cavalier blatancy, much to the chagrin of the New York official. "To such an extent is this course pursued that Southern merchants come continually to this city to make purchases of goods, and prepare for their being forwarded to their homes with contemptuous disregard of the restrictions sought to be imposed upon them." Though flagrant in their purpose, the smugglers were confounding the collector by, "of course, affording no such evidence of that purpose as to warrant me in detaining them."

While illegal cargoes funneled down by land, sea, and bay, the rebel ranks were gathering and growing on the lower Eastern Shore. "There is a camp of insurgents near Eastville, one at Horntown, one at Drummond Town, also at Pungoteague and Onancock inlets; they are, as far as I could ascertain, well supplied with arms," reported Budd. "The inhabitants of Tangier and Watt's islands are constantly threatened with attacks from marauding parties from east Virginia. They are able to give plenty of information, and would hail with delight the appearance of a couple of our small steamers, who, by cruising in Tangier and Pocomoke sounds, would effectually stop the passage of supplies and protect them at the same time."

Throughout the Chesapeake, goods were pouring south, and clearly, extreme vigilance was the only hope for at least fractionally staunching the flow. As an example of the importance of examining cargoes, Secretary Welles related to Craven the story of the schooner *Buena Vista*, out of Baltimore for St. Marys.

Craven's predecessor, the late Ward, had thought *Buena Vista* suspicious and had seized her. His instincts had been good: "Barrels purporting to contain whisky were filled with pistols."

To help stop the smuggling, the army sent out a boat-burning expedition from Fort Monroe up Back Creek by barge transport on July 24. The party destroyed and captured several smuggling vessels while rebel scouts looked on. It was the latest in a series of post–Big Bethel forays from Fort Monroe. Old Point Comfort was all hustle and bustle now, swarming with soldiers and ships. The new telegraph line linked the fort to the mainland for the first time in history. The grandiose Hygiea Hotel, the fort's neighbor, had been partially converted into a hospital for the troops, whose continual probing ventures on the York-James peninsula inevitably yielded clashes with the rebels, present in great abundance just a few short miles away.

SOLDIERS EAGERLY RECEIVE LETTERS AND PACKAGES AT
THE ADAMS EXPRESS OFFICE IN FORT MONROE.
Frank Leslie's Illustrated Newpaper

In a July 5 skirmish with the Louisiana and Georgia soldiers lying in ambush at Curtis's farm near Newport News, the Louisiana commander, Lieutenant-Colonel Charles Dreux, had lost his life. In another skirmish near Newport News on July 12, a wood-gathering party from the New York Seventh went farther than their orders allowed and had a run-in with Major John B. Hood's cavalry. Hood routed the patrol, killing and wounding some, capturing others. It gained for his commanding officer, General Magruder, the praise of Robert E. Lee, who called it a "brilliant skirmish" and instructed Magruder to "express to Major Hood and the gallant men who were engaged in the affair the pleasure which their conduct has given both myself and the President."

Any movements around Monroe were about to become subject to change. When the war's first big battle was waged on July 21 and the Federals retreated in sloppy haste from Bull Run, it left the capital feeling somewhat vulnerable. From a fearful Washington City came General

Scott's telegram to Butler ordering him to send troops right away, by steamer from Fort Monroe to Baltimore, then by rail from Baltimore to Washington. Butler sent the regiments on July 26 and, his own numbers now weakened, abandoned the town of Hampton. He feared a Federal reduction in the lower Chesapeake would encourage a Confederate advance, and on July 29 he was proven right.

Magruder sent a two thousand-man reconnaissance force down the peninsula. As the rebels advanced they were watched from above by John LaMountain, pioneer of airborne reconnaissance, in his hot-air balloon.

On the second day of the push, on his left flank, Magruder came across a copy of the *New York Herald Tribune* and read with disdain an (erroneous) article about how Butler planned to turn Hampton into a runaway-slave camp. Hampton "being under the guns of Fort Monroe, it could not be held by us even if taken," figured Magruder. "I determined to burn it at once."

The remaining inhabitants were warned. Those too old or feeble to evacuate were helped. Then the historic old Southern town was put to the torch by Southerners.

"A more wanton and unnecessary act than the burning, as it seems to me, could not have been committed," wrote Butler. ". . . I confess myself so poor a soldier as not to be able to discern the strategic importance of this movement."

Colonel J. W. Phelps of the First Vermont Infantry was also stunned: "The barbarous fierceness of spirit which they have exhibited in the destruction of Hampton, one of the oldest towns of Virginia, and which connects her history with a glorious past, cannot fail to injure their cause."

When not tangling with smugglers and ship-stealers, the Potomac Flotilla had another severe annoyance to deal with: the Confederate shore batteries. Rebel guns ruled the lower Potomac, effectively scotching the thought of any major waterborne troop movement from the capital and threatening all transport to and from Washington. Hot exchanges between flotilla vessels and Confederate cannoneers were frequent, such as on July 29, when *Yankee* and *Reliance* traded shots with an accidentally discovered rebel battery at the mouth of Potomac Creek. Heavy guns along the water routes kept the flotilla busy and weighed heavily on strategy decisions in Washington.

On August 10 Budd took *Resolute* into the mouth of the lower Machodoc River. As the boat entered, the musket fire began from shore. Budd had come to shut down a receiving depot where men and goods were being landed after crossing over from Herring Creek on the Maryland side. Amid gunfire, reported Budd, "I landed, destroyed the premises, and captured a large boat that arrived from Maryland the night before." A band of Maryland secessionists were on the premises; they tore off through the woods as the Federals approached, and Budd gave up the chase after about a mile. He did, however, come away with ten contrabands, who were slaves of Colonel Brown, owner of the home-cum-smuggling den. And with the freed slaves came information: "The foreman of the contrabands, who is a remarkably intelligent negro, informs me that an expedition is organized in Machodoc to capture any of the schooners that are anchored or becalmed in that vicinity."

On the other end of the Herring Creek–Machodoc smuggling route, another contraband was coming forth with information. At sunset on the eleventh the Southern Maryland slave came aboard *Yankee*, anchored off Piney Point. He convinced Commander Craven's steward to let him come before the commander. The slave had details, named names. "He stated that there was at Herring Creek one Maddox, an Irishman, who has been quite active in procuring supplies of men, munitions of war, clothing, etc., for the rebels, and that he has sent many boat loads of them over to Virginia; that on Tuesday last he sent eight wagons and sixteen horses to Maryland Point (one wagon was loaded with uniforms), and on the same day eight men, who came from Baltimore, were sent across the river," recounted the commander. The informant had more to tell: Maddox was in league with a Dr. Combe or Coombs, "who has appropriated an old outhouse as a barrack for the reception of volunteers for the rebel Army." Maddox and the doctor "employ their negroes, horses, and wagons in transporting recruits to the various landings, at night, watching their opportunity when our cruisers are out of sight." There were others in on it: the Hughes brothers; a man named Johnson, who harbored recruits; and a man named Bell, who floated from place to place. There were smugglers' boats in Herring Creek now, fresh from the Virginia shore. Johnson's house currently was harboring the boats' owners as well as "a minister who came from Virginia and acts as a spy." Craven welcomed such detail. "This statement, sir, although made by a negro, has every appearance of being truthful," declared the commander in his report to the navy secretary. "I am convinced that all these persons are active participators in the rebellion and are constantly engaged in traitorous acts." Spurred by the slave's story, Craven sent out an eight-man party to seize the boats in Herring Creek. Next day, the party returned with three captured vessels. The officers of the Potomac Flotilla were learning the value of listening to what the contrabands had to tell them.

And Craven was arriving at a conclusion: "From all I can see and learn of the people of Maryland I am convinced that along the shores of the Potomac there is not one in twenty who is true to the Union, and I sometimes think there are many hundreds of them thoroughly organized into companies, perhaps regiments, and prepared to act against the Government at any moment."

With the Maryland shore of the lower Potomac as hostile as the Virginia shore, the threat of an invading force crossing here—into a territory that would more welcome than resist it—was real. The fear of trouble coming up from here was exacerbated by a message, dated August 13 and sent to the assistant secretary of war, who forwarded it to Navy Secretary Welles, who passed it on to Commander Craven. The message quoted a statement made two days earlier by Jefferson Davis:

"Have no street fights; keep Baltimore quiet for the present; in ten days I shall command the Potomac and cross between Mathias Point and Aquia Creek into Charles and St. Mary's counties (they are all friends there) and march upon Annapolis. Then, having two of the approaches to Washington in possession, let Baltimore rise and burn the bridges. The movements in the upper Potomac are only feints."

The intercepted missive had come from an "unquestionable" source, Craven was informed. The same source had avowed that "a regular communication exists by means of the St. Marys steamboat line from Baltimore up the Patuxent and then in an open boat from Port Tobacco to the Virginia shore after the police boat has passed."

On August 16 Governor Hicks sounded the same alarm bell in a message to War Secretary Simon Cameron: "I am advised . . . that the Confederate forces south of the Potomac and the disloyal men of Maryland are acting in vigilant concert, with a design to make a descent upon Maryland at some point, most likely . . . to be from St. Mary's or Charles counties." The governor advised that the number of troops and patrol vessels be beefed up from Washington to the mouth of the Potomac. But his admonishments did not end there, for Hicks was convinced the invasion would be two-pronged, coming north up both sides of the Bay. Thus he was compelled to "advise an increased force of men and vessels to watch the two eastern shore counties of Virginia in General Butler's division. The 20th instant is the time designated by them for assault. Do not think me scared; I only wish to head off the rebels."

Two hundred marines would soon be sent down from the Washington Navy Yard to the lower Potomac, and the U.S. Army would soon plant its flag in Southern Maryland. All that the Potomac Flotilla could do, meantime, was keep on patrolling. On August 15 Budd took *Resolute* down past Mathias Point and spotted a schooner gone aground near Persimmon Point on the Virginia shore. He sent a six-man boat party to free the schooner, which was right up against the shoreline. The men from *Resolute* came up alongside and were making fast to the schooner when they were blasted by musket fire from the bushes just five yards away. Three men dropped, instantly killed; another was wounded. From *Resolute*, Budd opened fire, shell-bombing the bushes, routing the rebel snipers. "After four or five rounds they were driven out, running in parties of three and four in different directions, some of them running into some dwelling houses on the right," recounted Budd. As he continued throwing shell at the shore, the surviving crewmen in the boat party managed to get the schooner off. *Reliance* came upriver now, joined in on the shore-shelling, and sent out a boat to help take the schooner out.

The boat Budd had sent came back riddled with holes. Along a hostile waterfront, you never knew which bush was going to shoot at you.

Of course, not everyone along the border shore was a rebel. One Union bastion was St. George Island, a narrow spit running parallel to the Maryland mainland just below secessionist-friendly Herring Creek. The loyal citizens of St. George were being threatened by Captain

Edward Code—smuggler, cavalry company commander, and influential Maryland rebel. (He also happened to be the father-in-law of the Herring Creek smuggler Dr. Coombs.) The islanders petitioned the protection of the U.S. schooner *Dana*. Since this was the Maryland shore, searching private property was problematic. "Force, therefore, being out of the question, we determined to try a stratagem," recalled Acting Master's Mate Robert Ely of *Dana*. Accompanied by sympathetic locals, Ely and two of his men posed as Southern sympathizers and paid Captain Code a visit.

It was a rain-soaked August night; a boatload of armed men waited in St. George Creek in case Ely got himself into a jam. At Code's house, Ely pretended to be "Captain Williams, of the schooner *John Grant*, a good secessionist, and bound to Coan River with bacon and salt from Port Tobacco." After questioning his visitor on how he had eluded the flotilla, Captain Code was convinced. "He complimented me on my sagacity and said it rejoiced him to meet a man of my stamp and wished me all possible success."

The night wore on; the captain grew expansive. "He freely expressed his sentiments to me, offered us wine and cigars, and gave me much valuable information as to the state of feeling in his neighborhood; told me that several parties had crossed from his immediate vicinity and expressed his sympathy for them, and from the tenor of his conversation I was led to believe that there were organized companies of armed men ready to cooperate with any forces which might land from Virginia in an attack upon the Government. . . ."

Dawn was coming. Ely made ready to leave, and in a closing effort to entrap the captain, "offered to carry any goods or letters he might wish to send over to Virginia." The captain cannily said no, but told his guest he could acquire a smuggler's load up the St. Marys River. "I may speak to a Union man and get myself in trouble," Ely played along. Captain Code reassured him that with few exceptions (the St. George Islanders included), "You can not find a Union man from Breton's Bay to Point Lookout. . . ."

Down at the Norfolk Navy Yard, Flag Officer French Forrest of the bottled-up Confederate States Navy had a hankering to push the cork.

He told Ordnance Inspector Archibald Fairfax to take one of the rifled guns and thirty rounds of ammo and put it all on the steam tug *Harmony*. The target: the big Federal frigate *Savannah*, at anchor off Newport News. Their objective: "Do her as much damage as possible."

So they unfurled the Confederate flag on the little tugboat, bristling with a bow gun now, and steamed down past Craney Island, hugging the coastal shoal water to Pig Point. Then, at midday on August 30, coming close as she could while staying out of range, *Harmony* commenced firing on the Federal frigate. The rebs blasted away for forty-five minutes, their shot splintering *Savannah*'s mainmast, ripping into her rigging, smashing under the port forechains, knocking the bow off one of the launches, and exploding under the port quarter with a deck-jarring authority. The *Savannah* crew fired back with every gun they could bring to bear, but the fire fell short, "much to the mortification of all on board," said the *Savannah*'s captain. He watched as the little tug steamed off, cocky and unscathed, throwing her remaining two shells at the shipping off Fort Monroe.

At the fort, there was a new general in charge now. Butler had suggested that the lower Chesapeake was too crucial a theater to entrust to a citizen-soldier such as himself, and on August 16, per his wishes, he had been replaced. He remained in command of the forces encamped on the mainland fringing Old Point Comfort. On August 26, Butler shipped out in command of nearly nine hundred troops with an eight-vessel naval squadron under Flag Officer Silas Stringham, destination Cape Hatteras. Butler's departure signaled not only the beginning of a new phase of importance for Fort Monroe—as the embarkation point for operations along the Carolina coast—but the passing of Ben Butler from the Chesapeake, where he had played so big and varied a part since the war's outset. From Annapolis to Baltimore to Hampton Roads, he had made his presence felt. He had "saved" Annapolis and "conquered" Baltimore. He had seen to it that the railroad and the telegraph lines ran out to Fort Monroe, and he had set up the Union encampments on the mainland beyond the fort. Through his encouragement and endorsement, Butler had been instrumental in LaMountain's pioneering balloon ascensions. The political course of the war had been changed with Butler's legal-legerdemain logic conjuring up the far-reaching "contraband of war" ruling. With this string of accomplishments, the ungainly general with the keen brain had strode flamboyantly across the Chesapeake stage in 1861. He exited at the head of the land phase of the first combined army-navy amphibious operation of the war. He would be back.

Stringham, for his part, resigned amid criticism after his return. The Atlantic Blockading Squadron he had commanded was divided into northern and southern divisions, the Carolinas' border the divisional demarcation. Louis M. Goldsborough, whose long career's highlights included Mexican War service and a stint as Naval Academy superindendent, was named flag officer of the newly designated North Atlantic Blockading Squadron, effective September 23.

The Fort Monroe that Ben Butler left behind was in better shape than he had found it, better suited now for its increasingly crucial role. As an offensive base, it would only become more important. As a defensive position, it was choking the water route to the Confederate capital, which meant trouble in the form of C.S. Navy breakout attempts, blockade-running, and random destructive attacks such as the tug *Harmony's* David-Goliath episode with the Union frigate.

Major General John E. Wool, the hoary, efficient Mexican War veteran who was Butler's successor in command at Hampton Roads, declared, "This is the most important position on the coast."

He was right about another thing, too: "The rebels have several vessels which they are anxious to get to sea and only wait a favorable moment to accomplish their designs."

When Maryland didn't secede that spring, Franklin Buchanan sat in the Talbot County comfort of his self-induced retirement and had second thoughts. He wrote a letter to the secretary of the navy: "If my resignation has not been accepted by the President, I respectfully recall it; the circumstances which induced me, very reluctantly, to tender it no longer exist, and I cannot voluntarily withdraw from a service in which I have spent nearly forty-seven years of my life in the faithful performance of duty, as the records of the Navy Department will prove."

The reply was curt: "By direction of the President your name has been stricken from the rolls of the navy."

Major General John E. Wool said of
Hampton Roads: "This is the most
important position on the coast."
National Archives

That summer, as the thought of it—the cold sting of it—sank in, and
as Federal troops came plundering past his home and he had to angrily
chase them off, Buchanan decided. On August 31 he went before the
justice of the peace in Easton and signed over all his property and
possessions to his wife and children. If he left it in his name, the state
could confiscate it for what he was about to do. He said his good-byes
and went south.

John Taylor Wood and his father quit talking to each other that
summer. The father couldn't forgive the son's resignation from the

service. John Taylor Wood wandered around the state, staying with friends and relatives below Baltimore and on the Eastern Shore. He bought a Colt revolver, paid up his bills, buried his silver, and headed south with his wife and children on September 3. They crossed the Potomac at night in an open boat. A storm struck, and they lost baggage and were drenched when they reached the other country on the opposite shore.

A Deal Island schooner master named Potts told the Potomac Flotilla commander about a smugglers' vessel: the sloop *T. J. Evans*, Baltimore registry, anchored presently off Holland Island. Craven ordered Acting Master's Mate Ely on *Dana* to sail over to the Eastern Shore and seize the sloop. He found her aground off Clay Island, and her owner, George Henry, in the custody of the magistrate. Islanders in canoes had chased down the smuggler and detained him. Ely already had Henry's cohort captured. With his two prisoners and prize sloop, Ely headed back across the Bay to Piney Point. George Henry claimed to be too sick to eat the salt-heavy schooner fare and asked to go ashore for his supper. Ely consented, accompanying the prisoner to the hotel at Piney Point. They dined together, topping it off with tea. Then George Henry asked permission to step outside to "fulfill the call of nature." Ely honored the urgent request, but followed his prisoner outside, of course.

Nonetheless, he had to report, "Favored by the darkness and the thick growth of trees, I am sorry to say that he succeeded in making good his escape."

Based on information given by others on board *Dana*, Craven regretted to report that "there appears to be strong ground for suspecting Mr. Ely of having been bribed by the rebel to allow him to escape."

Friday, September 13, started poorly for Francis Key Howard, editor of the Baltimore *Exchange*. At around half past midnight or one o'clock in the morning his doorbell rang.

He went to the bedroom window. The man on the porch below said he had a message from Baltimore delegate Severn Teackle Wallis. Howard went down and opened the door. The man had lied. He had no message. What he did have was an order for Howard's arrest.

Armed men swarmed into the house and ransacked it. Howard's wife was by his side when the men told him he had to go to Fort McHenry. He was allowed to go back upstairs to dress and pack, one of the men accompanying him. Upstairs, a man stood guard in the doorway to the children's room. The outraged editor was taken outside and put into the waiting carriage. "Two men, wearing the badges of the police force which the Government had organized, escorted me to the Fort," recalled Howard. "It was with a bitter pang that I left my house in possession of the miscreants who had invaded it."

When he reached the fort, he found friends of his there, just roused from their beds as he had been, rounded up and locked up through the early morning hours and into the day. The state legislature was due to meet on the seventeenth—it looked like most of the Baltimore delegation would not be able to attend.

The order had come down from War Secretary Cameron: "The passage of any act of secession by the legislature of Maryland must be prevented. If necessary, all or any part of the members must be arrested." So here they were, crammed into a couple of adjoining rooms at McHenry: Severn Teackle Wallis, Ross Winans, Henry Warfield, Lawrence Sangston, Charles Pitts, John Hanson Thomas, Leonard Quinlan, T. Parkin Scott, William Harrison, Robert Denison—bankers, merchants, lawyers, the secession-minded members of the legislature. Joining them in incarceration were Mayor Brown, Congressman Henry May, physician and state senator Andrew Lynch, firebrand editor Thomas Hall of the *South*, and Howard of the *Exchange*. No charges were brought against any of them; their opinions, and the vociferous expression of such, had rendered them guests of the fort. "But neither I, nor those who were afterwards my fellow prisoners, ever violated in any way, the Constitution or the laws," declared Howard. "We defended the rights of our State, and criticized the policy of the Administration at Washington. We advanced our views with perfect freedom, as we had the right to do, and we did no more."

The *Exchange* and the *South* were two of the most outspoken, stridently anti-Lincoln papers in the city. They railed against the rail-splitter, his administration, and his war with untempered ferocity. Loudly and often, they argued for Maryland's secession. The *Exchange* had been in circulation since before the war. The *South* had first hit the streets in late April of 1861, existing to espouse the Confederate cause. In the context of wartime, and a borderland of volatile public opinion, the newspapers' clamorous vitriol was deemed pure treason. There were other sheets in town doling out like-minded diatribes; many of them, too, would eventually be silenced. But the *South* and the *Exchange* were the first to be made examples of.

Allan Pinkerton, who oversaw the arrests, also rifled through the two papers' newsrooms and pressrooms on Baltimore Street in search of damning material. He found plenty, including a list of pro-secessionist Baltimoreans and, in Howard's office, papers pertaining to the legislature and the possibility of secession. The Baltimore delegates comprised just part of the sweep; thirty-one members in all were arrested, many of them already in Frederick for the opening of the legislative session. There would be no vote for secession—nor even talk of secession, for that matter—at this stripped-down gathering.

Citizen John Merryman had been arrested back on May 25, charged with treason, and taken to Fort McHenry. A writ of habeas corpus was issued. Major General George Cadwalader—the post-Butler, pre-Banks Baltimore military commander—had tossed back Merryman's writ. Constitution or no, this was war. It was the start of the clampdown.

The Federal military authority was growing. Since taking over the Department of Maryland in July, General Dix had outlawed secession flags and rebel song sheets in Baltimore; had transformed Federal Hill into a formidable barricade to augment its neighbor, Fort McHenry; had built additional fortifications to further dominate downtown and the waterfront; and had arrested so many dissident citizens that Fort McHenry was bursting at the seams. Less than a week before the members of the legislature were rounded up into the fort, Dix had written General George B. McClellan to lament the overcrowding of prisoners. "What is to be done with them? Every room is full, and we had about fifty prisoners last night in tents on the parade ground with hardly room left for the guard to parade."

Somehow they found temporary space for the politicians and prose-lytizers arrested on September 13. The two rooms into which they were corraled shared a balcony. Guards were posted on it, and the prisoners

FEDERAL HILL, BALTIMORE, BARRICADED AND OCCUPIED BY DIX'S TROOPS.
Frank Leslie's Illustrated Newspaper

were allowed to come out on the balcony. As Francis Key Howard stood on the balcony, he thought about the man he was named after:

> When I looked out in the morning, I could not help being struck by an odd, and not pleasant coincidence. On that day, forty-seven years before, my grand-father, Mr. F. S. Key, then a prisoner on a British ship, had witnessed the bombardment of Fort McHenry. When, on the following morning, the hostile fleet drew off, defeated, he wrote the song so long popular throughout the country, 'Star Spangled Banner.' As I stood upon the very scene of that conflict, I could not but contrast my position with his, forty-seven years before. The flag which he had then so proudly hailed, I saw waving, at the same place, over the victims of as vulgar and brutal a despotism as modern times have witnessed.

Loved ones showed up at the fort and were permitted to talk to the prisoners on the balcony from the parade ground below while the commanding officer looked on. That afternoon the prisoners were told they were being sent to Fort Monroe. They were shipped out that evening on the steamer *Adelaide*. Through the night, as the steamer carried them down the Bay, the after-cabin where they were confined was actually quite comfortable. They were the last pleasant accommodations the prisoners would know for some time.

They arrived off Fort Monroe at dawn, but did not disembark until late afternoon. They were imprisoned in a pair of the thick-walled casemates. Contrabands were still cleaning out all the dirt and garbage as the prisoners were put in there. On one side, they had a view of the fort's grounds. On the other, through narrow embrasures in the thick stone, a view of the moat. The men were kept under constant guard. "For a week we never left our two casemates, for a single instant, for any purpose whatever," said Howard. "We continually remonstrated against the manner in which we were treated, and represented the fact that we were likely, under such circumstances, to suffer seriously in health. Our complaints were generally followed by some new restriction."

After a few days, the window shutters and venetian doors to the casemates were closed and sealed with iron bars and padlocks. Severn Teackle Wallis penned an entreaty to the fort provost marshal. "Some of our number are old men," the distinguished lawyer wrote, "others in delicate health; and the restraint which excludes us from air and exercise is painful enough without this new annoyance." Not only had they been largely shut off from light, the odoriferous funk of fifteen imprisoned men and no privy had been shut in. "You are aware of the disgusting necessities to which we are subjected," wrote Wallis, ". . . and you will, of course, know how much this new obstruction must add to our discomfort."

The letter garnered no response. The men wallowed in the dankness and darkness for ten days. Some light did get through, however, enough to read and write. Wallis had a copy of Byron with him, and his fellow inmates enjoyed it and understood it well when he read aloud "The Prisoner of Chillon."

On September 25 the Baltimoreans were placed on the steamer *George Peabody* and sent to Fort Lafayette in New York Harbor. They eventually ended up in Boston's Fort Warren along with the Baltimore Police Commissioners, with whom they were finally released more than a year later. The legislature, which hadn't had enough votes for a quorum when it went into session on September 17, was adjourned.

The same day the Baltimoreans were transported from Fort Monroe, a four-gun rebel shore battery at Freestone Point blasted a hole in the bow

THE STEAMER *GEORGE PEABODY* (*FOREGROUND*), WHICH TRANSPORTED THE
BALTIMORE POLITICAL PRISONERS FROM FORT MONROE TO NEW YORK.
National Archives

of the Federal steamer *Valley City* while carrying on a shooting match
with Federal gunboats in the Potomac. It all started with six shells fired
by *Jacob Bell*, breaking up a work gang that was strengthening the battery
position with shovels. When *Seminole* arrived and also started shooting,
the rebel battery began its barrage and kept it up nonstop on passing
boat traffic from sunrise to three o'clock in the afternoon. Some of the
rebel guns along the river were more nuisance than threat, making
thunderous noise but lacking the reach to wreak real havoc. The Freestone Point battery, though, had a rifled piece with some range: "Many
of their shots during their firing almost touched the Maryland shore,"
reported *Jacob Bell*'s lieutenant.

The rebel blockade of the lower Potomac was taking its toll. Washington was now having to rely almost exclusively on the railroads to get
any supplies through. It got to the point that on October 22, the day
before he exasperatedly requested a transfer, Commander Craven declared that the rebels controlled all key points on the river from Alexandria on down. General Joseph Hooker's division of the Army of the

Potomac, taking up winter quarters in Southern Maryland, stared across the river at an elusive agitator. Contemplating, then deciding against, crossing over to attack the rebel battery at Boyds Hole, Hooker realized that "the battery can be moved to the rear faster than the infantry can follow it."

The Confederate right at Shipping Point was occupied by the First Maryland Confederate Light Artillery, expatriate Marylanders manning guns pointed across the water at their home state. Like other Maryland rebs, they had organized that summer in Richmond, where a new broadsheet ballad had come out:

> We've left our homes in Maryland,
> Our friends in Baltimore,
> To take up arms for the gallant South,
> On old Virginia's shore.

While some Marylanders rallied for Dixie, some Virginians had no interest whatsoever in secession. They just wanted to sell their oysters.

In Chincoteague Inlet, a schooner was being fitted out as a privateer, and Lieutenant A. Murray determined to stop its bold career before it began. On the morning of October 5 he dispatched two boats and twenty-three men from the North Atlantic Blockading Squadron steamer *Louisiana* to go in and either capture or destroy the privateer in the making. The boats had to run in through a fierce fire thrown up by some three hundred of the enemy. They reached the schooner and she was aground; they used her as a breastwork and began firing back at the enemy. *Louisiana* pitched in with her long-range gun, and the rebels retreated, hauling their dead. Murray's sailors put the schooner to the torch. (Seriously wounded in the fracas was Acting Master Edward Hooker, who faced an eventful future in the Potomac Flotilla in particular and the navy in general.)

But the Chincoteague Inlet attackers had not been Chincoteague Islanders; the islanders, out of step with their fellow Accomac Countians, were loyal to the Union and welcomed the arrival of the Federal steamer. On October 15 they issued a signed oath of allegiance proclaiming that "by interest and affection we cling to the Union," that "we are united as one man in our abhorrence of the secession heresy," and that Murray's arrival had saved them from being overrun by their "secession neighbors." Pleading their case to the secretary of the navy, Flag Officer Goldsborough avowed that the Chincoteague Islanders were "beyond doubt, true and loyal," and pointed out that they had kept the U.S. flag flying and had allowed no other to wave over the island. "They are generally poor, and oystering is almost their sole occupation," explained Goldsborough. "They now not only ask for protection, but for permission to carry their oysters to Philadelphia and New York. . . ." Philadelphians and New Yorkers would soon have their Chincoteague oysters again. And the rest of the Virginia Eastern Shore—that contentious, dangerously located stretch that General Dix had been ruminating over since summer—would soon have its destiny decided.

The Maryland general election of November 1861 was secession's last chance. Augustus Williamson Bradford, a Harford County man, was the Unionist gubernatorial candidate. Benjamin C. Howard of Baltimore County was the candidate for the Peace Party, or State Righters, as they were called. Bradford won handily—57,502 to 26,700—and probably would have won anyway even if Federal troops had not been posted at polling places around the state to intimidate State Rights voters and to arrest them if they were too outspoken. General Hooker, making ready to maintain election order in the Howard hotbed of Southern Maryland, quipped: "I am informed that a secession barbecue will be given at what is called White Horse Tavern on election day, at which I shall take the liberty to invite a full company of Indiana cavalry."

The Unionist candidates swept into the state legislature as well as the governor's mansion. Maryland soldiers in the field were given three days' furlough to go home and vote. Maryland rebels who had left the state would be arrested if they showed up at their polling places. Bradford had a lot of support, he ran a good race, and he won all but four counties—Talbot on the Eastern Shore and St. Mary's, Calvert, and Charles in Southern Maryland. All in all, the election passed fairly peacefully, though some citizens were arrested for toting weapons to the polls, for drunkenness, and for "treasonable language." At Prince Frederick in Calvert

County, the Honorable Augustus R. Sollers, a former member of Congress, went a little bit wild, spewing rebellious invective while brandishing a large knife, slashing the air with it. He was arrested by Federal soldiers and taken to Lower Marlborough, but his gout had flared up so badly that they let him go.

Voter intimidation, illegal use of the military, and reports of illegal voting by nonresident soldiers had all been part of the day, but could not completely taint the Unionists' wide-margin victory. Only in the occasional isolated case could the state's pro-Southern element really cry foul. In Annapolis, nine U.S. Navy sailors came ashore from the Receiving Ship *Alleghany* and voted Union. The nine bluejackets were nonresidents, and their votes were illegal. They were also all that was needed to swing the election: The Union senatorial candidate for Anne Arundel County won by just six votes; the Union candidate for House of Delegates for Anne Arundel won by four. The sailors' unlawful votes were challenged. The challenge was overruled.

Two days before the election, General Dix had ordered Colonel Halbert Paine's Fourth Regiment Wisconsin Volunteers to take fifteen days' rations and head to the lower Eastern Shore. Also on board for the expedition were Captain Richards's Independent Cavalry and Captain Nim's Massachusetts Light Artillery battery, Boston soldiers with a half-dozen brass rifled fieldpieces. The general instructed them to make sure there was no mass migration of Virginia Eastern Shoremen across the state line "with a view to carry the election of the 6th . . . by spurious votes."

Beyond election day, the expeditionary force was acting as the vanguard of a larger deployment, some 4,500 men in all, coming from Baltimore on the steamer *Pocahontas* to invade the Eastern Shore of Virginia once and for all.

They assembled in Newtown, the closest Maryland hamlet to the state line, on November 13 under the command of Brigadier General Henry H. Lockwood. The brigadier general was a Delaware man, a mathematics professor attached to the U.S. Navy when the war broke out. He had resigned, gone home, and joined the state volunteer militia. Since August, when he was commissioned brigadier general of volunteers, Lockwood had been stationed at Cambridge, heading the camp of

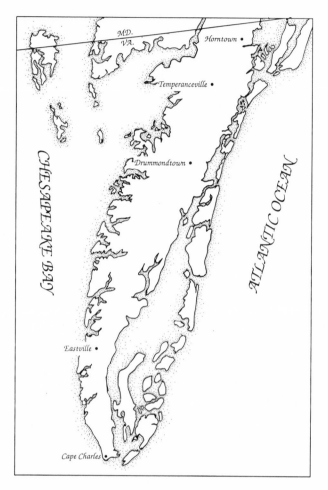

THE EASTERN SHORE OF VIRGINIA

instruction there while providing important information on the Eastern Shore state of affairs to Dix in Baltimore.

Before the Virginia invasion, Dix summoned Lockwood to Baltimore to personally hand him his instructions. Among the obvious objectives—breaking up the rebel force and reestablishing the sabotaged Cape Charles lighthouse—there was a larger, subtler aim: to invite these isolated Virginians back into the Union fold. To this end, Dix had written a lengthy proclamation and gave it to Lockwood to carry across.

Now, after steam transport and overland march, the force was ready. They were troops from Wisconsin, Michigan, Indiana, Massachusetts, New York, Delaware, and the Maryland Eastern Shore. They expected to face a rebel army of an estimated 1,500 to 3,000 men, under the command of Colonel Charles Smith, justice of the Northampton County court. The rebels were reportedly well armed and well stocked with ammunition and had six brass cannon smuggled across the Bay from Richmond.

Union cavalry moved out first, on Saturday morning, November 16. They carried a flag of truce, Dix's proclamation, and a demand for the surrender of Smith's troops. The colonel was gone, however, and his camp broken up. Captain Merrill's cavalry did come across 175 rebels armed with shotguns, and a few with old army muskets. The rebels informed the Union cavalrymen that Smith had disbanded his army, all but 400 of them, the core, who were going to try to escape across the Bay.

Union infantry now advanced, passing by felled trees, burned bridges, and abandoned, partially completed breastworks. The woods were filled with men and boys armed with shotguns, pistols, and old sabres. When the cavalry arrived in Drummondtown that evening, the secession flag had been lowered from the courthouse pole just fifteen minutes before. The Stars and Stripes was soon hoisted in its place.

By November 22 the bulk of Lockwood's force was encamped at Drummondtown, with a hefty advance force well on its way to Eastville. Colonel Smith, his officers, and main followers had fled across the Chesapeake Bay. They were already in Norfolk by November 17 and ended up serving under General Huger.

The Eastern Shore expedition was a bloodless success. General Dix's proclamation was distributed among the people of Accomac and Northampton Counties:

> If the calamities of intestine war, which are desolating other districts of Virginia and have already crimsoned her fields with fraternal blood, fall also upon you, it will not be the fault of the Government. It asks only that its authority may be recognized. It sends among you a force too strong to be successfully opposed—a force which cannot be resisted in any other spirit than that of wantonness and malignity. If there are any among you who, rejecting all overtures of friendship, thus provoke retaliation and draw

down upon themselves consequences which the Government is most anxious to avert, to their account must be laid the blood which may be shed and the desolation which may be brought upon peaceful homes . . . .

Once their greatest fear—that the Union troops were coming to confiscate all the slaves—was proved unfounded, the Eastern Shore Virginians were receptive to the army's overture-cum-polite threats. By the twenty-second, Lockwood was able to inform Dix, "All with whom I have conversed look to an annexation with Maryland as an event much to be desired whenever it can constitutionally be accomplished. This they think can be done by regarding themselves, together with Western Virginia, as the true State of Virginia, and inducing the State thus constituted and the State of Maryland to pass the necessary laws."

The people were, in short, more relieved than resistant. Lockwood, from his Drummondtown headquarters, could look around and safely assert: "Really I can scarcely perceive any traces of disloyalty among them, and they appear to receive the power of the Government as their deliverance from misery and great suffering; and I would most respectfully beg that all the advantages in the power of the Government may be speedily given them, that this once-deluded people may be again happy under our beneficent Government."

The Eastern Shore of Virginia, severed from the rest of the state by geography, had now been severed politically as well. Colonel Smith's unwillingness to fight had made for an easy expedition with far-reaching rewards. Traffic on the Chesapeake was no longer threatened by Virginia pincers acting in concert at the entrance to the Bay. Delaware and the Eastern Shore of Maryland were no longer under the gun. Smuggling would of course continue, but perhaps with a bit less flagrancy. In general, all one had to do was look at a map to see the importance of what had happened: The Chesapeake Bay was that much safer now, and that was nothing but good news for Washington.

It was with a renewed sense of optimism that President Lincoln, in his message to Congress on December 3, 1861, was able to say:

An insurgent force of about 1,500, for months dominating the narrow peninsular region constituting the counties of Accomac and Northampton, and known as the Eastern Shore of Virginia, together with some contiguous parts of Maryland, have laid down their arms; and the people there have renewed their allegiance to and accepted the protection of the old flag. This leaves no armed insurrectionists north of the Potomac or east of the Chesapeake.

But Chesapeake Bay remained contested, remained dangerous waters. The biggest threat yet was about to chug forth from the Norfolk Navy Yard.

CHAPTER 4

"A thousand years of battle and breeze"

IT WAS MIDDAY, Saturday, March 8, 1862, cold but clear, the storm of yesterday having moved off. People lined the shore and watched as the odd boat steamed down the Elizabeth River from Norfolk Navy Yard.

The erstwhile U.S. Navy steam frigate had metamorphosed into something hard and mean. USS *Merrimack* was now CSS *Virginia*. Under the supervision of an officers' board headed by Lieutenant John M. Brooke, the flagship of the Old Navy had acquired a new deadliness. They had cut her down to her berth deck, sealing it off for 70 feet fore and aft; the ends would be awash when she was afloat. And for 170 feet amidships, there now rose a sloping iron-covered shield bristling with cannon. The sides of this casement, rising at a 45-degree angle to 7 feet above the deck line, consisted of 24 inches of pitch pine and oak protected by 4 inches of iron plating. The plates had been rolled at the Tredegar Works in Richmond, the only foundry in the South capable of doing the job. They had been laid in alternately horizontal and vertical 2-inch layers.

The shield was rounded at bow and stern to allow for three different gun ports each for both the bow and stern gun, widening the sweep of their aiming range. The bow and stern pivot guns were seven-inch Brooke rifles with steel bands shrunk on to strengthen the breech. The armored hulk had eight more guns in broadside, a pair of Brooke 6.4s and six Dahlgren smoothbores, nine-inchers. A cast-iron ram—1,500 pounds of wedge-shaped hull-busting menace—was attached to the prow, adding four extra feet of nasty threat to the formidable war machine.

If she was deadly, she was also slow. New and impressively frightening on the outside, inside she still had the same old troubled engines of *Merrimack*, the tired, faulty pair of engines that had brought *Merrimack* to the Norfolk Navy Yard for servicing in the first place a year earlier before the war. Her subsequent burning and submersion hadn't done the already unreliable engines and boilers any favors. So the mighty *Virginia* was slow, only able to get up to six or seven miles per hour; turning around took her some thirty to forty minutes. But what she lacked in motive power, she could make up for, it was hoped, in sheer inexorability.

And she was quite a sight, a man-made sea monster on a sunny Saturday in March, descending the river to the sound of cheering crowds. Up to the very hour before her launching, overtime crews were still laboring heroically to ready her for her maiden outing. From her guns to her gears she was completely untried and untested, a floating experiment chugging down for her baptism under fire on the very first day she was ever afloat. For the Confederate States of America, a lot more was riding on her than her officers and crew.

There had been significant setbacks of late; the war in the West was being lost. Fort Henry had fallen, then Fort Donelson, with the capture of 1,500 Confederate troops. A Union general named Grant had made himself hero of the North with the fort victories. Back east, the Burnside expedition, a large-scale army-navy effort that had departed from Annapolis in January, had succeeded in capturing Roanoke Island, North Carolina, four weeks earlier on February 8. It was an important toehold on the rebel coast, threatening the back door of Richmond and Norfolk. At the same time, McClellan's well-trained and well-equipped grand army was making ready to descend into Virginia; it was just a question of where and when.

In the wake of reverses in the East and West, the just-completed *Virginia* chugged forth to wreak havoc and turn the tide of war. She posed a threat to Fort Monroe, the U.S. fleet in Hampton Roads, Washington City, and the whole East Coast. She was the South's great hope and the North's great fear.

FRANKLIN BUCHANAN, FIRST COMMANDER OF THE CSS
VIRGINIA. THE IRONCLAD'S ACTING CHIEF ENGINEER
CALLED BUCHANAN "ONE OF THE GRANDEST MEN
WHO EVER DREW A BREATH OF SALT AIR."
Special Collections, Nimitz Library, U.S. Naval Academy

As she steamed downriver toward Hampton Roads she was escorted by the gunboats *Beaufort* and *Raleigh*, vessels of the ad hoc James
River Squadron, of which the ironclad was now the flagship. And the
newly appointed commodore of the squadron, standing in *Virginia's*
pyramid-shaped pilothouse, was an Old Navy hero famed for bravery,
brains, and fierce moral certitude. He had a commanding presence, this
no-nonsense father figure, a Baltimore man by way of the Eastern Shore.

When he had arrived in Richmond from Talbot County the previous September, Franklin Buchanan instantly received his captaincy in the C.S. Navy. He'd spent the first autumn of the war overseeing the erection of batteries as chief of the Office of Orders and Detail, a top position in the nascent navy. Then on February 24 he received new instructions from Secretary of the Navy Stephen R. Mallory: Proceed to Norfolk and take command of the river squadron consisting of *Patrick Henry*, *Jamestown*, *Teaser*, *Raleigh*, *Beaufort*, and, of course, *Virginia*.

Because the ironclad was an unknown quantity, Buchanan was given license to exercise his discretion in how best to use her. But his orders did include the obvious suggestion: "Could you pass Old Point and make a dashing cruise on the Potomac as far as Washington, its effect upon the public mind would be important to the cause," wrote the navy secretary. "The condition of our country, and the painful reverses we have just suffered, demand our utmost exertions, and convinced as I am that the opportunity and the means of striking a decided blow for our Navy are now for the first time presented, I congratulate you upon it, and know that your judgment and gallantry will meet all just expectations."

The ironclad was a new weapon, and Buchanan had been chosen to wield it. Secretary Mallory summed up the weight of the moment: "Action—prompt and successful action—now would be of serious importance to our cause. . . ."

With Buchanan were about thirty officers, including, on the stern gun, Lieutenant John Taylor Wood. Since leaving Annapolis and crossing the Potomac the previous September, the Naval Academy professor had received his berth in the Confederate navy and had been busy helping erect and man the rebel batteries along the river border, particularly at Aquia Creek. The prospect of steaming into history on board the ironclad appealed to Wood, and with his Jeff Davis connection, he was able to secure a lieutenancy. It was Wood who had been charged these past weeks with assembling a crew for *Virginia*—no small task. The ironclad could boast "as capable a set of officers as ever were brought together in one ship," noted Wood. "But of man-of-war's men or sailors we had scarcely any. The South was almost without a maritime population. In the old service the majority of officers were from the South, and all the seamen from the North."

But by scouring Norfolk for beached Carolina gunboat crews and combing Magruder's army for men with maritime or gunnery skills, Wood had managed to muster a three-hundred-man crew. And though workmen still swarmed on *Virginia*, working feverishly through the weeks before her launching, Wood managed to give the raw crew at least some rudimentary on-board training and drilling. They were, said the lieutenant, "as gallant and trusty a body of men as any one would wish to command. . . ."

The ship's acting chief engineer was H. Ashton Ramsay. Late of the U.S. Navy, he had been an engineer on *Virginia* back when she was still *Merrimack*. He was on the engineering team that had converted her to her iron-plated incarnation. Having known her before, during, and after her radical redesign, Ramsay could say with authority, "I knew her every timber by heart." Now, as the vessel chugged downriver, Ramsay was watching the well-wishers crowding the shoreline when the boatswain piped to announce the midday meal. "A message was sent me by the caterer that I had better take a bite at once, as it might be my last chance to do so. He put it cheerfully," recounted Ramsay.

Hungry, the engineer headed for the wardroom, going through the gun deck to get there. "I was greatly struck by the countenance of the gun's crew as they stood motionless at their post with ram-rod and sponge in hand. These men looked pale and determined, standing straight and stiff and their nerves wrought up to a high degree of tension."

Down in the wardroom, officers were tucking into cold tongue and biscuit. Ramsay was all set to join them when he noticed that the assistant ship's surgeon was at the end of the table looking over his surgical instruments and bandages, making sure all was in order for whatever slicing, sawing, or staunching needs might arise during the day. "The sight took away all my appetite," said Ramsay, "and I returned to my post."

Soldiers waved their hats in the air and cheered as *Virginia* steamed past the Confederate battery at Craney Island. Ahead lay the deepwater channel where the rivers converged at Hampton Roads, flowing into the Bay. Anchored off Fort Monroe were the forty-gun screw-frigates *Min-*

nesota and *Roanoke, Merrimack*'s old sister ships, representing the apex of the man-of-war design. Also at anchor was the old fifty-gun frigate *St. Lawrence*, having just arrived two days earlier, as well as foreign vessels, store-ships, and transports.

Closer to the ironclad, across the channel at Newport News bar, lay the twenty-four-gun sloop-of-war *Cumberland*, which, unlike *Merrimack*, had escaped the destruction of the Norfolk Navy Yard, and the old fifty-gun frigate *Congress*. The two vessels had been off Newport News for months guarding the mouth of the James. At 12:40 P.M., as *Virginia* emerged from the Elizabeth River, the men could see the tall masts of the sloop and frigate, their first two targets, silhouetted in the bright distance. Beyond, they could see the neat, gleaming rows of white tents at Newport News, where the Union shore batteries lay waiting.

Now, on the gun deck, his crew assembled around him, stood Buchanan, "one of the grandest men who ever drew a breath of salt air," thought Ramsay. And as the ironclad made for *Cumberland* across the channel, the flag officer spoke: "Sailors, in a few minutes you will have the long-expected opportunity to show your devotion to your country and our cause. Remember that you are about to strike for your country and your homes, your wives and your children. Every man is expected to do his duty. Beat to quarters."

Ramsay would always remember the moment: "The surrounding shores for miles are lined with people. Norfolk and Portsmouth are emptied of their 18,000 troops. Nearly every one in the two cities rushed to the water's edge to witness the result of what many considered an ill-starred enterprise. No naval battle was ever witnessed by more people."

Virginia followed the south channel to Newport News. Across the way, sailors' laundry dangled damply from the rigging of the lazily at-anchor Union vessels. On *Congress* the quartermaster's spyglass caught sight of the approaching challenger. The ships cleared for action. On came *Virginia*. With smoke and flash, *Cumberland*'s heavy pivots roared and the battle was on. The guns of *Congress* joined in, as did the Newport News batteries, throwing futile fire at the oncoming monstrosity. *Virginia*'s guns held off as the iron-plated ship, impervious to the barrage, stayed on course for *Cumberland*. Now closer in at easy range,

Lieutenant Charles Simms, in charge of *Virginia*'s forward pivot, finally gave the order to fire. The first shot from the ironclad ripped *Cumberland*'s after-pivot gun crew to shreds.

Virginia passed alongside *Congress* and let fly a blistering starboard broadside. It was a devastating hit, garnering a furious response, said Ramsay. "The *Congress* belched forth a most terrific broadside against our shield, tons of iron rained on our casement. Hurrah and hurrah! The iron hail glances off like pebbles. The crew give cheer after cheer."

The pummeling was fierce and nonstop, recounted the engineer. "We are exposed to a very hailstorm of iron projectiles of all description from ashore and afloat. We are a target for 300 guns. The balls strike, glance upward, fall back on our shield and roll harmlessly into the water."

Buchanan sent for Ramsay. Ramsay rushed up to the pilothouse and got his orders: They were going to ram *Cumberland*. The engineer was to throw the engines in reverse as soon as the ship made impact—don't wait for the orders to do so, just do it when the time comes, Buchanan instructed. Ramsay saluted and hurried back to the engine room. As nonstop shot pounded a drumbeat on her hard outer shell, *Virginia* surged toward *Cumberland*'s black hull.

With sharp, stabbing authority the heavy iron ram crashed through the wooden body of *Cumberland*, and at the moment of violent splintering impact, *Virginia*'s bow gun barked at point-blank range. Timbers flew and masts rattled, and in the smoke and death the old ship rocked and flailed like a rag doll mauled by a bear.

Now the ironclad's engines strained in reverse, throttle wide open, as she sought to extricate herself from the gaping maw she'd just created in the dying wooden ship's starboard fore-channels. *Cumberland*'s gunners kept up their work; close-in shot found its way through *Virginia*'s gun ports, blasting the muzzles off two broadside guns and killing or wounding nineteen men. The double-decked guns of nearby *Congress* punched relentlessly, and an explosion wracked *Virginia*'s boiler room. But the boilers were intact; it was a shell going off in the stacks. The ironclad lurched and strained, tilting forward, sinking at the bow, but now, as she righted herself, the crew knew they had pulled free from *Cumberland*'s hull. They had lost their poorly attached ram in the bowels

CSS *VIRGINIA* RAMS USS *CUMBERLAND*.
Battles and Leaders of the Civil War

of the ship they had destroyed, but they had avoided going under like a lead weight. "The crew on the gun deck cheer and cheer again," said Ramsay. "We have crushed in the side of our adversary as a knife goes through a cheese, and she is sinking rapidly."

Water rushed into *Cumberland* where *Virginia* had pulled out. Observed Lieutenant Wood: "Our ram had opened up her side wide enough to drive in a horse and cart."

Virginia lumbered up the James. Blood poured from the ears of stunned men in the incessant, reverberant thunder of shot on shield. The injured were sent down to the cockpit, *Virginia* came back downriver, and the battle continued. "The exertions of the crew are superhuman," said Ramsay. "None flag. It's fire and cheer. Cheer and fire, as with unbounded enthusiasm the men work away at their pieces."

Cumberland was on fire, listing to port, and sinking fast, but Lieutenant George U. Morris, acting commander, refused to surrender. As the water rose, the wounded were moved to keep them from drowning. A shell soared through the hatch and exploded in sick bay, and four of the wounded didn't need to be moved anymore. The ship was a smoking hell of tangled wreckage and slain men, but those who were living stripped to the waist and kept on fighting. *Cumberland's* bow went under. The main hatchway was flooded. Wounded sailors were trapped amidships and drowned in the rising water. Those still in action were driven aft to the spar-deck where they continued to work the pivot and keep up small-arms fire. The water kept coming, and *Cumberland* was sinking faster now. Ramsay watched, incredulous, as her "crew leaped into the rigging, gave three defiant cheers and continued to fight their vessel." Finally Morris ordered that it was every man for himself, and the survivors jumped clear. With a roar, *Cumberland* went under, the Age of Fighting Sail dying with her, and 121 of the stubbornly fought ship's crew going down with her, too. Lieutenant Wood was moved to state, "No ship was ever fought more gallantly."

The sunken ship's spar still rose from the water, marking the spot, and above the roiling surface, her flag still flew.

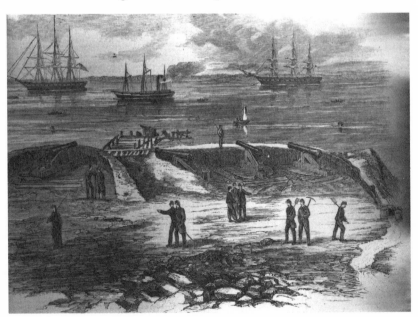

THE FEDERAL BATTERY AT NEWPORT NEWS.
Harper's Weekly

The Confederate twelve-gunner *Patrick Henry* came down the James at full steam, in the company of the small gunboats *Jamestown* and *Teaser*, running the shore-battery gauntlet to join the fray alongside their iron-clad flagship. "They all came nobly into action," Buchanan reported. As they stood down past Newport News, "they were under a galling fire of solid shot, shell, grape, and canister." A shot found *Patrick Henry*'s boiler. Four men were scalded to death; more were wounded. *Jamestown* towed her off, repairs were hastily made, and *Patrick Henry* returned to the action. *Cumberland* was down, and *Congress* was cornered. The latter had hoisted anchor, set jib and topsails, and with the help of her tugboat, had tried to hightail it into shore, where the water was too shoaly for *Virginia* to pursue and ram her. But in fleeing, *Congress* ran aground, still within the range of *Virginia*'s guns. The ironclad and her consorts circled the grounded frigate.

From 150 yards off, *Virginia*'s shells raked *Congress* fore and aft, while the other James River Squadron steamers pitched in on the pound-ing, "firing with precision and doing us great damage," reported Lieu-tenant Austin Pendergrast on *Congress*. The ship caught fire. The death toll mounted. Mud-stuck *Congress* could only bring her stern guns to bear, and they were soon blasted out of the picture. One gun's muzzle was blown off, the other dismounted, but no one could withstand the withering barrage and successfully man them, anyway. It was a blood-bath. "The men were swept away from them with great rapidity and slaughter by the terrible fire of the enemy," said Pendergrast. When word came to him that his commanding officer, Lieutenant Joseph B. Smith, had been killed, Pendergrast conferred with a fellow officer as the flames rose around them. "We deemed it proper to haul down our colors without any further loss of life on our part," said Pendergrast.

Buchanan ordered *Beaufort* and *Raleigh* to steam alongside *Congress* and help bring off her wounded. The gunboats were alongside the frigate under a flag of truce, accepting Pendergrast's sword and begin-ning to transport the injured, when Indiana soldiers on shore unleashed a heavy fire on the proceedings. *Beaufort* and *Raleigh* pulled off. Bucha-nan, "determined that the *Congress* should not again fall into the hands of the enemy," turned to Flag Lieutenant R. D. Minor and said, "That ship must be burned." Minor took a boat and some men and advanced

THE CREW ABANDONS SHIP AS USS *CONGRESS* BURNS.
Battles and Leaders of the Civil War

to within about fifty yards of *Congress* before he was fired upon. The flag lieutenant was severely wounded along with a number of his men.

"Vile treachery," an incensed Buchanan called it. Watching from *Virginia*'s upper deck, he snatched a carbine from one of his men and shouted below to Catesby Jones, his executive officer, "Burn that damned ship, Mr. Jones, she is firing upon our boat under her flags of surrender!" As *Virginia*'s guns cut loose on *Congress* with hot-shot and incendiary shell, an incendiary Buchanan stood there tall and in the open, impervious, firing the carbine. A minié ball ripped through his thigh and grazed his femoral artery.

USS *MINNESOTA*, ANOTHER *VIRGINIA* TARGET.
Harper's Weekly

He was taken below, and a pall fell over the men of *Virginia*: Fearless Buchanan had fallen. Flag Lieutenant Minor, himself suffering from wounds, came on deck with a message from Buchanan: He was not mortally wounded, and the fight would go on. The crew cheered. Buchanan transferred authority of the ship to Lieutenant Jones, "with orders to fight her as long as the men could stand to their guns."

Virginia went searching for more prey. *Minnesota* had run aground en route to the action. The Confederate batteries had fired on the frigate as she had passed, damaging her mainmast but not stopping her—it took the shallow bottom of Hampton Bar to do that. *Virginia* fired on *Minnesota* from too long a range to have much effect; *Patrick Henry* and *Jamestown* managed to move in closer and inflict some damage. But *Minnesota* wasn't going anywhere, and the light was fading. In the morning, the ironclad's pilot could better maneuver the middle channel and get them in closer to *Minnesota*. The Confederates had made enough history for one day.

Virginia retired across the twilit water to Sewells Point. The nonstop pounding she had received had not done any real damage to her iron armor. But she'd lost her ram, and two of her guns had been hit. And "nothing outside had escaped," noted Lieutenant Wood. "One anchor, the smoke-stack, and the steam-pipes were shot away. Railings, stanchions, boat-davits, everything was swept clean." As she headed home for the night, her flag flew from a boarding-pike, the flagstaff having been shot down. "Commodore Buchanan and the other wounded were taken to the Naval Hospital," said Wood, "and after making preparations for the next day's fight, we slept at our guns, dreaming of other victories in the morning."

The news spread fast. "The South went wild with joy," said Ramsay. "The hopes of the Confederacy were as high as the despondency of the North was deep." Telegraph lines burned with doomsday messages. The Confederate ironclad "threatens to sweep our whole flotilla from Chesapeake Bay," wired Assistant Secretary of War P. H. Watson to a New York acquaintance. War Department telegrams warned governors of coastal states and mayors of coastal cities to place obstructions at harbor entrances.

"Should the *Merrimack*, which did so much damage at Newport News, attempt anything at Annapolis, it is believed that the best defense would be an attack by a number of swift steamers, full of men, who should board her by a sudden rush, fire down through her hatches or grated deck, and throw cartridges, grenades, or shells down her smoke pipes," Quartermaster General M. C. Meigs advised Colonel Ingalls, Quartermaster at Annapolis. "Promotion, ample reward, awaits whoever takes or destroys her."

Panic prevailed when word reached Washington. The morning after *Virginia*'s exploit, Navy Secretary Welles visited a distraught Lincoln at the White House, and they were soon joined by other frantic cabinet members. The most unhinged was the new secretary of war, Edwin M. Stanton. Welles, who calmly contended that the probably unseaworthy ironclad was only "to be used in Hampton Roads and the Chesapeake," watched Stanton parade about the room, wild-eyed and accusatory. "He was at times almost frantic," Welles described the secretary of war. "The *Merrimac*, he said, would destroy every vessel in the service, could lay every city on the coast under contribution, could take Fortress Monroe."

But Stanton's root fear was undoubtedly that shared by the other terrified gentlemen on that Sunday morning, said Welles. "Likely the first movement of the *Merrimac* would be to come up the Potomac and disperse Congress, destroy the Capitol and public buildings; or she might go to New York and Boston and destroy those cities, or levy from them contributions sufficient to carry on the War." Stanton's mood was contagious. President Lincoln caught it. "Both he and Stanton went repeatedly to the window and looked down the Potomac—the view being uninterrupted for miles—to see if the *Merrimac* was coming to Washington."

So thick was the pall of worry in that room that it wasn't even lifted when Welles presented the best news of all: The Union's own ironclad had made it to Hampton Roads.

Stanton was entirely skeptical about this little floating battery he'd heard about, this contraption they called *Monitor*. "Stanton asked me about her armament," said Welles, "and when I mentioned she had two guns, his mingled look of incredulity and contempt cannot be described . . . ."

The North's answer to *Virginia* almost sank on her way to the action. The northwesterly wind was whipping up squally seas. The low flat vessel pitched and rolled as the waves smashed across her deck. Towed by the tug *Seth Low* and accompanied by the gunboats *Currituck* and *Sachem*, the USS *Monitor* had cleared New York on March 6. On the morning of the seventh the wind was raw. By noon it was a gale, and the cold, green sea was covering the sloping iron deck in foam and flooding into the ship in every possible place—through the turret, the pilothouse, the berth-deck hatch, the blower-pipe, the hawsehole, the smokestack. The engine room was a watery catastrophe. Engineering officers gagged on escaped gas and had to be brought above, nearly dead. By evening the weather calmed, and they got the engine working again. By midnight seas were rough again, and until daybreak it was an all-hands battle just to keep from foundering.

At 4 P.M. on March 8 *Monitor* passed Cape Henry. The crew hadn't slept in nearly thirty-six hours. Their greeting on arrival in Chesapeake Bay was the sound of heavy gunfire from Newport News. Lieutenant

LIEUTENANT JOHN WORDEN, FIRST COMMANDER OF THE
IRONCLAD *MONITOR*.
Harper's Weekly

John Worden turned to his water-logged and weary men and ordered them to strip *Monitor*'s sea-rig and ready her for action.

She was low to the water, a futuristic-looking creation. The iron-plated raft 172 feet long and 41 feet wide was topped by a revolving turret housing a pair of eleven-inch Dahlgrens. The raft set upon a 122-foot hull. The wrought-iron pilothouse peeked up out of the fore-deck, in the line of fire if the turret aimed dead forward; the gunners had to allow for six degrees or blast their own nerve center. The "ironclad floating battery" had a space-saving single-cylinder engine, the propeller protected from enemy fire by the raft's overhang. She drew 10 feet and weighed a nimble 776 tons, able to make a fast five-minute turn.

Built in just four months, the ship was designed by Swedish-born naval architect John Ericsson, attuned to the latest trends toward iron-plating in ship design. His *Monitor* plans, an evolved and improved version of a proposal he had submitted to Emperor Napoleon III in 1854, were approved by the president and studied by a congressional committee that convened in August and finally signed the contract on October 2, 1861. The keel was laid October 25 at the Continental Iron Works of Greenpoint, Long Island. The Federal government knew what the Confederates were up to with *Merrimack*, and the race to catch up commenced in earnest. Three mechanic gangs worked rotating eight-hour shifts around the clock, and a new breed of war machine was launched January 30, 1862. After three trial runs that pointed out problems there was no time to fix, the U.S. Steam Battery *Monitor* was commissioned February 25.

LIEUTENANT WORDEN, IN STRAW HAT, STANDS ON THE *MONITOR* DECK.
National Archives

She had a crew of sixteen officers and forty-two seamen. The men were volunteers culled from the receiving ships *North Carolina* and *Sabine* at anchor in New York Harbor. They had little time to learn the ropes of shipboard life on the odd, clanging craft on which they were suddenly serving. But they hungered for action and made a fine crew, and John Worden was proud of the group, declaring, "A better one no naval commander ever had the honor to command."

The admiration was mutual; the men loved Worden, a New Yorker whose naval career stretched back to 1840. In April 1861 Worden had been captured while making his way back through enemy territory after delivering secret orders to Pensacola. He was a prisoner for six months before he was exchanged, and when he was released he was ill. His return to duty came in the form of the *Monitor* assignment. Although his family pleaded with him not to leave his sickbed and his physician warned him he probably wouldn't make it back alive, Worden reported for duty anyway. The seasickness hit him hard as the ironclad pitched and heaved its way south.

Entering the Bay, *Monitor* learned of the day's disasters from a passing vessel. The bright blaze of the burning *Congress* licked the darkening sky as *Monitor* plied toward Old Point Comfort. At 9 P.M. she anchored alongside *Roanoke*, and Worden reported to Captain John Marston, in command of the Federal fleet while Flag Officer Goldsborough was off on the Carolina expedition. Marston had received orders to send *Monitor* packing straight to Washington. (Worden's orders to the same effect reached New York two hours after he had left.) To obey the orders would be to concede the lower Chesapeake to the Confederates, and to leave the ships at Hampton Roads to their doom when *Virginia* surged forth again on the morrow. The orders had to be broken. *Monitor* had to stay.

She would wait alongside *Minnesota* for the morning's onslaught. To get there she needed a pilot. Twenty Baltimore pilots all refused the job, claiming unconvincingly they didn't know the channel.

Acting Master Samuel Howard of the U.S. bark *Amanda* gamely offered his services. By the hellish yellow light of *Congress*, he piloted *Monitor* to *Minnesota*'s side. The great deliverer had arrived, the iron-shielded rescuer. She looked puny, almost silly, next to the tall, handsome ships she was there to protect. "An atmosphere of gloom pervaded the fleet," said Lieutenant Samuel Dana Greene, the young Marylander who was *Monitor*'s executive officer, "and the pygmy aspect of the new-comer did not inspire confidence among those who had witnessed the destruction of the day before." Now in position for the coming fight, the exhausted *Monitor* crew spent a tense, watchful night, punctuated at 1 A.M. by the strange, awful beauty of *Congress* as she finally exploded.

Through the dissolving fog of early morning, *Virginia* steamed out from Sewells Point to the surprise sight of the Federal ironclad they'd been hearing so much about for months. "She could not possibly have made her appearance at a more inopportune time for us," said Lieutenant Wood, expressing a view no doubt shared by his shipmates. But with the chagrin and disappointment of an opportunity lost overnight, there was also the raw-nerved anticipation of something new and horrible about to take place, of being part of a showdown like none ever before. "Now all was excitement," remembered Ramsay. "Greek was to meet Greek. For the first time in the history of the world ironclad was to battle ironclad."

Virginia was a mile off when her bow gun opened fire. The shell screamed over the heads of the *Monitor* crew and hit *Minnesota* below the waterline. Worden ordered his men below, the ironclad caught now in the wave-skimming crossfire between *Virginia* and *Minnesota*. *Virginia* steamed in closer to let fly a starboard broadside. *Monitor* came toward *Virginia*'s starboard bow. Worden gave the order to stop the engine, and as *Monitor* coasted slowly by, he sent back the command: "Commence firing!" Her eleven-inch Dahlgrens blasted *Virginia*'s armored hide at close range. *Virginia* roared back with a turret-rattling broadside.

The ships passed each other again and fired, and again. They pounded each other throughout the morning, the shot on iron raising a thunderous, deafening racket. In the *Monitor* turret, the gunners were stripped to the waist, powder-blackened, gushing sweat, smoke-shrouded, firing the guns as fast as they could serve them. Lieutenant Greene was in command in the turret, and the speaking-tube connecting him to his captain was destroyed early in the fight. So, in the thick of

THE DUEL OF THE IRONCLADS *MONITOR* AND *VIRGINIA*, MARCH 9, 1862.
National Archives

battle, men stationed in the berth deck had to constantly relay orders from Worden in the pilothouse to Greene in the turret.

"The situation was novel," remarked Greene. "A vessel of war was engaged in desperate combat with a powerful foe; the captain, commanding and guiding, was inclosed in one place, and the executive officer, working and fighting the guns, was shut up in another, and communication between them was difficult and uncertain."

The turret handled trickily; it was tough to get moving but then spun too quickly, and visibility was limited to the gun ports. But Greene's gunners, "sixteen brawny men," kept up a constant fire. Acting Master L. N. Stodder, in charge of the turret-revolving machinery, leaned against the turret wall as one of *Virginia*'s shells smashed against the outside. The eight-inch iron plating resounded and reverberated, and Stodder staggered back senseless, a concussion his reward for one unguarded moment.

It was *Virginia*'s ten guns against *Monitor*'s two, *Monitor* making up the difference with her superior maneuverability. While *Monitor* "could

THE IRONCLADS TRADE CLOSE-RANGE FIRE AS *MINNESOTA* LOOKS ON.
Harper's Weekly

take any position, and always have us in range of her guns," said Wood, the heavier, slower, deeper-draft *Virginia* "was as unwieldy as Noah's ark."

Getting nowhere against her iron opponent, *Virginia* again attacked *Minnesota*, whose captain, G. J. Van Brunt, barked orders. His men cut loose with "a broadside which would have blown out of water any timber-built ship in the world." The ironclad kept coming, firing, the shell from her bow gun ripping through the chief engineer's stateroom, the engineer's mess, amidships, into the boatswain's quarters, where it crashed and exploded two powder charges. *Minnesota* burst into flames, her men rushing to douse the blaze. *Virginia* hurled another shell, hitting the tug *Dragon* and blowing up her boiler. *Minnesota*'s guns kept raining down on *Virginia*. Gun deck, spar deck, and forecastle pivots all beat their futile tattoo on the ironclad. "At least fifty solid shot struck her on her slanting side without producing any apparent effect," noted an amazed Van Brunt. Now *Monitor* worked her way back in between the

Confederate craft and *Minnesota*. *Virginia* ran aground, and *Minnesota* again showered her with shot and shell.

Virginia got off, stood down with *Monitor* in pursuit, then came around, and Lieutenant Jones cried, "Go ahead, full speed!" *Virginia*'s cast-iron ram had been lost the day before in the hull of *Cumberland*—but the ironclad was still going to try to ram *Monitor*. Through the pilothouse sight-hole, Worden watched the oncoming giant and put the helm hard aport. *Monitor* sheered off, and the Confederate prow struck the starboard quarter a glancing, ineffectual blow, her impact diffused by *Monitor*'s deft angling. The target close, *Monitor*'s guns fired, seriously denting *Virginia*'s shield and sending her aft gunners flying from the sudden rocking blow.

It was as close as either got to piercing the other's armor. But *Virginia* keyed in on *Monitor*'s vulnerable spot—her pilothouse—and fired on it at close range, landing a direct hit on the sight-hole. With a roar and a flash, the pilothouse filled with smoke. Worden stumbled back, hands on his face. "My eyes," he cried. "I am blind."

The ship's surgeon and other crewmen helped their captain as blood poured freely down his blackened face, his eyes destroyed by hot powder and slivers of iron. He said, "Gentlemen, I leave it with you, do what you think best. I cannot see, but do not mind me. Save the *Minnesota* if you can." The men quickly conferred. They all agreed: keep fighting.

ON *VIRGINIA*'S GUN DECK.
Battles and Leaders of the Civil War

LIEUTENANT WORDEN OF *MONITOR* IS BLINDED
BY A DIRECT HIT.
Nimitz Library, U.S. Naval Academy

Worden put Greene in command. They helped Worden below to his cabin.

Monitor had drifted off in the meantime, her temporary meandering mistaken for a retreat. *Minnesota* braced for *Virginia*'s next attack.

But the Confederate ironclad was limping away, assuming, perhaps hoping, that *Monitor* was in retreat, and taking the opportunity to call it a day herself. Battered, operating roughly with her smokestack blown off, *Virginia* departed. Lieutenant Jones claimed he was concerned about beating the ebb tide.

Ready to resume action, *Monitor* came alongside *Minnesota*. But it was over. When the blinded Worden learned that *Minnesota* had been saved, he said, "Then I can die happy."

His eyesight was never fully restored, but John Worden had good years ahead of him. He was removed from *Monitor* on a tugboat and taken to Washington. *Monitor* and her crew remained in the Chesapeake, off Fort Monroe, where in the days following the battle they became the toast of all, lavished with gratitude and praise, the heroes, saviors, of the fleet and the fort. If they hadn't slain the dragon, they had at least halted its rampage.

And a similar heroes' welcome greeted the returning crew of *Virginia*. As the battle-scarred ironclad steamed back up the Elizabeth River, there was jubilation, recalled Ramsay: "Cheering, waving of handkerchiefs and flags, people yelling themselves hoarse, hundreds of small boats following in our rear." In Norfolk, Wood was summoned to Buchanan's bedside at the naval hospital. The commander, still in great pain, dictated a report for Secretary Mallory. He gave it to Wood to deliver, along with the surrendered flag of *Congress*. On the train to Richmond, Wood quickly discovered that "the news had preceded me, and at every station I was warmly received, and to listening crowds was forced to repeat the story of the fight."

Both sides claimed victory. *Monitor* had retired first, claimed the South. *Virginia* had been thwarted in her aims, claimed the North. Alban C. Stimers, chief engineer of *Monitor*, summed it up fairly: "Ironclad against ironclad. We maneuvered about the bay here and went at each other with mutual fierceness. I consider that both ships were well fought."

There was no denying it, though: *Virginia* had set out to sink *Minnesota* and wreak havoc on the rest of the lower Chesapeake fleet. And, the long day done, *Minnesota* was still afloat, likewise the rest of the fleet. "The battle was a drawn one, so far as the two vessels engaged were concerned," said Wood. "But in its general results the advantage was with the *Monitor*." And the South's joy over the results of the first day had to be tempered by the reality of the second day. As Wood stated, quite simply: "The *Monitor* was well handled, and saved the *Minnesota* and the remainder of the fleet at Fort Monroe."

The inconclusiveness did nothing to diminish the status of the Confederacy's great new naval hero. Franklin Buchanan had put the fear of God in the North and raised the hopes of the South when they desperately needed raising. If he was venerable before, he was venerated now. He was, said Wood, "an energetic and high-toned officer, who combined with daring courage great professional ability, standing deservedly at the head of his profession."

"A more gallant commander never trod the deck of a ship," Ramsay said of Buchanan. "He was without a peer, and his name must go down to posterity coupled with that of Collingwood, Stuart, Nelson, Decatur and Farragut." Buchanan's wound had created a nagging what-if in Southern hearts. The second day would have gone more successfully if bold Buchanan had still been at the helm, avowed Ramsay. If Buchanan hadn't been shot, "he would have forced the *Minnesota* to surrender before the *Monitor* came to the ground, and then run the *Monitor* down or forced her into deep water, where she could not have had the advantage of her light draft." If Buchanan hadn't been shot, said Ramsay, "We'd have compelled Fortress Monroe to evacuate and then leisurely steamed up to Washington and compelled the capitulation of that city just as Lincoln feared."

The Confederacy now had pride in its navy. Secretary Mallory wrote Jeff Davis: "It will be remembered that the *Virginia* was a novelty in naval architecture, wholly unlike any ship that ever floated; that her heaviest guns were equal novelties in ordnance; that her motive power and her obedience to her helm were untried, and her officers and crew strangers comparatively to the ship and to each other; and yet, under all these disadvantages, the dashing courage and consummate professional ability of Flag-Officer Buchanan and his associates achieved the most remarkable victory which naval annals record."

"I congratulate you, my dear friend, with all my heart and soul, on the glory you have gained for the Confederacy and yourself," the recuperating Buchanan read in a letter from Flag Officer Josiah Tattnall, CSN. "The whole affair is unexampled, and will carry your name to every corner of the Christian world and be on the tongue of every man who deals in salt water. . . . you proved yourself (as the old Navy always esteemed you) a man not of doubt or faltering when you had undertaken an adventure. . . . I hope that Congress will make you an admiral."

Congress did.

It had been an engagement rife with the coincidental ironies of internecine war. Samuel Dana Greene's old Naval Academy roommate, Walter Butt, was a lieutenant aboard *Virginia*. Two other *Virginia* lieutenants had brothers in the U.S. Army. Another *Virginia* lieutenant's father was in the U.S. Army, and a *Virginia* midshipman's father was in the U.S. Navy. While Lieutenant William H. Parker was escorting *Virginia* on the Confederate steamer *Beaufort*, his brother Foxhall was doing good work for the U.S. Navy farther up the Bay.

And, most nearly fratricidal of all, Franklin Buchanan's brother McKean was assistant paymaster aboard *Congress*. Both Buchanans knew of the other's presence, and both fought fiercely. McKean escaped unscathed from the ship his brother had ordered to be burned.

It was an engagement the impact of which went far beyond the waters of the Chesapeake and the worries of this war. As John Taylor Wood put it, "In this battle old things passed away, and the experience of a thousand years of battle and breeze was forgotten."

CHAPTER 5

Abraham on the water

ON MONDAY, MARCH 17, 1862, the largest army ever assembled in North America, the largest army ever led by one man in the history of the Western Hemisphere, began its journey down Chesapeake Bay. The waterfronts of Alexandria and Washington City were aswarm with stevedores and soldiers, livestock and cannon, noise and movement, as the largest amphibious operation ever launched got under way. From throughout the Bay country an eclectic armada of boats had been rounded up and gathered on the Potomac, some 400 vessels in all, steamers and schooners, brigs and barges, sloops and ferryboats, to carry 112,000 men, 25,000 horses and mules, 2,500 cattle, 3,600 wagons, 300 artillery pieces, and 700 ambulances down the Chesapeake to Fort Monroe and Newport News. From there it would be onward by land, through mud and blood and over and around anything that got in the way, on to Richmond. Major General George B. McClellan and his grand Army of the Potomac were going to crush the rebellion once and for all.

From St. Patrick's Day, when Brigadier General Samuel P. Heintzelman's division was the first to bid farewell to the Alexandria docks, on beyond April Fool's Day, when McClellan himself boarded the steamer *Commodore* and headed off down the Bay, the large-scale movement continued along the Chesapeake water highway. Assistant Secretary of War John Tucker had overseen the roundup of vessels, and Assistant Quartermaster Lieutenant Colonel R. Ingalls was in charge of the epic embarkation of men and matériel. McClellan was able to report proudly:

ARTILLERY IS LOADED AT ALEXANDRIA TO BE TRANSPORTED DOWN
THE CHESAPEAKE FOR THE PENINSULA CAMPAIGN.
Harper's Weekly

"Operations of this nature on so extensive a scale had no parallel in the history of our country."

Private Warren Lee Goss and his chums watched the excitement from their camp along the Potomac. "Numerous steam-tugs were pulling huge sailing vessels here and there, and large transports, loaded with soldiers, horses, bales of hay, and munitions for an army, swept majestically down the broad river. Every description of water conveyance, from a canal boat to a huge three-decked steamboat, seemed to have been pressed into the service." In the spring air the boys felt the fear and the nervous joy of pending peril, of finally setting out for another shore to prosecute the war. "At last, when drills and inspections had made us almost frantic with neatness and cleanliness," recounted Private Goss, "our marching orders came. We formed in two ranks and boarded a little steamer lying at the wharf near by."

The boys in blue crowded on board and jostled and joked and wondered out loud about God knows where they were going. "The general opinion among us was that at last we were on our way to make an end of the Confederacy. We gathered in little knots on the deck: here and there a party were playing 'penny ante'; others slept or dozed, but the majority smoked and discussed the probabilities of our destination, about which we really knew nothing, except that we were sailing down the Potomac."

It was a far less treacherous route to be trafficking on than it had been just more than a week ago. For on March 9, the same day *Monitor* and *Virginia* had dueled, something profound was taking place on Washington's river. The Potomac Flotilla steamer *Anacostia* shelled the rebel battery at Cockpit Point for a solid hour without a single reply. Landing parties from *Anacostia* and *Yankee* went ashore.

The Confederates had abandoned the battery.

The sailors spiked the rebel guns and hoisted the U.S. flag over Cockpit Point. Explosions and fire from Shipping Point battery spelled ammunition destroyed by the evacuating rebs. The next day a regiment of soldiers from General Joseph Hooker's division came across with the sailors, and they heaved cannon into the river. The Virginia shore was a deserted honeycomb of rifle pits, breastworks, and elaborately constructed batteries. Overnight, the Confederate artillery threat looming over the Potomac had vanished like a banshee. The chokehold on Washington loosened. The Potomac front was clear. The rebels had moved, and it was high time George B. McClellan did the same.

"Little Mac," who had ridden into Washington with such flourish and dash in the wake of Bull Run and molded the forces around the capital into a gleaming and impressive army nearly 150,000 strong, was making people impatient. It was 1862, the nation's war debt had risen to $600 million, and all the while the war effort had stagnated. In October McClellan had declared that a move to smash General Joseph E. Johnston's army headquartered at Manassas "should not be postponed beyond November 25." By December nothing had happened. Lincoln started postulating his own detailed strategy suggestions, while McClellan's own plans kept evolving. "We are still delayed," he wrote his increasingly anxious president on February 3. "I have ever regarded our true policy as being that of fully preparing ourselves, and then seeking for the most decisive results."

The movement on Richmond by way of the lower Chesapeake was the final version of one choice culled grudgingly from various invasion options. In December Congress had formed the Joint Committee on the Conduct of the War, three senators and four House members, to ride herd on the military. The influential committee was angered by the insulting fact that the capital was a virtual hostage to the rebels' Potomac batteries, and was disgruntled with McClellan's lack of action. The committee favored a straightforward overland invasion into Virginia. It was a simple plan, the least costly being put forth, and best of all, a defensive offense, keeping the Army of the Potomac between the Confederates and Washington.

But McClellan, led to believe that Johnston was camped along the front with a mighty army of 115,000 men, was loath to face the foe head-on. Better to outflank him, calculated McClellan. He had been poring over his maps and arguing for a more creative, and potentially more effective, maneuver: to boat-transport his men down to Urbanna, Virginia, near the mouth of the Rappahannock, and from there march on Richmond. The plan had a lot going for it. It took advantage of the water-laced geography. It led to a much shorter land route. And best of all, it avoided a direct confrontation with an enemy perceived to be amassed and waiting in large array.

There was wrangling back and forth, with the Joint Committee, the president, his cabinet, and McClellan all weighing in. A prime criterion for any plan, insisted Lincoln, was that McClellan leave back a large enough force to defend the capital city. While the Joint Committee and Secretary Stanton encouraged the president's growing uncertainties about McClellan, McClellan continued to push for his invasion plan.

On March 8, in his General War Order Number 3, Lincoln declared that no more than fifty thousand troops could move "until the naviga-tion of the Potomac from Washington to the Chesapeake Bay shall be free from the enemy's batteries and other obstructions. . . ." The presi-dent also gave McClellan a deadline, that any change-of-base operation "which may be intended to move upon Chesapeake Bay, shall begin to move upon the bay as early as the 18th of March instant . . . ."

Lincoln called for "an immediate effort" by both army and navy to sweep the Potomac clean of rebel batteries, once and for all. On the very next day, the Potomac Flotilla shelled Cockpit Point and discovered the rebel pullout. By March 11 Johnston's army had relocated to the south bank of the Rappahannock. Marching behind McClellan into Fairfax Courthouse and the former rebel position at Centreville, the Union troops were greeted by tree trunks fashioned into fake cannon—"Quaker guns." Soon came the humiliating realization that the North's shiny new army had been held in check for the last six months by a force less than one-third its size.

On March 11 Lincoln demoted McClellan from commander in chief of all the nation's armies to commander solely of the Army of the Potomac. On March 13 McClellan met with his division commanders (chosen by Lincoln without Mac's approval) to decide what course to take.

The Rappahannock was no longer the destination of choice. Since Johnston had pulled his army back to Rappahannock Station, "the Urbanna movement lost much of its promise," McClellan explained, "as the enemy was now in position to reach Richmond before we could do so." Farther down, however, where the York and James flowed into the

Bay, was McClellan's next best bet. The eighty-odd miles from there to Richmond constituted a longer hike than the Urbanna approach would have. But there was a compensating factor. The tip of the York-James peninsula was already a Federal outpost. "The alternative remained," concluded the general, "of making Fort Monroe and its vicinity the base of operations."

"It was with open-eyed wonder that, as part of McClellan's army, we arrived at Old Point Comfort and gazed upon Fort Monroe, huge and frowning," Private Goss recalled. Along the congested waterfront, amid the shouts of contraband workers, the transports anchored. And before the great Peninsula Campaign could begin, there was the matter of getting all the soldiers and supplies ashore. There weren't enough wharves to handle a disembarkation of this unprecedented scope. The Army Corps of Engineers, working with the Quartermaster Corps, rose to the occasion.

Canal boats brought down from the upper Chesapeake were used by the engineers to land the huge army, its animals, artillery, and everything else. The boats, sixty to seventy feet long and fourteen feet wide, were put twelve feet apart, connected by sturdy cross-timbers, and then covered with plank decking. Horses and fieldpieces were lowered onto the floating surfaces, pushed toward shore by tugboat, and linked to land by quickly assembled pontoon bridges. The end result was a wharf at which a transport could disgorge its cargo. For the disembark-ing soldiers, the engineers built ramps down to the waiting scows, and the troops were soon coming ashore at the rate of more than two thousand men an hour.

"Along the shore which looks toward Fort Monroe were landed artillery, baggage-wagons, pontoon trains and boats, and the level land back of this was crowded with the tents of soldiers," said Private Goss. "Here and there were groups frying hard-tack and bacon. Near at hand was the irrepressible army mule, hitched to and eating out of pontoon boats; those who had eaten their ration of grain and hay were trying their teeth, with promise of success, in eating the boats."

It was all noise and swirl and liveliness, a bayside boom town. "The scene was a busy one," Private Goss said. "The red cap, white leggins, and baggy trousers of the Zouaves mingled with the blue uniforms and dark trimmings of the regular infantry-men, the short jackets and yellow trimmings of the engineers; together with the ragged, many-colored costumes of the black laborers and teamsters, all busy at something."

The troops were still being landed when McClellan arrived on April 2. He met with Flag Officer Goldsborough to discuss the navy's role in the coming operations. It was doomed to be a misunderstood relationship on the part of both branches of the military.

Also on his arrival, McClellan received a telegram from the adjutant general's office in Washington: Major General John E. Wool's ten-thousand-man force stationed at Fort Monroe and its environs would *not* come under McClellan's command. The general was taken aback. He'd been counting on those men. Less than sixty thousand of his own men had been disembarked, but McClellan determined to get things moving, and on April 4 he did just that.

It was a two-pronged advance up the peninsula. The right column, led by General Heintzelman, headed up along the York River side to

GENERAL GEORGE B. MCCLELLAN IS CHEERED BY HIS TROOPS AS HE LEADS THE SOON-TO-BE-STALLED ADVANCE ON YORKTOWN, APRIL 5, 1862.
Frank Leslie's Illustrated Newspaper

engage the rebel entrenchments at Yorktown. The left column, under Brigadier General Erasmus D. Keyes, ascended the James River side, aiming to go around and behind Yorktown. There were rebel batteries both at Yorktown and across the York at Gloucester Point. The navy, already preoccupied with the *Virginia* threat, would send a flotilla up the York to bombard the batteries in concert with the land assault. McClellan's plan also called for a flanking attack by Major General Irvin McDowell with the First Corps, sweeping down from the north bank of the York to turn the rebel position.

But McDowell was still in Washington, the navy's cooperation was coming grudgingly at best, the troops advancing up the peninsula were relying on faulty maps, and the rebels up ahead had more extensive defenses than had been assumed.

With best-laid plans the march began. "It was a bright day in April—a perfect Virginia day," said Private Goss. "The grass was green beneath our feet, the buds of the trees were unrolling into leaves under the warming sun of spring, and in the woods the birds were singing." The soldiers stopped for the night and camped, and in the morning the rain was coming down hard.

The romance left the hike; the wagon teams that had gone before the soldiers had put the mud roads "in a state of semi-liquid filth hardly possible to describe or imagine." Outside Big Bethel, Private Goss approached a farmhouse in hopes of cadging something more palatable than field rations. The woman at the house cried as she talked about her son the rebel soldier. Private Goss opined that the Union army would get to Richmond with little resistance. The woman said, "You all will drink hot blood before you all get thar!"

The left column, meanwhile, was behind schedule after one day. Its destination: Halfway House, a landmark at the bottleneck of the lower peninsula, about midway between Yorktown and Williamsburg. From here, Keyes's men would be positioned to cut off any retreat attempt by Magruder from Yorktown. But in the rain the roads became downright rivers. The soldiers with their heavy loads bogged down in the slimy morass, and the artillery trains and supply wagons moved slowly if at all. Then another unexpected obstacle barred their way: Confederate gunfire.

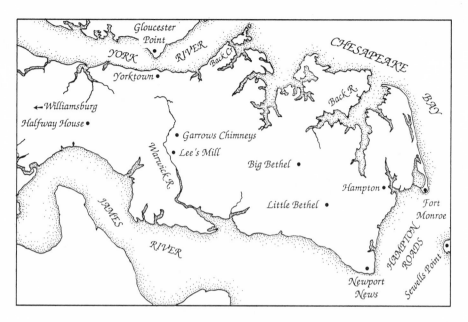

THE LOWER YORK-JAMES PENINSULA. MAGRUDER'S
DEFENSIVE LINE, WHICH RAN FROM YORKTOWN
DOWN THE WARWICK RIVER, STALLED THE ARMY
OF THE POTOMAC'S ADVANCE IN APRIL 1862.

On the map, the topography and the place-name were wrong, and
the spot where the Union troops hoped to cross Warwick River was
marked as a harmless rebel supply depot. In reality, Lee's Mill had a
harmful three-gun battery guarding the crossing, as Confederate shells
blasting at Keyes's advance force now indicated. The artillery fire was
quickly accompanied by the brisk and well-directed popping-off of
dug-in rebel sharpshooters. Keyes's troops halted in their muddy tracks,
stopped in the swampland fronting the Warwick.

The Warwick, beginning near Yorktown, cutting across the width
of the peninsula, and flowing into the James, was the line behind which
Magruder had built his defenses—defenses that McClellan had optimis-
tically assumed wouldn't amount to much. He had counted on the
Yorktown works being the only serious opposition to his move up the
peninsula. But Magruder had stitched a line of gun batteries and rifle
pits across the narrow land and flooded the already swampy terrain with
a series of dams in the Warwick. "Prince John" Magruder's being better

prepared hadn't been part of McClellan's plans. On the heels of this setback, McClellan was dealt another body blow. A telegram arrived from the adjutant general's office: McDowell's army, it had been decided, was needed to augment the defensive forces of Washington and would not be available for the Peninsula Campaign.

McClellan had left more than Lincoln's requisite fifty thousand troops to defend the capital (though the general had counted the troops in the Shenandoah as part of that total). Without McDowell and his forty-three thousand men, McClellan's campaign strategy as originally planned was a washout. Here he was, in the field, the enemy in front of him, and in Washington they pulled the rug out from under him. In the ruthless rain, as the Confederates displayed more defensive muscle than expected, and as the telegram in his hand bore news that felt like a knife in the back, General McClellan halted his advance. Talk of "rapid movements" was scotched after two days and ten miles. The protracted siege of Yorktown began. It was a curious sort of siege, really—one in which the besieged were free to walk out the back door whenever they saw fit.

On April 11, one of Fort Monroe's guns joined one of *Monitor*'s guns in firing off a morning-jarring alarm shot. What everyone at Old Point had been dreading, and expecting, was happening: Around Sewells Point came *Virginia*. Down into Hampton Roads returned the rebel ironclad, repaired and ready for trouble.

Out of deference to this eventuality, most of the Union fleet, *Monitor* included, lay at anchor out beyond the fort in the Chesapeake, and those squadron vessels that weren't sped there that morning. *Virginia*, now under the command of Flag Officer Josiah Tattnall, steamed toward Fort Monroe, trading shots with the fort, the Rip Raps, and the wary vessels. While *Virginia* kept them busy, two of her consorts, *Jamestown* and *Raleigh*, dashed across to Newport News. Having ignored Commodore Goldsborough's repeated warnings, some vessels in the service of the Quartermaster's Department were still dangerously at anchor there. The rebel boats took off two brigs and an Accomac schooner, capturing portions of their crews in the process. The rebels hoisted the captured vessels' colors Union-down—a taunt, a dare unanswered. The presence

of the English corvette *Rinaldo* in Hampton Roads to witness the flagrancy only added to Federal embarrassment. As *Jamestown* steamed
past with her prizes in tow, the English crew cheered with vigor.

Monitor and several men-of-war got up steam, but they all kept a
safe distance from *Virginia*, which retired, untouched, past Craney Island. The day before, Flag Officer Tattnall had written Secretary Mallory
for permission to try to run *Virginia* past Fort Monroe's guns. Permission
never came—a good thing, thought Lieutenant John Taylor Wood on
Virginia. The ironclad was serving a good purpose where she was, "and
any disaster would have exposed Norfolk and James River, and probably would have resulted in the loss of Richmond. For equally good
reasons the *Monitor* acted on the defensive; for if she had been out of the
way, General McClellan's base and fleet of transports in York River
would have been endangered."

Lieutenant E. M. Noyes of the Third Vermont Infantry slogged across
the waist-deep water of the Warwick, emerged dripping behind enemy
lines, and got within fifty yards of the rebel works without being seen.
He recrossed the river below Dam Number 1 at a place called Garrows
Chimneys or Burnt Chimneys. Reconnoitering, General William T. H.
Brooks's Vermont Brigade had been in a sharp skirmish since morning.
It was April 16, and as Lieutenant Noyes came back across, General
McClellan was moving to the front. Noyes reported his observations.
The Vermonters were going to try, right there, to break the Warwick line.

Two hundred of them charged, splashing across the river, a bold run
into enemy fire. They got across, hunkered down in some empty rebel
rifle pits, and started firing back. For half an hour, the Vermonters held
their tenuous lodgment on the rebel side of the river. The North Caro-
linians they tangled with lost their colonel, Robert McKinney. More
Confederate forces were rushed to the spot, including a Georgia regiment under Howell Cobb. The fire grew too heavy, and with losses
mounting, the four Vermont companies scooted back across the water.
They'd proven it could be done, and another attempt was made. This
time, eight companies reinforced by the division's twenty-gun battery
crossed in two places. But the rebels were riled to alertness now and

laying down too heavy a fire to allow for any second successful breach of the line. The Federals fell back. It was as close as anyone got to breaking through.

Chances probably would have been better back in those first siege days, when it was Magruder's eleven thousand stretched along the line holding back McClellan's fifty-eight thousand. By April 10, the advance

THE THIRD VERMONT ATTEMPTS TO GAIN A FOOTHOLD
ACROSS THE WARWICK.
Harper's Weekly

parties of Joe Johnston's army were arriving, and by the fourteenth Johnston's whole force had moved down from the Rappahannock to reinforce Magruder. Prince John, meanwhile, had been parading his troops up and down the line to create the illusion of more men.

The Union army continued to disembark, and McClellan continued to urge more troops from Lincoln, as April ticked by and the 101-gun siege train was brought up by land and barge to prepare for McClellan's big, decisive bombardment of the Yorktown fortifications. It was going to be a spectacle. Hell's own arsenal was being brought to bear on the historic little tidewater town, everything from standard siege howitzers on two-wheel mounts to thirteen-inch mortars and two-hundred-pounder Parrott guns—gargantuan, cumbersome seacoast artillery requiring special platforms. General Fitz-John Porter was named director of the siege, and with General J. G. Barnard, chief of engineers, and General W. F. Barry, chief of artillery, the Federal batteries were built outside Yorktown at ranges of from 1,500 to 2,000 yards. Behind their embankments, the rebels offered occasional token interference.

The North Atlantic Blockading Squadron, meanwhile, gave what support it could—nowhere near the scope of involvement McClellan had envisioned. The navy claimed it had been left out of the planning until the operation was already under way; McClellan claimed otherwise. In any case, the vessels in the lower Chesapeake fleet could only do so much against the high-perched rebel guns of Yorktown and Gloucester Point.

"The works of the enemy are excessively strong and powerfully armed," reported Commander J. S. Missroon of *Wachusett* to Flag Officer Goldsborough. "Their cannon are managed and served with surprising accuracy, exceeding anything I have heretofore known, and there is every indication of a most determined resistance. More than fifty heavy cannon bear upon this bay, and the destruction of vessels of this class is inevitable if taken under such a fire without their having the power to inflict any damage, or but trifling damage, to the enemy, owing to the superior and well-chosen position of their batteries."

Wachusett was one of the seven gunboats assigned by Goldsborough to patrol the York. Honoring McClellan's request "to annoy the enemy by firing a few shells by day and night," the vessels shelled the rebel works almost daily through the latter half of April. They hindered the extension of rebel fortification of Gloucester Point, dropped some shells behind the Yorktown lines, and maintained the Federal presence on the water during the siege buildup. And by May, preparations were just about complete for McClellan's big bombardment.

Sunday, May 4, was to be the date when the amassed siege guns would begin bludgeoning Yorktown with nearly 180 tons a day. On the

FEDERAL TROOPS ARE TRANSPORTED TO THE YORKTOWN
LINES ABOARD THE STEAMER *OCEAN QUEEN.*
Harper's Weekly

night of May 3, rebel artillery fire was unusually high. On the momentous morning of May 4, as McClellan's pickets tried to get things going, there was no reply from behind the rebel works. The word spread down the line: The Confederate army was gone.

After keeping McClellan stuck in the mud for an entire month making meticulous and elaborate preparations for his next move, the rebels had upped and left. They headed toward Richmond, with the Union army on their heels and Union gunboats running up the York to establish a supply base on the Pamunkey River.

Slowed by rain and bad roads, Johnston's army was forced into a rearguard action with the advancing Federals. Union cavalry under Brigadier General George Stoneman clashed with Jeb Stuart's horsemen east of Williamsburg. By the rain-soaked morning of May 5 both sides had a battle on their hands that neither had intended. On the Union left, Hooker's division stormed the Confederate forces that had thrown themselves behind a crossroads bastion that Magruder earlier had built—Fort Magruder, an earthwork surrounded by a ditch and a series of lesser earthworks. To attack it, the Union soldiers had to wend through a jagged quarter-mile maze of felled forest. As Hooker's first skirmishers ventured forward, artillery fire ripped across the tree-stump terrain and the rifle pits came alive. "The constant hissing of the bullets, with their sharp *ping* or *bizz* whispering around and sometimes into us, gave me a sickening feeling and a cold perspiration," a soldier related. "I felt weak around my knees—a sort of faintness and lack of strength in the joints of my legs, as if they would sink from under me. These symptoms did not decrease when several of my comrades were hit."

The survivors backed out of there "from stump to stump and from log to log," returning to the edge of the woods. Two Federal batteries were brought up and put in position, several battery men getting mowed down by rebel artillery in the process. The batteries blasted away relentlessly at the rebel works, clearing them out by nine o'clock in the morning. The Union soldiers poured over the rebel defenses around the deserted mud fort.

From an adjacent ravine, a howling Confederate horde surged, firing deadly shots and cutting loose with their terrifying rebel yell. The Union troops fell back. Fighting grew intense. General James Longstreet,

THE BATTLE OF WILLIAMSBURG, MAY 5, 1862.
Frank Leslie's Illustrated Newspaper

in command of the Confederate action at Williamsburg, threw his entire division against Hooker.

On the right of the Federal line, General Winfield Scott Hancock's brigade gained control of a rebel redoubt, tried to gain more ground, and was attacked by D. H. Hill and Jubal Early's brigades for their troubles. Hancock's troops retreated, the rebs in hot pursuit. Then, over the crest, the Union soldiers about-faced, and the chasing Confederates charged smack into a blistering musketfire. The Union soldiers then bayonet-charged across the open field. Early was wounded, and the Confederates were driven back, four hundred dead in the quick turn-around.

The fierce, disjointed fighting continued until the last Confederates evacuated Williamsburg that evening. The day's casualties had been around two thousand for each side—high for a rear-guard tangling. Around five o'clock in the afternoon, General McClellan arrived at the front. He had been at his new headquarters in Yorktown, overseeing the transport of part of his army upriver.

After the Battle of Williamsburg, Private Goss saw one of his fellow soldiers taking aim from behind a felled tree. "I called to him, but he did not turn or move. Advancing nearer, I put my hand on his shoulder, looked in his face, and started back. He was dead!—shot through the brain; and so suddenly had the end come that his rigid hand grasped his musket, and he still preserved the attitude of watchfulness, literally occupying his post after death. At another place we came upon one of our men who had evidently died from his wounds. Near one of his hands was a Testament, and on his breast lay an ambrotype picture of a group of children and another of a young woman."

The armies moved on, leaving the lower York-James peninsula, continuing their slow dance toward Richmond. "The 6th of May was a beautiful morning," Private Goss remembered, "with birds singing among the thickets in which lay the dead."

Abraham Lincoln stood on the quarterdeck of the sleek vessel steaming down Chesapeake Bay when he spied an ax on the bulwarks. He hefted the ax and held the butt of its handle between his thumb and forefinger, at arm's length, extended that way for several minutes. "The most powerful sailors on board tried in vain to imitate him," remarked Brigadier General Egbert L. Viele, one of the president's fellow passengers. The bizarre ax feat was something Lincoln had been impressing folks with since he was eighteen years old; proof, said Viele, that the commander in chief "had the strength of a giant."

For five days in May 1862, the U.S. Revenue Cutter *Miami* was the flagship of the nation, the "ship of state," as it were. It served as headquarters for President Lincoln during an expedition on the Chesapeake Bay. During those five eventful days, Lincoln assumed his role as commander in chief in active campaigning. The administration's ire at McClellan's sluggishness had peaked; Norfolk had yet to be turned, the Peninsula Campaign seemed to have more boondoggle than decisiveness about it. The cabinet met, the decision was made, and on May 2 Major General John Wool at Fort Monroe received a wire telling him to get ready.

Late in the afternoon on May 5 Brigadier General Viele, "with the somewhat mysterious caution to speak to no one of my movements," received orders from the secretary of war to be at the Washington Navy Yard within the hour. Viele got there just as Secretary Stanton himself was arriving. In the darkness Stanton led Viele through an enclosure, down to the Potomac wharf where *Miami* was moored. They boarded her and made for the cabin. There, to Viele's surprise, was the president, along with Secretary of the Treasury Salmon P. Chase. Their destination was the seat of operations, their mission to observe just what was going on down there. At 8 P.M. *Miami* got under way and steamed downriver in the rain.

She was a graceful craft, well built, well outfitted, and well suited to serve as the temporary floating headquarters of government: a 115-foot schooner-rigged screw steamer, 213 tons, ten sails, two oscillating engines. An elegant craft, she bore teak planking, copper fastenings, and a frame hewn from good English oak. Built in 1853 on Scotland's River Clyde, and christened *Lady Le Marchant*, she worked in the transatlantic trade for six years. In January 1862 she was purchased by the U.S. Treasury Department for the Revenue Marine Service. The government had her completely overhauled and fitted her out with a new screw and new fastenings—and a new name, *Miami*, by order of Secretary Chase. He had her appointed for comfort, with everything from spare bedding to champagne glasses to a silver-plated nutpick. She was armed with four brass howitzers, two to a side, and a rifled pivot gun on the bow. Captain Douglass Ottinger, considered one of the Revenue Marine Service's finest, was given the command. With him were three lieutenants, two engineers, and thirty-four crewmen. The cutter arrived in Washington from New York on April 7 and quickly became the toast of the town, especially among the top government officials and their wives who had the privilege of being invited to cruise on her.

On April 11 the Lincolns and the Sewards enjoyed a *Miami* excursion to Alexandria and back. On April 19 Lincoln was on board again, this time on business. The president, Stanton, Chase, and others steamed down to the Aquia Creek army headquarters, where Lincoln first received the news: McDowell had taken Fredericksburg. The next day the general and his officers came aboard and were congratulated by the president.

On May 5, after being scrubbed, provisioned, inspected, and coaled up, *Miami* headed out for the lower Chesapeake. Ensconced from the dreary downpour, Lincoln, Chase, Stanton, and Viele reclined in comfortable chairs in the cabin described as "neat and cozy" by Viele. "A

THE U.S. REVENUE CUTTER *MIAMI*, THE VESSEL THAT CARRIED
ABRAHAM LINCOLN DOWN THE CHESAPEAKE BAY IN MAY 1862.
Nimitz Library, U.S. Naval Academy

shaded lamp suspended from the ceiling threw a cheerful light over the table, upon which a tempting supper was spread." Chase had brought along his butler, who waited on the men with great panache. The gracious Chase "seemed to feel that we were his guests, as the steamer belonged to the Treasury Department," said Viele, "and he treated us as if we were in his own house."

The dishes were cleared, and the men sat in the cabin lamplight discussing the war into the wee hours. "It was a most interesting study to see these men relieved for the moment from the surroundings of their onerous official duties," Viele said. "The President, of course, was the center of the group,—kind, genial, thoughtful, tender-hearted, magnanimous Abraham Lincoln! It was difficult to know him without knowing him intimately, for he was as guileless and single-hearted as a child; and no man ever knew him intimately who did not recognize and admire his great abilities, both natural and acquired, his large-heartedness and sincerity of purpose."

Visibility was bad that night on the water, and the captain brought them to anchor just below Mount Vernon. "The driving rain outside only served to make our little cabin seem more cozy," said Viele "and the small hours of morning came before there was any disposition to retire." Lincoln, Chase, and Stanton had never been to Fort Monroe; Viele had, and he answered their questions as they hovered over maps of the region. They were inquisitive about Norfolk. Viele had taken part in the Port Royal expedition, and while "lying rather listlessly at Hampton Roads in 1861," he had wished an attempt could be made to capture Norfolk. "We had nearly 20,000 men on board the transports at that time, destined for a descent on the Southern coast, and we could readily have struck the blow and re-embarked during the time we were lying there idle in the ships." Beneath the cabin lamp, Viele pointed down at the map and showed the men "what I regarded as a feasible route to the rear of Norfolk. . . ."

They called it a night. The president's berth was too small for his elongated stature, but he lay down as best he could and slumbered on the waves not far from George Washington's home. *Miami* set sail in the predawn darkness at the invitation of a northwest wind too good to pass up. In no time the cutter was doing 10 knots on sail power alone, and with squaresail and topgallant aloft she raced from the river into Chesapeake Bay.

Lincoln and his party came above and spent much of the day idling on the quarterdeck as *Miami* made her way down the Bay. The president was engaging company, a font of backwoodsy, always apropos anecdotes and great, long memorized passages of Shakespeare, Browning, and Byron. Viele showed Lincoln a humorous verse in *Harper's Weekly*. Lincoln loved it, and "instead of requesting me to cut it out for him, he borrowed my knife, and, extending himself at half length on the deck, spread the paper before him and cut the piece out, remarking at the same time that it was not precisely the attitude for the President of the United States to assume, but it was a good position for a man who merely wanted to cut a piece out of a newspaper."

Wind died, progress slowed, and an awning was put up on the deck for the president and his party. Being out on the Bay prompted Lincoln to reminisce at length about his earlier maritime experience, when as a

A CONFERENCE IN THE CABIN OF *MIAMI*. *FROM LEFT*: BRIGADIER GENERAL EGBERT L. VIELE, PRESIDENT LINCOLN, SECRETARY OF THE TREASURY SALMON P. CHASE, AND SECRETARY OF WAR EDWIN M. STANTON.
Nimitz Library, U.S. Naval Academy

young man he traded whiskey and tobacco down the Mississippi on a flatboat. But the deck conversation naturally kept winding its way back to the war and the governmental woes thereby created. Offering bemused lamentation over the large number of political favors he was always being asked for, Lincoln said, "If I have one vice, and I can call it nothing else,—it is not to be able to say no! Thank God for not making me a woman, but if He had, I suppose He would have made me just as ugly as He did, and no one would have tempted me."

Night fell. *Miami* reached Fort Monroe. "The outlines of the grand old fortress were dimly visible along the horizon as we approached," Viele recalled, "and around and about it in the adjacent waters was a cordon of floating videttes, whose thousand lights glimmered like stars in the mirrored surface." Around nine o'clock the revenue cutter tied up

THE USS *VANDERBILT*, A "LEVIATHAN" THAT HOPED FOR A
CHANCE AT BATTLING CSS *VIRGINIA*.
Harper's Weekly

alongside the old Bay steamer *George Washington*. General Wool and his
staff boarded *Miami*, greeted their distinguished guests, and held a
conference. After midnight *Miami* cast off, and they all went over to meet
with Flag Officer Goldsborough on *Minnesota*, anchored nearby. By
dawn, the conference had moved to *Vanderbilt*, "that leviathan of ocean
steamers, a million-dollar gift" from her owner, Cornelius Vanderbilt,
to the government for the war effort. If *Monitor* could coax *Virginia* out
for another fight, the hope was to have the mighty *Vanderbilt* come on
full-steam and run the rebel monster down.

After this nightful of floating conferences, Lincoln finally stepped
ashore and breakfasted in Quarters Number One at Fort Monroe. Then
he set out to visit some people to whom he felt a good deal of gratitude:
the *Monitor* crew.

As the tug came alongside, the dignitaries boarded the ironclad.
Chase was there, and Stanton, and General Wool with his staff in
full-dress uniform. And the president. The mood was celebratory, joy-
ous, patriotic, yet Lincoln wore a sad, troubled look. His gaze was turned

away from *Monitor*'s assembled officers, and when he finally turned to look upon them his lip was trembling and his gaunt form shaking, betraying some deep emotion. He toured the vessel with evident curiosity and interest, obviously well versed in its construction and mechanics. The crew was mustered on deck, and he slowly walked down the line with his tall hat in his hand. He was offered whiskey. He accepted ice water. As he departed from the iron deck, the crew's farewell was a rousing three cheers.

After the presidential party left, a boatload of congressmen arrived to tour *Monitor*. Their visit was curtailed by the sudden shrillness of the bosun's whistle and the call to clear for action. The congressmen rushed back to the tug. At the mouth of the Elizabeth, in a black smokestack cloud, *Virginia* appeared. She remained off Sewells Point for a while, making her presence felt, then vanished.

Lincoln ordered Goldsborough to send some boats up the James, *Virginia* or no *Virginia*. Goldsborough accordingly dispatched the new six-gun ironclad *Galena* and the gunboats *Aroostook* and *Port Royal* with instructions "to harass the retreat of the rebels wherever they can be reached," thereby assisting McClellan's advance. On the morning of May 8 the three vessels steamed up the James with no interference from the rebel ironclad. They clashed with a couple of batteries, silenced them, and chased CSS *Jamestown* and *Yorktown* up the river. While the three-boat squadron was stirring things up on the James, a six-boat squadron was carrying out Lincoln's other orders for the day: the bombardment of Sewells Point.

Shortly after noon the vessels—including *Monitor* and the new one-gun ironclad *E. A. Stevens* or *Naugatuck*—took position in Hampton Roads and commenced their heavy cannonade. They were out to test the current strength of the Confederate position, to ascertain if a troop landing would be viable thereabouts. Their other goal, particularly *Monitor*'s, was to lure *Virginia* down far enough that she could be rammed by *Minnesota* or *Vanderbilt*, waiting hopefully under the guns of Fort Monroe.

That morning, a little tug called *J. B. White* had come steaming down hell-bent-for-leather from Norfolk and crossed over to Newport News. She'd been sent out to retrieve a couple of Southern schooners lying off the mouth of Tanners Creek. But the tug's officers had long wanted to defect and knew their main chance when they saw it. With them they brought big news: Norfolk was being evacuated. Much of General Huger's army had already pulled out; maybe two thousand remained, but they too were exiting rapidly. It was timely information, and the troops of Fort Monroe were making ready to cross the water as the Sewells Point shelling continued.

The vessels blasted away at the Sewells Point battery for hours while President Lincoln viewed the spectacle from the deck of a steam-tug and then from the Rip Raps ramparts. The Sewells Point soldiers' quarters went up in flames. The Confederate flag was shot down, and as it was replaced with another one, the new flag and the rebel raising it were both blown to oblivion. Then, amid the shells and smoke, another defiant flag rose on another makeshift flagstaff. By midafternoon the Confederate return fire was diminishing. Then out came *Virginia*.

She waited, inviting an attack just by showing herself. The Federal squadron likewise waited, hoping *Virginia* would dare to come closer. She advanced far enough for the Rip Raps' guns to thunder off a shot at her, which soared past overhead. The Federal vessels held back—withdrew speedily, according to Confederates—and after a while an exasperated Commodore Tattnall on *Virginia* turned to his lieutenant and said, "Mr. Jones, fire a gun to windward, and take the ship back to her buoy."

Norfolk had to be turned, and now was the time. But the landing was going to have to be out of *Virginia*'s range. On May 9 *Miami* transported Secretary Chase, Brigadier General Viele, and General Wool to inspect the shoreline of Lynnhaven Bay. Below Old Point Comfort, it would be shielded from *Virginia* by the Fort Monroe Rip Raps gauntlet. It was also where, in 1861, Viele claimed to have favored a Norfolk-aimed deployment.

Wool had brought along his aide, Colonel T. J. Cram, chief of topographical engineers, the man responsible for McClellan's faulty peninsula map. Accompanied by an armed crew, Colonel Cram took a boat in to sound fathoms and reconnoiter closer to shore. Soon the boat came racing back, Cram having spotted a sizable picket guard.

Secretary Chase scanned the land with a spyglass. "Instead of defiant warriors he saw some people waving a white sheet as a flag of truce; a longer scrutiny revealed a white woman, a negress, a child and a dog, as the sole cause of the colonel's terror, . . ." said Viele. Cram's rowboat headed back in, this time in company of Chase and Viele in another boat. The white woman said her husband had lit out for the woods, dodging Confederate conscription. She gave the landing party much valuable information about road conditions to Norfolk. The water depth here

PRESIDENT LINCOLN RECONNOITERS POSSIBLE LANDING
SITES FOR THE ADVANCE ON NORFOLK.
Nimitz Library, U.S. Naval Academy

could handle the transports: a natural harbor, a gently sloping beach, eight miles or so to the back door of Norfolk—here was a good place to land the troops. Situated below Willoughby Spit, it was a popular destination for Norfolk outings called Ocean View.

Miami returned to the location with President Lincoln. Earlier, he and Stanton had combed the same coastline by tugboat; they, too, had thought it promising—in fact, they'd warmed to a spot just a mile or so away. But Lincoln wanted to see firsthand the *Miami*-chosen site. He walked along the beach in the moonlight—the president of the United States leaving large footprints behind enemy lines. Remarked Viele, "How little the Confederacy dreamed what a visitor it had that night to the 'sacred soil'!"

When *Miami* returned to Fort Monroe, the ready-to-move troops cheered heartily at the sight of Lincoln. By horseback and by boat, the commander in chief had been in continual motion on his sojourn, lighting a fire under the boots of army and navy alike, lifting men's spirits by his presence, making things happen, and getting things moving. The president, enthused the Baltimore *American*'s Old Point correspondent, had "infused new vigor in both naval and military operations here."

The troops began moving out at midnight, nearly six thousand of them in canal boats towed by steamers. The soldiers rode in the boats, while cavalry steeds and fieldpieces filled the steamers. The guns of the Rips Raps bombarded Sewells Point to foster the illusion that the landing would be made there. Meanwhile, the first troop transports were arriving at Ocean View by 1:10 A.M. The march began while the disembarkation continued through the morning. Old General Wool was given the honor of command; under him were General Max Weber and Brigadier General Joseph Mansfield. Wool remained at the beach, overseeing the landing, while the infantry marched down the road. The advance force, New York and Massachusetts regiments led by Weber, got to the Tanners Creek bridge to find howitzers aimed at them from the opposite bank. The retreating rebels torched the bridge and fired their cannon at the vanguard Yankees.

Secretary Chase and Brigadier General Viele were riding toward the front with a half-dozen dragoons. Confusion reigned; soldiers along the roadside were unclear whether they were under the command of Weber or Mansfield. Men were straggling back from the boom of cannon up ahead. When General Wool finally arrived with a bodyguard of mounted rifles, Chase rather harshly inquired what was going on. Wool answered that apparently General Mansfield "had felt some delicacy" in taking the reins of command in the presence of General Weber, and Weber felt likewise toward Mansfield.

"Talk of delicacy, with the enemy firing in front!" Chase shouted. "What absurdity! Let General Mansfield go to the rear and bring up reinforcements, and that will settle all questions of delicacy."

As Wool and Mansfield repaired to the shade of a sycamore to discuss at length their next move, Chase remarked, "Two cackling old hens!" Then he turned to Viele and said, "Sir! I order you in the name of the President of the United States to take command of these troops and march them upon Norfolk."

Viele got them moving on the double-quick, throwing out advance skirmishers ahead of the march. Wool soon caught up, indignant. Chase smoothed ruffled feathers, and the advance progressed. A native helped them out with a detour in lieu of the burnt Tanners Creek bridge. An eight-mile march on the Princess Anne road around the head of the creek would get the army to Norfolk. Outside the city, they came upon extensive fortifications. Thirty heavy guns were mounted in lines of earthworks three miles long. "These works could have been defended by five thousand men against an army of forty thousand," a reporter observed. But the ramparts were deserted and the guns were spiked. Instead of dug-in resistance, the advancing army was met by a flag of truce.

It was brought out by Mayor William W. Lamb and a select committee of the municipal council of the city of Norfolk. With great decorousness and official flutter, the mayor surrendered Norfolk into the hands of General Wool and the U. S. government, pleading for protection of citizens and property. The ceremonious welcome was "a most skillful ruse to gain time for the Confederates to secure their retreat from the city," figured Viele. He described the scheme.

> The mayor, with all the formality of a mediaeval warden, appeared with a bunch of rusty keys and a formidable roll of papers, which he proceeded to

read with the utmost deliberation previous to delivering the "keys of the city." The reading of the documents—which embraced a large portion of the history of Virginia, the causes that led to the war, the peculiar position of the good citizens of Norfolk, and in short a little of everything that could have the remotest bearing upon the subject and exhaust the longest possible space of time in reading—was protracted until nearly dark. In the meanwhile the Confederates were hurrying with their artillery and stores over the ferry to Portsmouth, cutting the water-pipes and flooding the public buildings, setting fire to the navy yard, and having their own way generally, while our General was listening in the most innocent and complacent manner to the long rigmarole so ingeniously prepared by the mayor and skillfully interlarded with fulsome personal eulogium upon himself.

Chase politely cut short the speechifying. The troops bivouacked on the outskirts while the officers and officials climbed into carriages and proceeded to city hall, where the mayor succeeded in further dragging out the formalities. Wool appointed Viele military governor, then Wool and Chase departed, leaving Viele to deal with the conquered populace. A crowd of several thousand had gathered around city hall, getting boisterous, shooting off pistols, calling for a speech by the mayor. According to the correspondent from the *New York Times*, Mayor Lamb told the crowd that "the citizens of Norfolk had been deserted by their friends, and all the city authorities could do was to obtain the best terms possible. . . . He was happy to assure them that in this he had been successful. . . . If the decision had rested with him, he would have defended the city to the last man. . . ." The crowd cheered the speech and gave three cheers for Jefferson Davis and then three groans for Abraham Lincoln. The darkening sky was lit up by the glare of the burning Norfolk Navy Yard.

By morning the yard lay in ruins, more efficiently destroyed by the evacuating Confederates than it had been by the evacuating Federals a year earlier. Even the great stone dry dock had been damaged this time, crippled by a mine blast after being stripped of its engine and pump. The yard was a wasteland of blackened, broken building husks and lone-standing chimneys amid rubble and residual flames. Nonetheless, Sunday, May 11, was a day worth savoring for the Federals. The U.S. flag flew over the abandoned Sewells Point battery and atop the cupola of Norfolk's customhouse. Ships of the North Atlantic Blockading Squad-

ron sat in the harbor. *Monitor*, the first one in, was moored off old Fort
Norfolk. Bands played "Hail, Columbia" and "Yankee Doodle" beneath
a clear sky. The waterfront was crowded with blacks, working-class
whites, and the soldiers of occupation. Much of town, though, was quiet
this Sunday, houses tightly shut, particularly among the wealthy portions.

At 11:30 A.M. the steamer *Baltimore* arrived with President Lincoln,
Secretaries Chase and Stanton, General Wool, and Flag Officer Goldsborough. Entering the harbor, the president removed his stovepipe hat
and bowed to his navy. In an hour *Baltimore* departed, first for Fort
Monroe, then on up the Chesapeake, carrying Lincoln back to Washington. The USRC *Miami*, her boiler blown while she assisted the troop
landing at Ocean View, was laid up for repairs, and the president had
to return now. It had been a fruitful journey. It was underscored by the
best news of all: *Virginia* was no more.

The crew of the rebel ironclad knew something was wrong on May 10
when they no longer saw the flag flying on Sewells Point. Up on the other
side of the river, the Confederate colors still waved over the Craney
Island battery. Commander Tattnall put his flag lieutenant ashore there
to find out what was going on. And Pembroke Jones came back with
disconcerting information. The Yankees had landed in force out on the
Bay shore and were on the march to Norfolk. Sewells Point had been
evacuated; the army was in retreat. The lieutenant was sent to Norfolk
to find out more, and he did: General Huger and all the other army
officers had left, as had all the officers of the navy yard. The navy yard
was in flames. The enemy was right outside the city. All the river
batteries, even Craney Island, were being quickly abandoned now. The
railroad cars to Richmond were packed with the pursued, and suddenly
Virginia was all alone. Commander Tattnall called all hands on deck.

If diligent and fast, they had a fighting chance. The pilots assured
the commander that if the vessel's draft could be reduced to eighteen
feet from its current twenty-two, they could get the ironclad up the
James as far as City Point or Harrisons Landing. Once there, *Virginia*
could be re-outfitted and continue to protect Richmond from the river.
To succeed, they would have to scoot past Newport News before day-

light to evade the Federal fleet, and there was much lightening of the ship to be done. The crew gave three cheers and got to work.

Into the night they jettisoned with great spirit, stripping the vessel of ballast, water, stores, throwing overboard anything not nailed down, sparing only the powder and shot. By midnight, *Virginia*'s wooden hull was exposed above the waterline. There was hope, until the pilots spoke again.

They now said that considering the unfavorable wind factors, even with eighteen feet of draft they couldn't get the boat as far as James-town Flats. Tattnall was flabbergasted at the pilots' change of story, and the crew shared the chagrin. Now stripped, *Virginia* was no longer fit for battle; they no longer even had the option of running past Fort Monroe and going down fighting. "It will be asked what motives the pilots could have had to deceive me. The only imaginable one is that they wished to avoid going into battle," stated Tattnall. "Moral: All officers, as far as possible, should learn to do their own piloting," commented John Taylor Wood.

Josiah Tattnall was out of choices and out of time. He landed his crew with weapons and two days' provisions. It took three hours to debark them all at Craney Island. Wood and Catesby Jones were the last off the vessel. She was torched fore and aft and was soon blazing lively, and by the fire's glow the lieutenants rowed to shore. Two minutes before 5 A.M., the great rebel ironclad was blown to bits.

Tattnall reported, "The *Virginia* no longer exists, but 300 brave and skillful officers and seamen are saved to the Confederacy."

The beached crewmen hiked the twenty-two miles to Suffolk, then took the train Richmond-bound. The Confederate capital was in a panic. The Federal fleet was moving up the James. The city was ill-prepared to repel an attack from the river because there had been *Virginia* to bank on. *Virginia* could help Richmond no more, but her crew could. They made haste for Drewry's Bluff.

The bluff was seven miles down, a high overlook at a bend in the James. Augustus Drewry, the landowner, had put up a three-gun battery on the bluff and had a volunteer defense unit to man it. Fort Darling, as it was called, was now being buttressed by river obstructions, more gun emplacements, and an influx of additional men. If the Union boats got past, Richmond would fall. "Here, for two days, exposed to constant rain, in bottomless mud and without shelter, on scant provisions, we worked unceasingly, mounting guns and obstructing the river," said Wood. Then on May 15 they rounded the bend: *Monitor, Naugatuck, Aroostook, Port Royal.* At the head of the flotilla was the new ironclad *Galena,* its Commander John Rodgers. The boats came in range, the defenders on Drewry's Bluff fired their guns, and a four-hour battle ensued.

The fort's elevation was a definite advantage; *Monitor*'s guns, for example, just couldn't angle to a high enough trajectory. Confederate sharpshooters lined the steep riverbanks below the bluff. Wood and some of his shipmates were among those stationed in the rifle pits. "The enemy were excessively annoyed by their fire," Catesby Jones reported. The position held by the *Virginia* shooters "was well chosen and gallantly maintained in spite of the shell, shrapnel, grape, and canister fired at them." The big guns on the bluff concentrated much of their pounding on *Galena,* which Rodgers had boldly brought up well within range and proceeded to maneuver masterfully in the narrow, shallow water, positioning for a broadside with calm precision while the high artillery pounded away on the experimental vessel. "It was one of the most masterly pieces of seamanship in the whole war," an enemy officer on the bluff had to admit.

But the fort was unpassable. Ammunition spent, armor pierced in several places, *Galena* retired, a floating hell of flung body parts and blood and groaning men. The other boats retired with her. The rebels at the bend in the river had saved Richmond.

With its boiler repaired, the U.S. Revenue Cutter *Miami* steamed back up the Chesapeake Bay, anchoring at Washington on May 18. She had brought something along for her former passenger. The gift for President Lincoln came from an admirer in Norfolk.

It was the safety valve from the late CSS *Virginia.*

CHAPTER 6

Smugglers and travelers

BALTIMORE STREET WAS mobbed. It was May 25, 1862, a Sunday, and a volatile mix of pro-Union and secessionist elements had packed newspaper row. News was coming in from the upper Potomac, which was terrible or terrific, depending on which side received it. The Union forces under General Nathaniel Banks had been beaten by Stonewall Jackson's troops and chased across the Potomac. Banks, who less than a year ago had been military overseer of Baltimore, had among his force the First Maryland Regiment, the favorite sons of Baltimore's Union faction. The First Maryland's founder/colonel, John Kenly, had been wounded and captured. Jackson, on the other side, had Marylanders in his ranks, too. It was the first battle in the war where Marylanders had faced off.

Standing on the crowded corner of Baltimore and South Streets, an old man named Robert Morrow chose now to utter the sentiment that "every one of the First Maryland Regiment ought to be killed." He was knocked down and beaten, and the police had to fight the crowd to get him out of there. Old Morrow's face was covered with blood as the lawmen hustled him off to the central station house, where it was determined, reported the Baltimore *Sun*, that the arrested secessionist had "made use of expressions calculated to excite a riot. . . ." The police had their hands full thereafter, as a Mobtown street version of civil war seethed and erupted and lasted for days. And if the secessionists had started it with their gloating or, with what the Baltimore *American* called "their inopportune rejoicings over the defeat and slaughter of a regiment raised from our own population," the riot soon became retaliation time, a bloodletting for the city's Union faithful, who set upon the rebels among them with ferocity.

Though the Robert Morrow beating sparked Sunday's violence, the trouble really had begun Saturday night, as word of Banks's retreat and the First Maryland's defeat had first started pouring in. Secessionists congregated on street corners and boisterously celebrated. In West Baltimore a butcher strode up to a Union man and said, "Well, your great cock has fallen in the first pit."

"Who do you mean?" the Union man asked. "John Kenly," the butcher replied. Right away, words turned to blows, and the butcher was knocked to the sidewalk. The donnybrook became more general as the neighborhood Union men "declared their determination to whip every secessionist they could find who uttered a word of rejoicing. . . ."

Next morning, with Morrow's blunt utterance, the storm center of mob violence shifted to the business district. A pair of Union men spotted the lawyer Thomas J. Warrington at the corner of Baltimore and Frederick Streets. Warrington was said to have sons in the Confederate army. The Unioners knocked the lawyer's hat off, chased him a few blocks, and beat him up. Another secessionist, one Mr. Kirk, was riding his carriage up Baltimore Street when the mob swarmed. He got as far as Calvert Street before they yanked him down from the carriage and proceeded to attack him. Bolivar D. Daniels, Esquire, was being beaten on the head by an enthusiastically enraged throng when the police finally managed to pull him out. As they escorted him to the Office of Police Commissioners, a crowd of five hundred to six hundred followed, brandishing rope and chanting, "Hang him! Hang him!"

A gang stormed the house on the corner of Baltimore and Harrison, where a pro-Southern association kept upstairs rooms. As their furniture was being smashed, the members of the association jumped from the second story. In front of his home on High Street near Lombard, a Mr. Passano was bashed on the head with a brick while the women of the house watched from the windows and screamed. Caleb Sawyer was on Calvert near Baltimore Street when he was singled out for being a reb, and he fired his revolver as he fled from the attacking mob. James Knox, a British shipping merchant who owned Knox & Company on Smiths

Wharf, got in a brawl on North Street. The crowd was making ready to hang him near the Chesapeake Bank when police came to the rescue.

The central station jail was filling up. It was past 5 P.M. when Samuel Hindes, a police commissioner, climbed up on a box on Baltimore Street and urged the unruly mob to disperse, appealing to their ostensible support of "the Union, the Constitution, and the enforcement of the laws." The commissioner's presence and his impassioned address worked to break up the crowd. But by the next morning trouble was brewing again, and Monday became bloodier than Sunday.

By 9:30 A.M. a huge crowd had again gathered on Baltimore Street between South and Calvert. By shortly past ten people were being pointed out as secessionists, attacked, and severely beaten. Part of the throng headed up Fayette Street, another down South Street. On Baltimore Street the newspaper offices were "visited" and forced to fly the U.S. flag. Marshal Van Nostrand had to rally almost the entire city police force to the Baltimore-Calvert-South-Street area, and they rushed along with the ebb and flow of the mob. At 2 P.M. the Board of Police Commissioners issued a special proclamation: "All persons are warned not to congregate on the street. All public demonstrations will be promptly dispersed. All bar-rooms, restaurants, and other drinking saloons are required to be forthwith closed for twenty-four hours." Men were being attacked and beaten in the southern, southwestern, and eastern portions of the city as well as in the main center of disorder. In the railroad yard at Mount Clare Station, several workmen were assaulted, and others had to flee to avoid the same vicious roughing-up.

By day's end, it was again clear that while the mob rule had been that of gone-wild Union men, there were Southern supporters who had done nothing to calm matters. The new guests at the central lockup included, among others, one Alexander Ramsay, arrested "for inciting a riot and huzzaing for Jeff Davis."

Major General Dix, whose headquarters adjoined the Board of Police Commissioners' office, had summoned Marshal Van Nostrand early on in the unrest and asked him if the police needed help quelling the disturbance. The marshal gave his assurance that the police had things under control. The major general made it clear that if need be, he would call out the military.

John Adams Dix's last week in command at Baltimore was turning out to be a frisky one. (On Sunday, June 1, he would be transferred to the Fort Monroe–Norfolk command, trading positions with General Wool, who was ordered to Baltimore.) The volatile city was exploding in street warfare as it had always been threatening to do. And while the Mobtown throng swirled, Major General Dix had another situation on his mind as well. By his orders, Deputy Provost Marshal James McPhail and four officers had cleared Baltimore Saturday on the steamer *Balloon*. They were expected to return with a certain prominent, and problematic, individual from the Eastern Shore.

The Honorable Richard Bennett Carmichael, judge of the Seventh Judicial District of Maryland, was the august and distinguished product of an august and distinguished Eastern Shore family lineage. A former congressman and son of a well-remembered lawyer, Judge Carmichael was venerated, widely popular, a gentleman farmer-cum-legal sage whose judiciary circuit encompassed Talbot, Caroline, Queen Anne's, and Kent Counties. He had the big beard, little spectacles, and balding pate of the archetypal man of intellect, and since last November he had been political dynamite.

The state elections of fall 1861 had taken place with the accompaniment of Federal troops at voting sites. Whether it was viewed as keeping the peace or voter intimidation, one result of this polling-place policing was a number of arrests of citizens branded "disloyal," by dint of their not supporting the Unionist ticket. Judge Carmichael charged the grand jury, first of Queen Anne's and then of Talbot, to regard any warrantless arrest as a crime in itself:

> Violent and dangerous injuries have been committed, upon your citizens, whilst the process of law has been forbidden to reach the offender. Arrests have been made, utterly groundless as it turned out; but whether with cause or not, by persons having no legal competency to make arrests, and without 'warrant of law,' or process from legal authority. A squad of soldiers, with no pretence of authority but their arms, it is said, have invaded the homes of your fellow-citizens, and dragged them to their camp. There they have been detained as long as it suited the pleasure of their captors.

He quoted the Bill of Rights, and he repeatedly stressed how sacred was Americans' freedom from arrest without due cause:

> Exemption from the exercise of such power, is the birthright of Americans. They trace it back in the musty scrolls of the mother country for ages long past. It is inscribed, in letters of light, in the Constitution of Maryland. This right may yet be found in the Constitution of the United States—the Supreme law—before which every person, potentate, and power in the United States must give place.

The Queen Anne's County grand jury kicked forth with bills of presentment against the soldiers who had performed the arrests, but the soldiers were transferred out of Maryland before any court action could be taken. Then, likewise charging Talbot's grand jury at that county's November term, Judge Carmichael had the charge printed and published to clarify his position. It was the kind of documentary evidence that could get a fellow in trouble. Six months passed, and Talbot's spring court session had just recently convened before the powers that be finally got around to punishing the dissenter.

McPhail and his men barged in on the middle of a trial at the Talbot County Courthouse in Easton on Monday, May 26, 1862, and told Judge Carmichael he was under arrest. The judge asked by what authority they disrupted the proceedings. "By the authority of the United States" was the reply. James Bishop, one of McPhail's men, came forward and grabbed the judge's beard and told him to get moving. Judge Carmichael kicked Bishop; Bishop took his revolver butt and started chopping, pistol-whipping the judge until he lay bloody and unconscious on the floor of his own courtroom. The 125 men of the Second Delaware Regiment, McPhail's reinforcements he had wired Dix to send, arrived and took the now-bandaged judge to the steamer waiting at Wye Landing. Prosecuting attorney Isaac C. W. Powell, the prominent Eastonian who had tried to help the judge while he was being beaten, also was roughed up, arrested, and shipped to Baltimore. He and the judge were imprisoned at Fort McHenry for six weeks; then it was on to Fort Lafayette and finally Fort Delaware. They were prisoners for six months and never formally charged. Judge Carmichael wrote the president twice, but never received a reply.

Across the harbor from Fort McHenry there were other prisoners. Campbell's Slave Jail, on Pratt Street three doors east of Howard, was the current residence of seventy-two captured runaways from all parts of the state, boarded here for safekeeping until their masters wanted to take them home. Campbell's Slave Jail had a yard where the prisoners could go during the day. At 7 P.M. they all had to repair to their rooms and were awoken at 5 A.M. That was the routine. On Saturday, May 31, Baltimore's week of violent disturbances culminated with the slaves' refusal to clear the yard at seven.

B. M. Campbell, proprietor of the slave jail, ordered them to obey. "They offered him violence," the *Sun* reported, "and he was compelled to leave the yard." The slaves began to raise a ruckus, filling the May night with a fearful noise. Alarmed neighbors flocked to the jail front. Inside, the slaves were shouting, swiping the air with makeshift clubs.

Captain Manley and a twenty-man squad from the Southern District police station showed up at about 9 P.M. and charged into the yard. As soon as they entered, the blacks attacked them "with what weapons they had, and it was not until after a severe struggle that they were overpowered." Police gunfire was scattershot and ineffective. Lawmen and slaves alike were battered, cut, and bruised in the melee. Campbell the jailer was clobbered on the back of the head with a shovel and suffered "a severe blow in the left eye" when he tried to stand up.

The slaves, reported the *Sun*, had loudly and repeatedly declared "that the time had come for them to go free, and do as they pleased. . . ."

In addition to the high-profile arrest of Judge Carmichael, Deputy Provost Marshal McPhail came very close to another notable nabbing. He probably never knew just how close he came to catching Levi White.

McPhail had it in for Baltimore's prince of smugglers, and on a hot summer evening he dispatched nine detectives to White's McCulloh Street home. Acting on a tip that the elusive White was actually there at present, "the provost thought he had me this time for sure," recounted White. The agents surrounded the house, some of them jumping the fence from the back alley, others going in the front door. For three hours they searched, "over and over again from roof to cellar, including the bathroom." They questioned and requestioned White's family and servants, to no avail—the servants didn't know and the family wasn't talking. McPhail's men left frustrated and empty-handed. Thorough as they'd been, they hadn't paid much notice to the man of the house's vest hanging on a peg in the library, the gold watch in the vest pocket.

Levi White hadn't meant to leave it hanging there; it tended to indicate he was still on the premises. But it was hot, he'd removed his vest, and when the time came to disappear he forgot it in his haste. And as he listened to the detectives on the other side of the wall, he kept worrying that any minute one of them might notice the vest. When he finally heard them leaving, he waited only long enough to be sure the coast was clear before emerging, sweat-soaked and hungry. He tucked into his supper with zeal.

It wasn't the only time the artful hiding place had saved White. One of his cohorts had built it, a "false bulkhead" behind the back room, "and it was so carefully made that no one unacquainted with it could detect it." For the life White was leading, it was a home improvement that repeatedly proved its worth.

Since becoming a special agent of the Confederate States Ordnance Department in 1861, Levi White had kept hazardously busy as locater, purchaser, and smuggler of materials needed for the Southern war effort. So regular were his risky trips to and from Richmond that he became relied upon as a mailman as well as deliverer of goods. "Sometimes there would be 300 to 500 letters from Marylanders in the South to their friends in the North," recalled White. "I carried so many letters both ways during the war that the Marylanders in Richmond declared that when the Confederacy had been established I should be made postmaster at Baltimore."

From potassium to block tin to gutta-percha to uniform buttons, White acquired what the Ordnance Department needed whenever and wherever he could. With the daring of a spy and the shrewdness of an entrepreneur, he became a far-ranging and resourceful procurer. "Obtaining supplies at first was the most difficult part of my operations, but experience soon broke up all obstacles," said the man who claimed to have set up large transactions even with merchants who had sons in the Union army. "In a very short time I had but little difficulty in getting any materials either in Baltimore or New York, but more caution was necessary in Baltimore, as detectives were constantly watching. . . . In New York I could purchase almost as readily from a Union man as from a 'sympathizer.' No questions were asked. They had the goods and I had the cash. They took my money and I got the goods."

Making a buy in New York or Philadelphia was one thing; getting the shipment past heavily guarded Baltimore and across the border was the dangerous half of the venture. To skirt the guards patrolling the Long Bridge where Light Street ran southward out of the city, White and company loaded goods on small boats and secreted them across to Curtis Creek. From there the options opened up: to the Potomac via land route; down the Bay in larger boats to the Potomac; down the Bay to the Patuxent and from there, overland to the Potomac. There were scads of variations, and all routes led to Richmond.

White's preference became Middle River, northeast of town. It was a well-situated rendezvous for shipment, vessel, and crew. Once they'd developed a routine based on healthy amounts of caution, "we ran upon this schedule as regularly as some railroads do on their timetables." It was all quite choreographed: First in motion was the wagonload of cargo, hauled out of town by the trusty Biddison, eschewing the obvious Philadelphia Road. Outside Baltimore limits it was well guarded, "but it never occurred to the military in charge at Baltimore that goods for the Confederates could be hauled by other roads," said White. "I maintained the route and rendezvous until near the close of the war and lost but one load." Out the York Road, to the Harford Road, to the Bel Air Road, and crossing the Philadelphia Road farther out, Biddison transported the goods to the drop-off point at Middle River. His circuitousness avoided the main guard, but he nonetheless occasionally had to pass by Union encampments. And the White gang's very first time on this route had almost ended up being the last time, too.

With two million musket-caps in tow on that maiden run, Biddison was on the Harford Road when two Union soldiers jumped out in front of him and halted his team. The game is up, feared Biddison. But when the soldier boys handed him an empty bottle, their purpose became clear. They needed the civilian to go in the store up ahead and fill the bottle with whiskey for them. They sent him ahead on foot and drove his wagon for him. Biddison came out of the store and gave the Billys

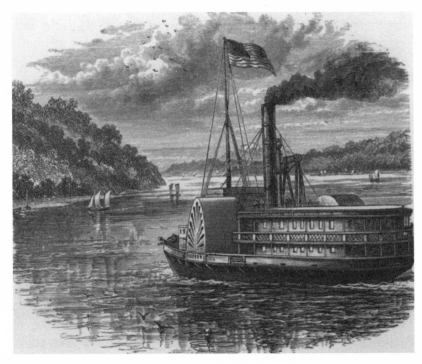

A POTOMAC FLOTILLA VESSEL ON PATROL. SAID ONE BALTIMORE SMUGGLER,
"WE COULD WATCH THEM EASIER THAN THEY COULD WATCH US."
Nimitz Library, U.S. Naval Academy

their whiskey. They gave him a dollar for his efforts and went merrily on their way. Biddison rode on with the two million musket-caps for the Confederacy and an extra dollar in his pocket.

"I am a temperance man," Levi White later reflected, "but have experienced the fact that sometimes whisky is a valuable ally."

Biddison would be met by another operative at the Middle River rendezvous. "I had a careful, sharp, wide-awake agent there named Bowers," said White. Once the goods were out of the city, it was White's turn to follow along separately. The sought-after ringleader needed the most precaution. At exactly 4 P.M. a carriage would turn off Biddle Street onto McCulloh, clip-clop past White's house, then turn onto Preston. White would peek out; his aide Rogers would be on the block. If Rogers had a white handkerchief it was safe to come out; a red handkerchief meant wait. Given the all-clear, White would slip out of his house and go around the corner to Preston Street. The carriage door opened, White jumped in, and with his friends Forester and Sharrets he lit out, borne by briskly trotting horses to Middle River.

Last but not least came the smuggling vessel. "I had purchased a good schooner and placed her under the command of Captain Bennett, a nervy old Chesapeake pilot." Forester had built a spacious false bulkhead with a secret entrance from the schooner's cabin. On the appointed night, Captain Bennett would bring the schooner down from Havre de Grace with a load of coal, the cover-story cargo, bound for Washington. He put in at Middle River, they loaded her hidden compartment with the shipment, Levi White came aboard, and off they sailed. There was one time they didn't depart on schedule—thanks to Deputy Provost Marshal McPhail.

McPhail had gotten wind of the Middle River goings-on. He dispatched a boatload of detectives to catch the smugglers in the act. "They 'played off' as a fishing party and remained there three or four days," White said. A load of ordnance stores was there ready to be loaded and shipped out, Captain Bennett was up at Havre de Grace just waiting for orders to sail, and in between sat that bothersome boatload of McPhail's men.

A lone fisherman, meanwhile, had befriended the surveilling "fishing party." He showed them the good spots to fish and was cheery company. He found out that the men were planning to leave Friday afternoon. The lone fisherman was Bowers, White's Middle River lookout man.

After McPhail's men left and Bowers declared the coast clear, the smuggling schooner came on. "The goods were securely stored on board, and we went sailing down the Chesapeake Bay," said White. "We left Middle River about eight hours after the detectives had gone."

White and the illegal cargo would be debarked somewhere along the rebel shore. As a matter of course, any boat passing the mouth of the Potomac could be expected to be boarded and searched by the guardboat officer. When any flotilla vessel came near, White repaired to the false bulkhead with the stash. "It would imperil the expedition for me to be seen."

It was up to Captain Bennett and some relaxing libations to entertain the boarding officer. "I always had some prime whisky on board," said White, "and when the boarding officer came Bennett would meet him courteously and ask him to 'take something,' which, of course, he did." Whiskey was a valuable ally on sea as well as land. "From my conceal-ment I could hear the boarding officer praising the quality of that whisky. It was really of good quality and on board for that very reason. Our papers being declared all right, the boarding officer would 'take another' and then depart for the guard ship."

On all the runs they made, they "never had any trouble with the guard boat on the Potomac," White said. "In fact, our schooner got to be well known to the boarding officer, and especially the prime whisky which was sure to be in her cabin."

The goods would be landed in darkness. White had made arrange-ments for the wagon teams that would get the shipment to Richmond. Captain Bennett would take the coal to Washington; White would be waiting along the riverbank when Bennett returned. From Smiths Point at the mouth of the Potomac to twenty miles upriver, there were certain favorite landing points. But, said White "When these points became dangerous we could easily find other points that were unguarded."

"Gunboats plied about the Chesapeake and along the shores of the Potomac. . . . These gunboats gave us little concern," Levi White said. "We could watch them easier than they could watch us."

"That an extensive carrying of clothing, provisions, etc., is going on upon and across the lower Potomac I am thoroughly satisfied," for-mer Governor Hicks wrote from his Cambridge home to Washington Navy Yard Commandant Andrew A. Harwood on August 1, "as I am in the receipt of a letter from a man that I had employed for six or eight months as a spy on the Potomac. . . . This man is entirely reliable and has been down to St. Mary's County, and assures me by letter that a constant going and coming over the Potomac is kept up by Confed-erate persons. . . ."

With the capitulation of the Virginia Eastern Shore, the evacuation of Yorktown, the recapture of Norfolk, and the destruction of CSS *Virginia*, the Federal forces had more strongly solidified their control of

Chesapeake Bay than they had since the outbreak of war. But no matter how bottled-in the water became, there remained smugglers to raise all sorts of hob along the inland sea's porous edges. The Potomac Flotilla was being kept busy. On April 17, as McDowell was advancing toward Fredericksburg, the flotilla's realm of jurisdiction had been expanded to include the Rappahannock River, previously part of the already spread-thin North Atlantic Blockading Squadron's bailiwick. On April 20 Commander R. H. Wyman headed an expedition up the Rappahannock to Fredericksburg. Sporadic gunshots greeted the sailors going upriver. About seven miles down from Fredericksburg, stone-laden schooners had been sunk across the channel, but it was still passable. At Fredericksburg, just surrendered to McDowell's forces the day before, Wyman saw the bridges demolished by the departing rebels. On the waterfront were the black remains of some forty schooners, burned along with two steamers, one of which was the celebrated prize *St. Nicholas*.

The Potomac Flotilla captured several small boats on this initial Rappahannock run. These shores were now theirs to patrol. The neck of land formed by the Rappahannock, the Chesapeake Bay, and the Potomac—the Northern Neck—was stalwart guerrilla-and-smuggler country, as the flotilla would constantly be made aware.

Wyman soon was pushing the boundary of the Potomac Flotilla's patrols below the Rappahannock to the Piankatank River, at the invitation of shore sharpshooters firing on his boat. With the York-James peninsula no longer Confederate-controlled, the Piankatank and Mobjack Bay (Wyman started sending vessels there, too) seemed likely to become even busier contraband and communication conduits. On April 28 the flotilla took five prisoners, caught on a smuggling run from the Virginia Eastern Shore. During a Piankatank reconnaissance on April 29, flotilla vessels exchanged fire with masked shore batteries in two locations. During a Mobjack Bay reconnaissance on May 2, more Eastern Shore trafficking was in evidence.

Avowing that "the county of Mathews is largely Union in sentiment," M. P. Morse, Esquire, pleaded for "a legitimate trade under proper restrictions" in an August 7 petition. "The illegal traffic to the eastern shore of Virginia is not confined to the secessionists. We are suffering terribly for many of the necessaries of life; necessity knows no law." Grant Mobjack Bay's Union faithful the privilege to engage in legitimate commerce, argued Morse. Then, "a gunboat stationed in our harbor would, we think, have the effect to a great extent of stopping the present illegal traffic carried on with the eastern shore of Virginia, and which for a month past has been almost unimpeded. The mode is to pass and repass in canoes when there is no gunboat in our harbor, letters and spies having thus a free course to Richmond."

One of wartime Richmond's reigning belles decided to get out of the city for a brief spell in that battle-surrounded summer of 1862. Hetty Cary hadn't seen her Baltimore in nearly a year and felt like paying a call. She made her way across the border and reached Baltimore. As she strolled the streets of downtown her celebrated auburn hair was concealed beneath a black wig. Someone recognized her anyway.

Luckily it was a friend, who in hushed tones warned her that the Federal authorities knew she was back in town and had issued a fresh arrest order in honor of the occasion. By that night Hetty Cary was Philadelphia-bound. From there it was on to the Eastern Shore, where friends gave the far-famed "fair rebel" aid and comfort. She found passage on a blockade-runner and set sail across the Chesapeake. Nearing the western shore, the vessel was spotted, chased, and fired upon, but she scooted through. Hetty Cary went ashore on the Northern Neck and returned to Richmond.

Others, too, wished to get to Richmond and were willing to pay a Bay pilot to run them across. Henry Hollyday was one of them.

Like his mother's notoriously imprisoned cousin, Judge Carmichael, Henry Hollyday was the product of an old and distinguished (if a bit tangle-branched) Eastern Shore family tree. The handsome estate that Hollyday was in line to manage someday was "Readbourne," dating back to around 1731 and located along the Chester River in Queen Anne's County. On a late-summer evening in 1862 Hollyday and another cousin gathered at Readbourne to finalize their dangerous plans. Both young men had lived in the North, but their hearts were with the South, and that's the direction they were heading; they were going to sign up and fight. Even here, cozily seated in the family mansion, they made their preparations with surreptitiousness, leery of being found out by the house servants, "for they were tampered with constantly by extra zealous supporters of the Northern cause, who were seeking an opportunity to entrap Southern sympathizers."

In the morning, "full of hope for the future, but full of sorrow at leaving," the two said their farewells and began their journey. They had lined up a driver they could trust, and rode off across a sparsely populated, nondescript, flat landscape to Smyrna, Delaware, where a sympathizer was expecting them and lodged them for the night. In the morning they rode on to Dover, where they would catch the train to Seaford. They arrived at the Delaware capital around noon; the train didn't leave until three. A state convention was in town, and the two young strangers ate at the hotel and blended in with the crowd. When it came time to head to the station, they had to amble past the provost guards. Henry recalled it as a nervous moment. "The soldiers stationed at the depot to intercept and arrest suspicious characters little realized that the train as it steamed off contained two incipient Confederates."

They chugged into Seaford at sundown. The sympathizer's house was a mile outside of town. The cousins gave the password and were welcomed in. The sympathizer had friendly daughters; their company brightened the evening, and the Hollyday boys enjoyed the last really fine-quality supper they would have for years. The sympathizer gave them the name of their next contact, a doctor in town. Later that night the cousins went there, gave the password, and the doctor let them in. They quickly had his trust. As the clandestine route's chief agent in Seaford, the doctor had his share of stories to tell, "for quite a number of men who bore an active, some a conspicuous, part in the service of the Confederate States had passed over this route."

The doctor gave them their next set of instructions: A man would call on them at the Seaford Hotel the next day and invite them to go for a ride, and of course, they would accept, no questions asked. In the morning the innkeeper handed the cousins each a buckshot, "a talisman of safety," as they departed. The escort, a dentist from Salisbury, picked them up in a one-horse buggy and they set out for Dorchester County. Just over the state line they stopped at Johnson's Crossroads to water the horse and slake their own thirsts as well. They entered the Cross Head Inn, and there among the crowd was the sheriff, "a Union man of the ultra stripe." They assiduously avoided the lawman and quickly were back on their way.

They lay low at a farmhouse on the road to Vienna, running out to hide in the cornfield whenever anyone passed by. After some close shaves near New Market, the cousins parted company with their guide and continued on the road past Vienna to the home of "a gentleman whose whole soul was wrapped up in the Southern cause," a Mr. Raleigh, who lived on the north bank of the Nanticoke. From here the boys were ferried across in a dugout, and on the other shore food, rest, and directions to the rendezvous point were waiting for them. They were led down into the broad marsh, where twelve others also had been led, to gather and wait.

Since the wait was going to last until sundown, "shelter from the scorching rays of a summer sun and protection from the searching eye of the provost guard was sought in potato holes or bins, places used for storing sweet potatoes during the winter, but under the undisputed sway of mosquitoes during the summer," said Henry. "These potato holes are like the bombproofs built by soldiers as protection against cannon balls and shells from mortar guns. They are dug under the ground, like vaults. . . . Fortunately, the stay here was not very long, else the mosquitoes would not have left blood enough in the fourteen for them to be of any use as soldiers. These mosquitoes were voracious feeders."

Here amid the marsh grass the cousins met the others with whom they were about to run the Chesapeake blockade. There were "two stout Irishmen from Dorchester County" and a pair of young farmers from the same quarter, eager to enlist in the Second Maryland Battalion of Infantry, CSA. There were six Delaware fellows, and a Washingtonian prone to excitability.

"The whole party was under command of a brave little captain named Turpin," said Henry. "The boat used in conveying this party across to the Virginia shore was a canoe about thirty-three feet long, such as can now be seen on the tributaries of the Chesapeake employed by that class of oystermen known as tongmen. Captain Turpin owned this boat and was regularly engaged in the blockade-running business, carrying passengers and contraband goods. Though a very hazardous

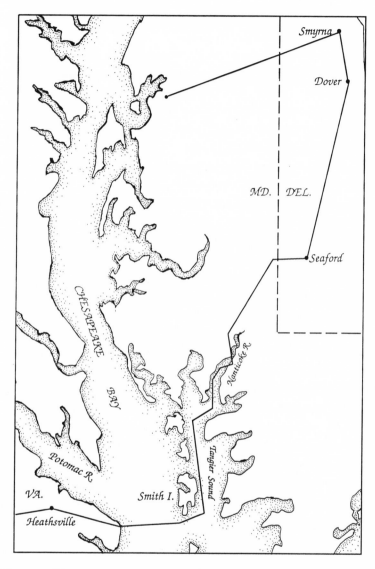

HOW THE HOLLYDAYS WENT SOUTH: AIDED BY A NETWORK OF SOUTHERN
SYMPATHIZERS, THE EAGER-TO-ENLIST COUSINS SECRETED THEMSELVES
TO RICHMOND IN THE SUMMER OF 1862. THE ROUTE TOOK THEM FROM
QUEEN ANNE'S COUNTY, MARYLAND, THROUGH SMYRNA, DOVER, AND
SEAFORD, DELAWARE, ON THROUGH DORCHESTER COUNTY, MARYLAND.
THEN THEY SAILED BY NIGHT DOWN THE NANTICOKE, THROUGH
TANGIER SOUND, AND ACROSS THE CHESAPEAKE ABOARD CAPTAIN
TURPIN'S BLOCKADE-RUNNING LOG CANOE.

business, it was very profitable, twenty dollars in gold being the fare each passenger had to pay. . . ."

The sun went down and Captain Turpin called them aboard. They shoved off and rowed down the Nanticoke until they hit wider water, "and night had thrown its mantle over nature so that sails could be used without being seen from land."

Out Tangier Sound, around Smith Island, across Chesapeake Bay southwesterly to Little Wicomico River: The captain was familiar with the course. As the log canoe entered Tangier Sound, "a dark cloud rose in the west, causing Egyptian darkness, from which soon burst upon the party a terrific thunderstorm and drenching rain," Henry said, "and the boat, which had been gliding along so smoothly, was brought to a sudden halt aground upon the flats, miles from either shore." They had to be across by dawn. All hands climbed out and pushed. "Although the water was shallow, the mud was deep," remarked Henry. They finally got her clear and were sailing with good speed across the broader Bay, when in the distance, bearing down, came the light of a large vessel.

The Washingtonian, fearful of execution as a traitor if caught, fell into a right panic. "For God's sake don't let them capture me! Anywhere, captain; up the bay, down the bay, only don't let them capture me!" It turned out to be no gunboat, however—just a steamer on its routine Baltimore-Norfolk run.

The sky was the eerie gray of night becoming dawn as the boat neared the Little Wicomico. Something moved, a dark object, coming toward them from shore. No Norfolk steamer, this. "As for the captain of our craft," said Henry, "he trimmed his sails and handled his rudder so skillfully that, with the aid of a friendly breeze, he soon found his boat with its human cargo rapidly nearing land." The obscured vessel came closer with the sound of muted voices and muffled oars.

This was it; the chase was coming. "Captain Turpin understood thoroughly the situation in which he was placed; knew the qualities of his boat, the navigation of the surrounding waters, and that land would soon be reached." He told the men to lie down in the bottom of the boat.

"Boat ahoy! Heave to!" The barked order broke the dawn quiet. The boat was more defined now: a Federal barge, armed marines, a howitzer mount. Captain Turpin played deaf and kept inching toward shore.

"Boat ahoy! Heave to!" The log canoe crossed the barge's bow at one hundred yards, and the Federal officer shouted, "Heave to, or we'll fire!"

"Fire and be damned to you!" someone on the log canoe blurted back.

"And fire they did," said Henry, "the sharp report of the howitzer being followed quickly by the whizzing sounds of the leaden missiles which it sent forth. This left but little doubt that unless the canoe could rapidly sail out of reach its passengers would soon be battling with the bold waters of the Chesapeake as well as an armed enemy." With the wind cooperating, the log canoe was making distance. The oarsmen in the barge were unable to keep up. The first shot ripped through the canoe's sails. The second shot fell alongside, and the men in the canoe felt the splash. The third shot went high. Turpin brought her around a sharp point of land, and they were in the river. Some of the men jumped overboard, scurrying to shore and scattering through the woods and cornfields.

They needn't have jumped; the chase was over, and Captain Turpin landed the rest of the men. It was sundown by the time they had all regrouped in a farmhouse. They spent the night in Heathsville, noticing there were no young men about, just the crippled, the elderly, and women and children. The blockade runners were treated hospitably, refreshed by a popular local drink of homemade peach brandy mixed with honey. In the morning they secured wagons, teams, and guides and made their way to Richmond. After watchfully crossing the Rappahannock at Bowlers Wharf and riding through battle-scarred Mechanicsville, they arrived at the capital. After a night of much-needed rest at the Spottswood Hotel, the Hollyday cousins enlisted as privates in Company A of the Second Maryland Battalion of Infantry, Captain William H. Murray commanding. They wouldn't see the Eastern Shore again until after the war, one "but a wreck of himself by reason of exposure and want of proper food and clothing while in active service," the other "maimed for life in the battle of Gettysburg. . . ."

On July 6, 1862, Captain Charles Wilkes was ordered to the James to take command of a new flotilla. Earlier, on November 8, 1861, he had caused an international stir with the "Trent Affair." Wilkes, commanding the USS *San Jacinto*, had seized the Confederate diplomats Mason and Slidell on their way to London aboard the British mail packet *Trent*. The prisoners were brought to Fort Monroe, then shipped up the coast to Boston's Fort Warren. The affair sparked tense diplomatic debate. In the wake of the affair and amid both praise and condemnation of Wilkes, Secretary Welles ordered him to proceed to Norfolk, take command of the vessels in the James, and "hoist your broad pennant upon any boat you may select." A new temporary division of the North Atlantic Blockading Squadron, the James River Flotilla, had been created to meet the exigencies of the Peninsula Campaign. McClellan's base of operations had shifted from White House on the Pamunkey to Harrison's Landing on the James.

The captain arrived at Hampton Roads on July 8, and General Dix supplied him an army tug to take him upriver. Wilkes had just missed President Lincoln, who had gone to Harrisons Landing to review the troops and confer with McClellan. In the morning, when Wilkes finally met with the general, Lincoln had already departed on the steamer *Ariel*. Wilkes introduced himself to McClellan and got to work. The Confederates had vessels up the river beyond Drewry's Bluff; there was constant fear of a downriver aggression by them that never came. In the ensuing weeks, as the Peninsula Campaign petered out, Wilkes and his James River gunboats kept the river open. Most rebel threats came from the south shore; they were kept in check by Wilkes's threat to blast any house in the area from where a shore battery dared fire. In addition to rebel containment, Wilkes had to police his own herd, as Federal transports were getting into the habit of going ashore and plundering civilians of everything from lamps to pianos.

Meanwhile, the captain who had managed to stir things up internationally was apparently managing to stir things up from Harrisons Landing to Hampton Roads. Flag Officer Goldsborough huffed in a July 15 communiqué to Secretary Welles: "The appointment of Captain Wilkes to the independent command of the flotilla in James River has, as I apprehended it would do, subjected me to the most scurrilous and unmerited attacks on the part of public prints. . . . In this state of things I have arrived at the conclusion that I ought to be relieved from my present position. . . ." On August 1 an irked McClellan wrote Captain

PENINSULA CAMPAIGN MATÉRIEL CROWDS THE YORKTOWN SHORE.
National Archives

Wilkes about the captain's reaction to some soldiers loaned for service aboard the screw sloop *Wachusett*: "It was certainly intended to give you good men, and we thought it had been done, but from the fact that you considered these ten, who have served with credit through the battles of the peninsula, as 'not even food for gunpowder,' I fear that the standard of the Navy is, perhaps, higher than the land service will be able to meet."

But the general had heavier woes than a jack-tar insult weighing him down. Two days earlier Henry W. Halleck, Lincoln's new appointee as general in chief of all U.S. land forces, had ordered McClellan to remove all the sick and wounded from Harrisons Landing. If it seemed like the thin end of the wedge, like the precursor to ordering the entire Army of the Potomac off the peninsula, it was. On August 3 the next order came: McClellan was to get out of Harrisons Landing, leave the peninsula, and move his army up to Aquia Creek and Alexandria. Major General John Pope, fresh from success in the West and now at the head of the recently created Army of Virginia, stood between the rebels and Washington. McClellan's new role was a supportive one, to buttress Pope and help defend the capital. Fighting and moving and fighting and moving near Richmond since May, McClellan wasn't ready to give up his campaign yet, and did so under protest. He wanted more reinforcements to get the job done; Washington wanted more troops for its defense—the arguments that clouded the opening of the Peninsula Campaign were still there to define its finale.

With the help of the York River squadron, McClellan had established his supply base at White House on the Pamunkey by May 15. "The troops do not like to move in the neighborhood of the rivers unless accompanied by a gunboat, and we accommodate them as much as we possibly can," Commander William Smith had reported. By May 24 the army was within six miles of Richmond, and McDowell was on the march from Fredericksburg to join in on the attack. But Stonewall Jackson's bold successes in the Shenandoah heightened Washington's fears, and McDowell was held back. McClellan, meanwhile, had his army precariously split by the Chickahominy River, three corps on the northeast side, two on the south. Johnston attacked the two south-bank corps, intending to knock them far enough back that he could destroy

THE ARMY OF THE POTOMAC AT YORKTOWN.
Harper's Weekly

the York River railroad—McClellan's lifeline to the Pamunkey supply base. The Battle of Seven Pines, or Fair Oaks, a vicious, poorly coordinated affair, was fought on May 31. The Confederates gummed up their attack, but nonetheless succeeded in corralling Union momentum. The fight's most far-reaching result was that Johnston was wounded and taken from the field. Jefferson Davis named his chief military advisor to the command of the Confederate forces. And as he took the reins, this new leader, General Robert E. Lee, gave his troops new hope and a new name—the Army of Northern Virginia.

Lee wasted no time. He put the soldiers to work digging an elaborate trench-line protecting Richmond. While he made ready to defend, he also made ready to attack, sending 1,200 cavalry under Jeb Stuart to reconnoiter McClellan's right flank; they ended up riding a circle around the entire Union army. Alarmed, McClellan moved the bulk of his army south of the Chickahominy and began relocating his supply base from the Pamunkey to the James. The roads became impassable muck and the swamps overflowed in the heavy June rains. McClellan pined for reinforcements. Lincoln yearned for McClellan to move. And Robert E. Lee

RECEPTION OF WOUNDED SOLDIERS AT FORT MONROE.
Frank Leslie's Illustrated Newspaper

swiped the initiative. He sent for Stonewall Jackson to hit the Union right flank. As Jackson's forces were on their way, the Seven Days' Battles began on June 25. Oak Grove, Mechanicsville, Gaines Mill, Savage Station, Frayser's Farm—the Confederates kept pushing and McClellan kept withdrawing. His was too strategic a retreat to be called outright defeat, but to a relieved South, the nomenclature didn't matter. The Union army was being forced back farther and farther from Richmond, was being pushed down to the river's edge. The Confederate advance was anything but flawless. Jackson never factored in as efficiently as had been hoped, and casualties were high. On July 1 the Seven Days culminated at Malvern Hill. McClellan's troops fought bravely, holding the hill against a series of sloppily managed and costly Confederate assaults. But the Army of the Potomac had won nothing except more time to continue its withdrawal to the James, to Harrisons Landing. There it remained, through a month of occasional skirmishes, mounting controversy, and growing animosity between McClellan and the Lincoln administration.

When the order to withdraw from the peninsula came on August 3, McClellan's troops had just succeeded in reoccupying Malvern Hill the day before. Skirmishing continued there until the Federal troops were pulled out on August 7. By August 15 McClellan's First and Fifth Corps were disembarking at Aquia Creek. By August 16 the evacuation of Harrisons Landing was complete, and the troop transports continued to steam north from Fort Monroe, where the Sisters of Charity had come in late June to care for the wounded boys of the Peninsula Campaign.

"The Army of the Potomac was accordingly withdrawn, and it was not until two years later that it again found itself under its last commander at substantially the same point on the bank of the James," noted McClellan. "It was as evident in 1862 as in 1865 that there was the true defense of Washington, and that it was on the banks of the James that the fate of the Union was to be decided."

CHAPTER 7

Gunboats and oysters

WHILE INVADING MARYLAND, Captain Harry Gilmor of the Twelfth Virginia Cavalry figured he might as well visit some friends. Being a Marylander himself, it seemed a good idea, at least until he found himself surrounded by Federals with their pistols drawn.

The son of a Baltimore business leader, the cavalry captain had grown up in comfort and grace at "Glen Ellen," the family estate near Loch Raven in Baltimore County. He had gone west to seek his fortune and came home in time for the war. He became a corporal in the Baltimore County Horse Guards, based in Towson, and rode with them into the city when the trouble broke out on April 19, 1861, and afterward when they rode north burning bridges. He was arrested and sent to Fort McHenry, and after he was released, he crossed the Potomac on August 30, 1861, and signed on with Colonel Turner Ashby the very next day. Harry Gilmor scouted and rode picket up and down the Shenandoah, was made captain of Company F, Twelfth Virginia, in March 1862, and was active throughout Jackson's storied Valley Campaign. Strapping, mustachioed Harry Gilmor was a ladies' man, every inch the cavalier, but right now, the soldiers and policemen marching him into the Western District station house in Baltimore had a different word for him: spy.

The Army of Northern Virginia had trounced Pope's forces at the Battle of Second Bull Run on August 29–30 and began crossing over into Maryland on September 4. Jackson occupied Frederick on the sixth; the advance continued with daily fighting. On the night of the twelfth Captain Gilmor was on the hoof down Reisterstown Turnpike to a relative's house when Lieutenant Grafton Carlisle, the captain's riding

HARRY GILMOR, SCION OF BALTIMORE SOCIETY
AND CONFEDERATE CAVALIER.
National Archives

companion, suggested they stop by and see their old friend, Dr. Luke Williamson, since they were on the Reisterstown road, anyway. The doctor lived about seven miles outside Baltimore. The rebel riders had picked a bad night to come calling. Soldiers and city police, on the hunt for a southbound contraband shipment, surrounded the house. Gilmor and friend rode into the yard and right into the thick of them. The cavalrymen were unsaddled and marched into the city, where Gilmor was written into the arrest book as a "spy." The false charge followed him to Fort McHenry, where he was taken, again a prisoner as in 1861— but for more than two weeks this time.

The combustible city was in alarm, of course, over the rebel invasion. A mortar-boat fleet late of the James River was amassed in Baltimore Harbor, ready to wreak downtown destruction if the Confederates came capturing. Ward militias were called for. Partisan street violence erupted again. A special force of four hundred extra policemen was formed to maintain order. On September 8 Governor Bradford issued a proclamation calling for citizens to arm and organize and "assist in

defending our homes and firesides against the assault of the invader."
Baltimoreans were urged to sign on with the First Light Division of
Maryland Volunteer Militia or to register at the post office to join a new
independent outfit, the Maryland Line, to help defend the city. General
Wool had the soldiery on high alert and made ready to build more
defensive works. The popular John Kenly, now a general and recovered
from his Front Royal wound, was put in command of the city infantry.
It was all understandable precaution, but all for naught; the Army of
Northern Virginia didn't come as close to Baltimore's outskirts as the
errant Captain Gilmor had. The clash came to the west on September 17,
the bloodiest day of the war, at Antietam Creek.

When Secretary Welles ordered the mortar boats from James River to
Baltimore Harbor, he also ordered several vessels to Washington—and
with them, Commodore Wilkes. The northward shift of armies spelled
the disbandment of the James River Flotilla and the rapid augmenting
of the Potomac Flotilla. Wilkes was appointed to the Potomac command
on August 29; since Commander Wyman's late-June reassignment the
flotilla had been led by Washington Navy Yard Commandant Andrew
Harwood. It was to be a season of quickly shifting commands, redefined
territory, and an expanding flotilla. On September 2 Welles officially
stretched the Potomac Flotilla's area of operation to include the Piankatank
River, which Wyman had been patrolling since spring, anyway. Also on
the second, Flag Officer Goldsborough was relieved of duty at Hampton
Roads as Rear Admiral Samuel Phillips Lee was assigned command of
the North Atlantic Blockading Squadron. On September 9, after little
more than a week in command, Charles Wilkes was ordered out to the
West India Squadron, and the Potomac Flotilla's commodore was once
again Andrew Harwood.

On September 25 the Potomac Flotilla was split into two divisions.
The First Division (seven vessels under Lieutenant Commander S. R.
Franklin) patrolled from the lower Potomac south to the other tributar-
ies; the Second Division (six vessels under Lieutenant Commander
Samuel Magaw) covered the Potomac up to Washington. The late Com-
mander Ward's little gunboat navy continued to grow.

Concomitantly, smugglers, partisan raiders, profiteers, and sundry other outlaw travelers continued to frequent the waterways. Levi White had many kindred spirits darting back and forth with clockwork regularity among the creeks and coves, and like Levi White, knowing about them was one thing, catching them was another. "There is a person, whose name I glean to be Sable," Harwood informed Magaw. This Sable was making twice-weekly runs from the Virginia shore to a creek between the mouth of the Potomac and St. Marys River. Harwood had plenty of information about the smuggler, who posed as a waterman and had a three-man crew. Harwood could describe the smuggler's vessel in detail. "The individual has a large canoe, capable of carrying fifty or more persons. She has a white bottom, dark gunwales, two leg-of-mutton sails, foresail bright and new, mainsail not more than half as large as the fore, of dark color, mildewed and old." Harwood could point with precision to the smuggler's haunts and collaborators. "The depot on the Maryland side is in Smiths Creek, up a long, unfrequented cove, to Mr. Edward Able's landing. From this point he goes to St. Inigoes, where he is said to be supplied with various articles from a store kept by two persons—Taylor and Bean. One of them is a postmaster and the other collector of the county taxes, but both are spoken of as rank rebels." Harwood had plenty of information about the smuggler, but he didn't have the smuggler. Magaw was forewarned: "I would recommend you to proceed cautiously with this wary rogue. . . ."

Roguery could be perpetrated by both sides. On August 26 the crews of the U.S. steam transports *Telegraph* and *Rotary* came ashore at the mouth of the Rappahannock and went on a looting romp. Jewelry, clothes, and even beds were among the plunder stolen from the homes along the water. Along with the transport-vessel crews, the Potomac Flotilla sailors were likewise capable of occasional lapses in judgment, to the extent that by December, Harwood was compelled to lay down the law: "Several complaints have been made against the conduct of the boats' crews and the officers in charge. In future any accusation against men and officers of the flotilla by persons on shore will be rigidly examined, and the offenders will suffer the extreme penalty if found guilty."

Searching for arms in a rebel household in Southern Maryland.
Chesapeake Bay Maritime Museum

But allegations of rankled citizenry were only part of the story. With a vast, labyrinthine shoreline and just a baker's dozen boats to patrol it, flotilla activity was constant and various. Acting Master William Street on *Jacob Bell* sent a spy disguised as a rebel soldier onto formerly friendly St. George Island on September 16, picked him up the next day, went up every branch of the Yeocomico, captured five prizes, and exchanged fire with a cavalry detachment—a good day's work by the measure of most. Now, with the late part of the year coming on, the work often took on a distinctive flavor—the flavor of oysters.

Magaw seized a log canoe going into Smiths Creek on September 6. It fit Harwood's description of the twice-weekly smuggler's boat, but there was no "Sable" aboard her. The two men who were brought off, Thomas Richardson and William Allen, were known smugglers suspected of having run ammunition and recruits into Virginia. Mollusks were their mission, they claimed. "I have detained them until I can further investigate the matter," Magaw reported to Harwood. "They state they were oystering, which is improbable, from the fact that they were without tongs."

In the lower Chesapeake the oysters *themselves* were smuggled goods, not merely a smuggler's favorite excuse for being on the water. Oystering "for the consumption of the army, navy, and inhabitants, all in the immediate vicinity, may be allowed within reasonable limits," declared Rear Admiral S. P. Lee on October 4. But Richmond demanded oysters, wartime or no, and contraband bivalves were secreted to the Confederate capital. Sometimes they didn't make it. Commander Foxhall Parker went up the York River on November 27 and intercepted more than one hundred bushels en route inland on smugglers' boats. On another run up the York on December 23, he torched a shucking shack "in which, on the approach of our force, a number of men were engaged in opening oysters for the Richmond market." What became of the confiscated oysters is the stuff of conjecture.

It was autumn on the Chesapeake, so it was perhaps forgivable when a Yankee soldier stationed at Fort Monroe caught the waterfowling itch. In the October 24 crime and court-martial proceedings of Private Thomas J. Gill, Company C, Third New York Volunteers, it came out in testimony how Private Gill, "in violation of positive orders," strayed off limits and fired his Enfield rifle three times at some ducks out on the water. He missed the ducks but nearly killed three sailors on the quarterdeck of the USS *Wyandotte*. "I have examined the man myself," Major General Dix assuaged Rear Admiral Lee, "and am satisfied from his statement that it was an act of mere carelessness, and that it did not occur to him that anyone aboard the gunboat would be in danger. Indeed, he says, what I have no doubt is true, that he was not thinking of the gunboat at all."

Private Gill, cleared on more serious charges, was found guilty of disobedience for firing his weapon within a mile of the fort. He returned to duty and the standard rations inherent therein.

On a late October day Peter Smith was oystering in the York when he was hailed from shore. He went in, and Lieutenant Doggett, CSN, told him to come along. They went to Mobjack Bay, through Mathews Courthouse, on toward New Point Comfort. Deep in the woods, they stopped. There were other men gathered there, seventeen of them. Smith

JOHN TAYLOR WOOD: FROM NAVAL ACADEMY PROFESSOR
TO STERN GUNNER ON CSS *VIRGINIA* TO ONE OF THE MOST
FEARED RAIDERS OF CHESAPEAKE SHIPPING.
Battles and Leaders of the Civil War

was welcomed and told to wait until the leader arrived. A black-bearded
naval officer soon showed up.

John Taylor Wood had a job for Peter Smith.

With the Union threat gone from the upper James, Lieutenant Wood
grew desirous of more interesting work than that which Drewry's Bluff
now afforded. He wanted to strike at Federal shipping, to come alongside quietly, board quickly, and take ships in the dead of night at the
point of a gun. Secretary Mallory liked Wood's thinking, and at the

Rocketts Navy Yard near Richmond, boarding cutters were soon being built specially for the raiding venture. They looked like whaling boats and fit onto army wagons converted for the purpose. On the morning of October 1, 1862, as discreetly and invisibly as possible, Wood set forth with his wheelborne boats and about twenty hand-picked men from the James River service. They slogged and tumbled over rutted, ruined roads toward the Potomac, and when they finally arrived they fanned out for thirty miles, eyes peeled for a first victim. At midnight on October 7 they regathered and shoved off, rowing stealthily toward the Maryland side, toward the schooner *Frances Elmor* at anchor off Popes Creek.

They got in close and Wood rasped the command. The bow hands dropped oars and heaved grappling hooks at the schooner. Wood rose now, and the men followed him over the side. With sword and pistol they stormed the deck and quickly forced the captain and his six men to surrender. Wood ordered them down to the boats, stripped the schooner of valuables, and put her to the torch. As the raiding boats made for the Virginia shore, *Frances Elmor* with her cargo of hay sent up a high blaze, catching the attention of the Potomac Flotilla's USS *Yankee*, which arrived in time to do nothing much more than watch the flames eat the schooner.

Wood and his raiders braced the boats to the wagons and rolled back into Richmond with their prisoners in tow. Spirit high and seeking new ships to conquer, Wood had another cutting-out expedition organized in less than a week. This time, instead of north, he pointed his boat-wagons due east. Mathews County would be his base of operations, the wide-open Chesapeake his hunting ground. With Lieutenant Sidney Lee as his second in command and a party of crewmen from CSS *Patrick Henry*, John Taylor Wood set up camp at the Bay's edge and made ready to strike. All he needed now was a native pilot, someone who knew every nuance and opportunity for elusive rascality the coastline hereabouts could afford.

Wood asked Peter Smith if he knew the Bay. "I told him I did," Smith later testified. Wood asked him what places along the shore he could guide a vessel into. "I told him almost any river between here and Baltimore," Smith said.

It was just what Wood wanted to hear. He "said he was very sorry to deprive me of being with my family," related Smith, "but he wanted me to accompany him."

They camped in the woods by day and went out by night, heading north-northeast a dozen miles from shore in nasty, rainy weather. Wood, Lee, and Smith each commanded a boat. For two nights they went out, finding no prey in the cold October storminess. On October 28, the third night out, their luck changed.

The New York merchant ship *Alleghanian*, 1,400 tons' burden, out of Baltimore and bound for London with a load of guano, met a headwind in the Chesapeake and came to anchor off Gwynns Island. Seaman James Jackson was on watch. Shortly before 10 P.M. he spied three dim shapes nearing. He hailed them to identify. "Arabs" was the reply. Over the rail they came, the bearded leader flashing blade-steel, a gang of assailants brandishing cutlasses, muskets, and French revolvers surging up behind him. They charged on deck, grabbed Jackson by the throat, and tied his hands behind his back. They waylaid the other watchman, jumped down to the forecastle, and flooded into the cabin. This ship, John Taylor Wood told the dazed captain, was a prize of the Confederate States of America.

Peter Smith was put in charge of the prisoners, while for two hours the raiders stripped the ship, capturing her colors, bringing off the barometer and chronometer, pilfering the sugar, tea, and coffee stores, and rifling through the chests for clothing. *Alleghanian's* captain, first mate, and pilot were going to be seeing Richmond; the nineteen other crewmen were unbound one by one, lowered into the ship's boats, and set adrift. The raiders set fire to the ship from below, clambered back into their boarding cutters with prisoners and plunder, and stood up the Bay.

The cast-off crewmen were soon rescued as the nearby Potomac Flotilla vessels *T. A. Ward* and *Crusader* made haste to the site where $200,000 worth of ship and guano-cargo were lighting up the Chesapeake. The flotilla crews had the fire out by midmorning; *Alleghanian* had burned to within six feet of the waterline aft. What was left of her was towed to Yorktown.

The raiders sailed five miles up the Bay before veering west-south-west. They made land and hugged the coast back to their starting point, marked by signal fire. They lay low in the woods for a while before loading the boats on the wagons, getting breakfast, and pushing on for Richmond. At Gloucester, near his Capahosic home, Peter Smith was allowed to part company. On November 10 he was arrested, put in double irons, and hauled aboard the USS *Brandywine*. His captors told him he would be charged as either a pirate or a partisan civilian. Pleading that he had been pressed into service, he gave a helpful deposition and managed to garner treatment as a prisoner of war, a less unhealthy designation than pirate or partisan.

On October 31 John Taylor Wood entered Richmond with his prisoners, his boats, and a new notoriety. If crews plying the Chesapeake were wary of him now, the wariness was warranted. He would be back.

Mobjack Bay, its reputation rising as a paradise for troublemakers, was attacked by Union army-navy forces on November 23. Foxhall Parker left Yorktown harbor on the twenty-second with three boats and three hundred infantrymen of the Fifty-second Pennsylvania Volunteers under Major John Conyngham. Next morning the infantry battalion disembarked with twenty seamen and a Dalhgren twelve-pounder two miles from Mathews Courthouse. While they took up the march for New Point Comfort, *General Putnam* accompanied by a howitzer boat delved up East River with orders "to capture or destroy all vessels and boats that could be used in running the blockade." The river detachment destroyed a saltworks, burned three schooners and various smaller boats, and captured a lighter and twenty-four log canoes. Conyngham's troops, meanwhile, wrecked eleven saltworks and three hundred to four hundred bushels of precious salt. On the twenty-fourth, soldiers marched on Mathews Courthouse while more boats were destroyed. On the twenty-fifth, Parker, with two vessels and no soldiers this time, returned to Mobjack Bay, probed North River and destroyed more boats, one of which, on the stocks and partially built, had the timber strength and construction design of a privateer gunboat in the making.

While Parker quashed potential privateering, a fall-line face-off loomed imminent as land forces massed along the Rappahannock. The Army of the Potomac, for the moment under the command of General Ambrose E. Burnside, had begun arriving on the bluffs across the river from Fredericksburg on November 17. The Army of Northern Virginia was occupying the hills above the town by the nineteenth, and Robert E. Lee rode up on the twentieth. As the buildup continued on both riverbanks, the Union gunboats on the Rappahannock found themselves afloat on the dividing line, a target for south-bank artillerists.

Major General D. H. Hill, CSA, was ordered to move his division to Port Royal to thwart any attempted crossing in that area. The Confederates spied four Yankee gunboats at anchor off the town. Captain R. H. Hardaway opened fire with his Whitworth gun from Pratts Bluff more than two miles downriver. As the solid shot flew past, the Potomac Flotilla vessels *Currituck, Anacostia, Jacob Bell,* and *Coeur de Lion* got under way and returned fire until sundown. Another battery above Port Royal then opened up on them, while small-arms harassment added even more incentive to seek safer anchorage. The boats headed downriver, having to pass below the Pratts Bluff battery that had started it all. But it was another gun emplacement, closer to the river's edge, that managed the parting shot. Major John Pelham, Jeb Stuart's "gallant Pelham," waited until the flotilla boats were within three hundred yards before ordering the two nine-inch rifled guns to let fly. *Jacob Bell* was hit but kept moving. The boats replied with grape and took a rebel gunner's leg off. The boats tangled with shore batteries again on the tenth and eleventh, when *Currituck,* returning from the mouth of the river, was fired on thirty times from Brandywine Hill; she beat to quarters, returned fire, and made it upriver relatively unscathed. A mile up, in company with the other vessels now, another battery opened fire and the boats gave it back. On the eleventh, in the morning fog, the big push came.

At General Burnside's request *Satellite* and *Jacob Bell* attacked the Pratts Bluff battery, while *Anacostia* opened up on the battery that harassed them the day before. Both sites were evacuated; something was happening up at Fredericksburg. "The general wished us to make a noise and we did," reported Samuel Magaw that afternoon. "Heavy firing has been heard up the river all day, and we are anxiously awaiting news."

Slowed but not stopped by rebel sharpshooters, the Union troops had laid pontoon bridges across the river. Burnside had occupied Fredericksburg. The sense of success was short-lived. On December 13 the Army of the Potomac was decimated in a series of bloody and futile assaults

MONITOR MEETS HER FATE, DECEMBER 31, 1862.
Harper's Weekly

on the rebel line. On the fifteenth, the defeated Union troops completed their withdrawal back across the Rappahannock.

Magaw was aboard *Yankee*, at anchor off Bristoe mines in the Rappahannock, when a commissioned officer delivered a message from General Burnside on the night of December 18: "Tell Captain Magaw that for the present the Army is brought to a standstill. . . ."

At 2:30 P.M. on December 29, with a light wind out of the southwest and clear weather, the USS *Monitor*, towed by the USS *Rhode Island*, left Hampton Roads bound for duty off Cape Hatteras. The surface of the water was smooth as the ironclad passed Cape Henry at 6 P.M., departing the waters of the Chesapeake for the first time since arriving there on her maiden voyage on March 8. In rising seas off Hatteras, with a loss of sixteen officers and men, *Monitor* sank between midnight and 1 A.M. on December 31, 1862.

CHAPTER 8

Death's ditch

LEVI WHITE WAS wrapped in a shawl, walking in bitter cold behind four wagonloads of contraband. It was January 8, 1863, before daybreak, below the Rappahannock. White's partner was in the front wagon and White brought up the rear, "totally unconscious that our movements were known and that the biggest kind of a trap had been set for us."

Less than a week before, they had loaded up the schooner and sneaked down the Bay with big blocks of gutta-percha and three thousand pounds of block tin, "the largest lot of goods I had ever carried," stated White. The Rappahannock gunboats prevented the Baltimore smugglers from using their preferred crossing to Bowlers Rocks. They crossed farther downriver and hired wagons for the next leg from a man named Fisher. They were held up at Fisher's for a few days waiting for some of his teams to return. It gave one of the black men there time to get word to the Federals.

So the Confederate Ordnance Department's chief Baltimore purchasing agent was on a cold, dark Virginia road on January 8 when all of a sudden the wagons stopped. Levi White stepped out from behind the last wagon to see why. More than one thousand Federal cavalrymen had them surrounded.

White moved up alongside his partner in the front wagon and told him he was going make a break for it. His partner told him to go ahead and he'd try to get away too and rejoin. A cavalry officer came forward with raised sabre. "Who has charge of these wagons?" he demanded.

"I have, sir," Levi White said.

"Bring them up in front of the troops," the officer said.

"I am under obligation to that officer," White later reminisced. "His question and his order enabled me to escape."

White complied, keeping his face toward the officer and walking backward, giving each wagon's teamster a loud, distinct order in turn. "Jim, come on with your team. Not too fast. You other boys hold on until I tell you to move. . . . Now, Caesar, come on with your team; not too fast. . . . Now, Henry, come on with your team. . . . Now, Bill, come on with your team."

He was cooperating, a servile saint. "But all the time I was walking backward, and the soldiers were riding forward, and by the time I reached the rear wagon the wheelhouses of that wagon were abreast of the last soldier. That was my time, and I embraced it. . . ." White threw himself under the last wagon and lay flat. The wagon moved on; no one noticed him missing yet. He rolled into the roadside ditch, waited for the sound of the wagons turning off, then jumped a fence and high-tailed it for the woods. He could hear horses coming back as he reached the woods. He hid and watched as the cavalry squad took the wrong man, a lone traveler along the road, into custody. "I did not linger in that region," said White.

He later learned the fate of his partner, imprisoned at Norfolk for four months. The man mistaken for Levi White was quickly released. And as for the real Levi White, he would look back and remark that "this was the narrowest escape I ever had during the whole war. . . ."

"It is impossible to maintain inviolate the blockade of a coast so extensive and so indented with navigable waters as the western shore of the Chesapeake," Rear Admiral Lee wrote the secretary of the navy on January 19, pointing out "the frequent operations of the naval force in that vicinity, in the destruction of boats, canoes, and other craft which might be used in carrying on such illicit trade. . . ." During that particularly cold winter, while a major ironclad fleet was assembling at Hampton Roads for a spring attack on Savannah and Charleston, there were joint army-navy thrusts up the York and Pamunkey. The Potomac Flotilla destroyed Oscar Yerby's big salt manufactory on Dividing Creek, Virginia, depriving Richmond of one of its major salt sources. Fast-firing rebel riflemen came close to capturing a flotilla sloop that

The gunboat USS *Commodore Barney*, one of numerous such vessels charged with an "impossible" task: "to maintain inviolate the blockade of a coast so extensive and indented with navigable waters as the western shore of the Chesapeake."

National Archives

strayed on a canoe chase near the mouth of the Rappahannock. And Mobjack Bay, by virtue of location, layout, and local temperament, remained a first-class lair for recalcitrants. It was spidery with tributaries, and with spring came another Federal raid up one of them.

Acting on an informant's word, Lieutenant Commander J. H. Gillis on the gunboat *Commodore Morris* ascended Ware River on March 31 and arrested Patterson Smith, a farmer suspected of stashing weapons and selling grain to the rebels. Returning to Yorktown with the prisoner at 10 P.M., Gillis conferred with Major General E. D. Keyes at Fourth Army Corps headquarters. Keyes agreed: It was either remove the grain or destroy it. Rebel cavalry was stationed at Gloucester Courthouse, so Keyes availed the naval officer of one hundred infantry. *Commodore Morris* returned to Ware River on the morning of April 1, accompanied by *Delaware*. There were about 1,000 bushels of wheat to bring off from Patterson Smith's plantation. They hadn't removed 250 before the rebel cavalry arrived.

"The men were immediately formed," reported Gillis, "and we prepared to give them a warm reception as they charged down upon us, and a few well-directed shots caused a wavering in their ranks, and a cheer and a charge on the part of both sailors and soldiers turned an attack into a retreat, and they fled until out of range of our muskets. . . ." The rebel horsemen halted and regrouped, and the one hundred-pounder on *Commodore Morris* blasted a shot right through the thick of them. Those still able galloped off around the bend in the road. The Federal force followed. "I discovered indications of the effect of our firing, there being quite a quantity of blood in the road," said Gillis, "showing that some of the party had paid dearly for their temerity."

The soldiers and sailors burned the bulk of the grain and moved on to the home of an absent army officer, whose barns were brimming with corn. They ignited the barns. Through the acrid, billowing smoke, rebel cavalry came charging down. A gunboat howitzer shell exploded among the horsemen, squelching their attack. The raiding party continued torching with impunity; by expedition's end it was "altogether some 22,000 bushels of grain that the rebels have thus been deprived of."

A general springtime movement was afoot, soon evident as the Confederates drove the Federal troops out of Williamsburg, cut the wires, set fire to the camp of the Fifth Pennsylvania Cavalry, and pushed down the lower peninsula to within five miles of Yorktown on April 11. Major General Keyes urged S. P. Lee to send gunboat assistance. Lee did what he could, dispatching *Commodore Morris* back to the York to join *Crusader* already patrolling there. The North Atlantic Blockading Squadron was spread desperately thin, with vessels off supporting army movements in the North Carolina sounds. And closer to home base, concomitant with the Williamsburg attack, there was trouble stirring on the Nansemond River.

USS *Stepping Stones* Acting Master T. A. Harris's February prediction that "sooner or later there will be an attack upon Suffolk in force" was being proven correct, thanks to General James Longstreet's First Army Corps, which laid siege to the city on April 11. The Federal force there under Major General John J. Peck was cornered. To prevent the Confederates from getting across the river, S. P. Lee quickly sent two flotillas up the Nansemond, commenting to their commanding officers

The USS *Commodore Perry*. Like so many gunboats patrolling Chesapeake waters, she was a reincarnated civilian vessel. An old New York ferryboat, she was outfitted for naval service with an 11-inch Dahlgren on the port side and a 100-pound Parrott rifle on the stern. Note the canine mascot on the starboard rail.

National Archives

that "the army should cease the impolicy of occupying so many detached and weak positions, and relying upon what are called ferryboats in New York and gunboats here to make such positions tenable." The upper Nansemond flotilla under Lieutenant R. H. Lamson got caught up in a pitched firefight on the fourteenth; at Hills Point near the mouth of Western Branch the Confederate battery reduced the grounded *Mount Washington* to a riddled, disabled hulk. She was towed off by *Stepping Stones* amid a galling barrage as the tide rose. The channel came within fifty yards of the Hills Point guns; they had to be silenced for the river to be passable. Lamson had a plan, which he carried out on April 19.

Soldiers of the Eighty-ninth New York Volunteers and the Eighth Connecticut Volunteers, nearly three hundred men under Brigadier General George Getty, boarded *Stepping Stones*. Just before 6 P.M. her steam whistle sounded—the prearranged signal for the already in-position gunboats to unleash in unison a heavy fire on the Hills Point battery. Getty's two batteries on the opposite shore also joined in. Then, slowly, with the troops on deck concealed behind a canvas screen, *Stepping Stones* steamed downriver, as if about to run the battery. Now came Lamson's next signal; the gunboats ceased firing as *Stepping Stones* veered hard and ran for shore, straight for the battery, getting too close for its guns to be able to hit. Up came the canvas, out went the gangway boards, and with a roar the soldiers charged.

They ran right over the first line of works, but there was a second line and a ravine in the way. The Eighty-ninth ran around to skirt the ravine, and the rear-line rebels swung their guns and discharged grape into the onrushing New Yorkers. Lamson, meanwhile, had brought up four boat howitzers and perched them atop the ravine's crest; he threw canister into the rear of the battery, and the Eighty-ninth took the works. They came off with five artillery pieces and more than 120 prisoners. More importantly for the gunboats that had been trapped upriver, the way was now open.

Fighting continued up and down the Nansemond. Four Potomac Flotilla vessels were sent down on temporary duty. The Confederates were reported to number ten thousand, ready to pontoon over as soon as they'd won an opening. Batteries and sharpshooters kept the gunboats hotly engaged. On April 22, hoping to rescue five sailors lured into capture by a waved white handkerchief, Lieutenant W. B. Cushing led an attack on the village of Chuckatuck. Cushing, commander of the lower Nansemond flotilla, stated his object was "to recapture our men and to punish the rebels for their cowardly conduct." He rounded up about ninety sailors from various vessels. They loaded into seven boats for shore. Gunboat fire covered them as they landed with a twelve-pounder in tow. Chuckatuck was a three-mile march inland and reportedly occupied by four hundred cavalry. Cushing's men chased off the first squad of pickets more than a mile outside of town. Now the expedition had acquired a mule cart; they tied on the howitzer rope and started to make good time. They rolled back two more picket squads and reached Chuckatuck by late afternoon. Cavalrymen drew their sabres and charged down the street. The sailors fired the howitzer and their muskets. The

mules were spooked. Carting the sailors' howitzer ammunition, they ran
wildly through the rebel line. The howitzer was already loaded for the
next volley. The sailors fired, cheered, and advanced. They retrieved the
ammunition cart. The rebels were in retreat. "We remained masters of
the town," reported Cushing. But the captured crewmen weren't in
Chuckatuck after all, and the expedition skirmished its way back to the
boats.

Next day, Lamson joined forces with Major General Peck to sweep
the Nansemond-Western Branch peninsula. A five-thousand-man force
with cavalry and artillery crossed over, ran the rebels out of their rifle
pits, and pushed them back to the woods. A four-gun battery opened up
on the attackers now; heavy fire pinned them down for an hour before
both sides withdrew.

The action along the Nansemond ended almost as abruptly as it had
begun, when the Confederates pulled back on May 3. "Thus ends the
present investment or siege of Suffolk," Peck was relieved to report,
"which had for its objects the recovery of the whole country south of the
James, extending to the Albemarle Sound in North Carolina, the ports
of Norfolk and Portsmouth, 80 miles of new railroad iron, the equip-
ments of two roads, and the capture of all the United States forces and
property, with some thousands of contrabands." It would have been a
plum turnabout, but Longstreet was wanted elsewhere. He was being
recalled to the Army of Northern Virginia's main body, currently em-
broiled at and around the town of Chancellorsville.

By the time he got there it was over. When the Army of the Potomac,
presently and briefly under the leadership of General Joseph Hooker,
retreated across the Rappahannock on May 6, it marked another
stinging victory for the Confederacy. Robert E. Lee's and Stonewall
Jackson's finest hour—the rule-breaking tactics, the brilliant payoff at
the Battle of Chancellorsville, May 1–4—was more than soured by the
accidental wounding of Jackson on the night of May 2; he died May 10.
The South's sorrow over the loss of Jackson was concurrent with the
North's chagrin over the loss of another battle, the failure of another
general.

On the Eastern Shore, the news of Hooker's retreat from Chancellorsville gave much joy to Tom Robson—he reportedly was in a very good mood over it at the time of his arrest.

The firebrand editor of the Easton *Star* had been relishing each Southern victory, lavishing generous amounts of ink on them in the pages of his newspaper. No one could call Thomas K. Robson shy about his opinions, which ran ardently pro-South and anti-Lincoln. The *Gazette*, a rival sheet, said of the *Star*, "There is no paper this side of Charleston that has been more severe upon the cause of the Union." Robson, with his newsprint invective, had been courting trouble throughout the conflict. In January 1862 he had been hauled into Camp Kirby, the Federal troop station east of town, because of a satirical piece insulting to the soldiers, particularly the men of Company E, who didn't much appreciate being called "Caroline county sand diggers." In November 1862 a gang in Union uniforms pulled a nocturnal raid on the *Star* office, breaking in, smashing furniture, damaging the press, hurling type into the street. No one was caught, but it was widely held that drunken cavalrymen from Camp Quaker on the Trappe Road had perpetrated the act.

Whoever sacked the *Star* no doubt felt it a blow struck against sedition. Robson harangued regularly and heartily. He railed against the Judge Carmichael arrest, of course; even the pro-Union press had voiced discontent then. Robson called Easton's Union faithful "eavesdroppers, spies and informers," and the local occupation troops "Mr. Lincoln's pet lambs." When the inevitable last straw fell, the arrest was ordered by President Lincoln himself, the nominal reason being publication in the *Star* of "Noble Ashby," a locally penned elegy to the fallen Turner Ashby. But Robson's flirtation with incarceration had been an onrunning one. On the night of May 8, 1863, the steamer *Balloon*—the same vessel that had carried off the bloodied Judge Carmichael—docked at Easton Point. Robson was given fifteen minutes to pack and say goodbye. He was shipped to Fort McHenry and a few days later taken to Harpers Ferry. He was banished, dropped off beyond Federal lines on a Shenandoah road. He made his way to Richmond, where he became an aide to General Winder, another expatriate Eastern Shoreman, in charge of Federal prisoners. The office of the Easton *Star* was shut down.

Major General Robert C. Schenck, military
commander at Baltimore for the better part of 1863.
National Archives

The paper had gone the way of the *St. Mary's Beacon*, the Southern Maryland newspaper whose press had ground to a halt and whose editor had been arrested on April 15. "The War Upon Women" was the editorial that caused the fuss in the *Beacon*; it ran in the April 2 edition. Under the new military governance of Major General Robert C. Schenck and Provost Marshal William S. Fish, Baltimore women found "guilty of disloyal acts" were being exiled that spring, and the *Beacon* attacked the practice.

> Our first revolution gave to history its score of women patriots, and the Frenchman still remembers with a commendable pride the names of Charlotte Corday and Madame Roland. The advent of these Maryland women at Richmond will not be without its influence upon the Southern heart. Driven from their homes and families by the unrelenting hand of a fanatic [Schenck] and a ruffian [Fish], they will be welcomed to the South with outbursts of generous sympathy, and their wrongs will become identified with the great cause in which her sons are battling. . . . Is Mr. Lincoln a man? And has he a wife and children and, yet, will sanction this conduct from

Gen. Schenck? If so, he does not deserve to be ruler over free men, nor is he entitled to either obedience or respect from any Christianized or civilized people.

Deemed treasonous, the diatribe landed editor J. S. Downs into the custody of the Federal forces at Leonardtown. The *St. Mary's Beacon* was suppressed, and Downs was taken to Baltimore.

The Schenck-Fish era was in full flower there—as Miss Fanny James came to appreciate firsthand when she was arrested on May 11. Miss James was hauled in on a treason charge; if she was guilty of aiding the enemy, she was also clearly guilty of possessing a letter that made fun of Fish, altogether not a healthy letter to be caught with in Baltimore in the spring of 1863.

When General Wool was replaced as general in command of the Maryland Department on December 23, 1862, Baltimoreans rejoiced, for the old warhorse had been even more dictatorial, more arrest-fervent, than his predecessors. During the Wool months, even well-known Union men could find themselves jailed on specious suspicions. Wool's replacement, Major General Robert C. Schenck, was welcomed with joy, at first. An Ohio lawyer, a former Whig congressman and minister to Brazil, he was praised by the pro-Union papers and feted at a January banquet presided over by Governor Bradford. It wasn't long, however, before Schenck was making Wool look pretty good.

Lieutenant Colonel William S. Fish, Schenck's choice for provost marshal, was a man who brought a certain virulent zeal to his duties. In February he ordered a Methodist-Episcopal congregation to worship with a large American flag displayed at the head of the gathering. In March the sale of South-leaning broadsheet ballads was outlawed, likewise the sale of portrait photographs of popular Confederate leaders. In April former Mayor Jesse Hunt, president of the Eutaw Savings Bank, was arrested for doffing his hat to Confederate prisoners of war. It was also in April that Baltimore women suspected of disloyalty were banished southward, inspiring the editorial that put the *Beacon* out of business.

One of these ousted ladies was Mrs. John James, the mother of Fanny James. The daughter too had attracted the suspicious Fish's eye, which led to an evidence search, which led to the discovery of the incriminating letter from a Richmond friend.

The letter contained such damning lines as "we can rely on your dispatching the goods at the earliest possible moment . . ." and "if we only had more such as you in Maryland, how many of our brave soldiers would be supplied with all their wants. . . ." The description of the provost marshal as "a mean, cowardly villain" and "a mighty *little Fish*" surely did nothing to alleviate Fanny's predicament, either.

The letter-writer, "N.," expounded further on Fish. "Any man that would make war upon women is beneath notice. But I acknowledge he's right in one respect—that the Baltimore ladies are more dangerous than the men. I'm of the opinion that if the men were like the women the villainous Yankees would have been obliged to make a retrograde movement long ago."

Baltimore's pro-Union citizenry, meanwhile, held mass meetings almost every month, remained true to the Stars and Stripes, supported the war effort, and continued to belie the notion perpetuated by "N." and others that the Federal troops were entirely unwanted here. On June 15, when the Army of Northern Virginia invaded Maryland again and the city once more prepared for an onslaught, it prepared with even greater elaborateness than it had the previous September. Major General Schenck called for the "Loyal Leagues" to help defend, and more than six thousand men quickly rallied in response.

The city council appropriated emergency money for fortifications on June 20. The police rounded up black men from around the city and put them to work erecting a perimeter of street barricades. Hogsheads, wagons, and carts were lined up, the road shoveled up and piled to form earthworks. By the twenty-first all approaches to Baltimore had been plugged by the barricade lines. The guns on Federal Hill and other militarily manned high spots were ready. Commodore Thomas A. Dornin, senior naval officer at Baltimore, positioned his war steamers at Schenck's request. The eight-gun *Eutaw* waited for trouble at the foot of Thames Street, *Daylight* at the foot of Broadway, *Maratanza* up the harbor, *Seymour* covering the B&O railroad and western Baltimore. North of the city, gunboats were sent into the Gunpowder and Bush Rivers to protect the railroad bridges. Then, fleeing Federals came into the city on the night of the twenty-ninth bearing the news: Stuart's cavalry was less than ten miles away. The word spread fast and with it the panic. The general alarm was sounded, arms distributed, the barricades manned. When morning came, Schenck declared martial law.

The orders were sixfold: no arms sales without a permit from Schenck. No leaving the city without a signed pass from Fish. No passing in or out from the barricades between 10 P.M. and 4 A.M. without giving the proper countersign. No clubhouse open without permission from Schenck. All saloons closed from 8 P.M. to 8 A.M. A 5 P.M. curfew on all businesses except apothecaries and newspapers, so the workers could practice arms drills. The martial law applied to Baltimore and all the western shore counties. "Traitors and disaffected persons within must be restrained, and made to contribute to the common safety," proclaimed Schenck, "while the enemy in front is to be met and punished for this bold invasion."

The rules quickly expanded. Possession of any weapon was forbidden except by citizens in organized defense militias. Soldiers of the

BALTIMORE CITIZENS BRACE FOR INVASION AND BARRICADE
THE STREETS, JUNE 29, 1863.
Frank Leslie's Illustrated Newspaper

Fifty-first Massachusetts joined with police in a citywide search of suspected secessionist households on July 2. Squads made rounds with furniture wagons and piled them with pistols, muskets, old swords, and fowling pieces. A huge crowd meanwhile flocked to newspaper row. Soon word started coming of a major struggle raging to the north. Soon wounded soldiers, Union and Confederate alike, began straggling into Baltimore from the Battle of Gettysburg.

The Union victory came on the Fourth of July. Lee's defeated army skirmished its way back to the Potomac with General George Meade, the Gettysburg victor, in pursuit. The Confederate army crossed the Potomac on July 13. The momentum was with the North now; the great battle had changed everything, and from it flowed a frightful inundation of dead, wounded, and prisoners of war. It created a huge new demand for more hospital beds and more prison camps. One camp that would be among the Union's largest was on a low-lying sand spit in Chesapeake Bay, and it was born in the wake of Gettysburg.

A fashionable resort occupied the site first. It opened in 1857 and had become quite successful by the time of war. There were four hundred acres with a main hotel and several cottages leased on a twenty-year subscription plan. Perched narrowly between a priceless view of the Bay and a priceless view of the Potomac, and catered to by regular steamboat service, the resort attracted such leaseholders as magnate Cyrus McCormick and Chief Justice Roger Taney. When war came, business dropped off. The property was mortgaged and then sold to the U.S. government. A military hospital, Camp Hammond, opened here in August 1862. On July 20, 1863, a prisoner-of-war camp was proposed for the site. It would be built to hold up to ten thousand prisoners. In honor of Colonel William Hoffman, commissary general of prisoners, it would be officially designated Camp Hoffman. But in general, people just called it by its location: Point Lookout.

Brigadier General Gilman Marston was assigned to run the prison camp, and St. Marys County was detached from the Middle Department and made its own separate district on July 23. On July 31, Navy Secretary Welles wrote Potomac Flotilla Commodore Harwood: "Point Lookout having been designated as a depot for rebel soldiers captured by our forces, you will direct a sufficient naval force to be always in close vicinity and in communication with the senior Army officer at that point." The first shipments of prisoners arrived from Baltimore and Washington. By August 31 there were 1,827 prisoners at Point Lookout. By October there were 7,585; by December 9,153; by July of 1864 nearly 15,000; and by the end of the war more than 20,000.

The camp compound was rectangular, about twenty acres, surrounded by a twelve-foot board fence with the sentinels' platform running along the outside of it three feet from the top. Inside the compound, fifteen feet from the fence, there was a ditch. It became known as the dead line.

The prisoners were on the Chesapeake shorefront, a half-mile across the jutting spit of land from the wharf, which lay just inside the mouth of the Potomac alongside the hospital. The hospital buildings fanned out circularly like wheel spokes and stood on the point's extreme tip. Be-

THE STAFF POSES BEFORE THE OFFICERS' QUARTERS AT POINT LOOKOUT PRISON CAMP. BRIGADIER GENERAL JAMES G. BARNES, COMMANDING OFFI-CER AS OF JULY 2, 1864, IS IN THE CENTER WITH HAND ON BELT.

Review of Reviews Co.

tween the prison stockade and the hospital were a growing camp of contrabands, an artillery battery, officers' quarters, and the old hotel, now seeing service as additional hospital wards. Past the prison pen, between the captured rebels and where the point widened and met the mainland, the prison guards were encamped.

The rebel officers were kept in a separate compound adjacent to the rank and file. The main prison area was a filthy hell, a cramped cesspool fecund with disease. The men lived in tents, neatly aligned in military rows, and it was a festering oven in summer, a barren tundra in winter. The food wasn't bad—hardtack and coffee morning and midday, a meat ration at night. The water reeked and turned things brown.

Among the rows in the tightly packed tent city ran a main thoroughfare. The men called it "The Change," and it was where they gathered to trade and gamble, playing cards and keno, and wagering money, tobacco, or a day's rations. Three narrow gateways led down to the Chesapeake beach. The prisoners were allowed to go there during the day.

Their clothes were falling apart, and it was three men to a blanket. Chronic diarrhea, scurvy, fever, pneumonia, and smallpox thrived in the miasmic environment. The mortality rate climbed as the prison grew more crowded. Drainage ditches were pointless; they soon filled with rancid water and the effluvium of too many humans too closely corralled. "They live, eat, and sleep in their own filth," reported W. F. Swalm, a Sanitary Commission inspector who toured Point Lookout in November 1863. The inspector blamed the prisoners' own indolence and hygiene apathy for much of their deplorable state. But he stressed that there was a dangerous deficiency of clothing and medicine and suggested the commission send more of these along for the prisoners. "I know they are our enemies, and bitter ones, and what we give them they will use against us, but now they are within our power and are suffering."

The inmates of Campbell's Slave Jail in Baltimore were paid a visit by Federal officers that July. The police had come here in the spring of 1862 to stomp down a breakout attempt. When Colonel William Birney came calling in the summer of 1863, he let the slaves go.

The women and children were sent on; it was the men Birney had come for. "These all expressed their desire to enlist in the service of the United States, and were conducted to the recruiting office on Camden street," the colonel was pleased to report. He was the son of the abolitionist James G. Birney, and Secretary Stanton had appointed him mustering officer for the U. S. Colored Troops in Maryland. Colonel Birney ostensibly was only supposed to be recruiting among the state's large free-black population; Maryland's being in the Union had exempted her from the Emancipation Proclamation. But be the recruit free man or slave, the abolitionist's son was being blissfully indiscriminate. Campbell's was one of five Baltimore slave pens he hit, and each slave who signed on for service was another blow for abolition. For the espouser of the cause, this was freeing people from bondage in the most literal sense. At Campbell's Slave Jail, stated the colonel, "Sixteen of the men were shackled together by couples, at the ankles, by heavy irons, and one had his legs chained together by ingeniously contrived locks connected by chains suspended to his waist. I sent for a blacksmith and had the shackles and chains removed."

Throughout that summer and fall Birney's enlistment steamboats, often replete with black marching band and impressive black troops, plied the rivers of the Eastern Shore and Southern Maryland, and hundreds of slaves left the plantation to fight. Two hundred left Easton on the steamer *Champion* in September, and more followed on the steamer *Cecil*. When one steamer came to Kent County in September, it seemed that "the negroes had previous notice of the coming of the boat and flocked to the shore in such crowds that many had to be left behind," reported the *Chestertown News*. "The number carried off is estimated at from 150 to 200, including nearly every able bodied slave in Eastern Neck." Hundreds more flocked to the steamers *John Tracy* and *Meigs* on the lower shore, another 130 to *Balloon* and *Cecil* tapping the Chesapeake oyster fleet from the mouth of the Patuxent to Tangier Sound. There was rising indignation in some quarters.

Governor Bradford met with Stanton in late September. Reverdy Johnson and other state luminaries met with President Lincoln. On October 3, with the issue of War Department General Orders Number 329, the regulations for border-state negro recruitment were more clearly defined. Free blacks of course could be enlisted, and slaves, too, if the master agreed. For consenting, the master would receive up to three hundred dollars' manumission compensation. If a county's recruitment quota wasn't filled in thirty days, the Bureau of Colored Troops had the power to recruit slaves *without* the master's consent, but the master would still have up to three hundred dollars due him. The manumission offer applied only to slaveowners loyal to the Union.

In late October the Bureau of Colored Troops established recruiting stations at Baltimore, Annapolis, Leonardtown, Havre de Grace, Chestertown, Queenstown, Oxford, Princess Anne, and eleven other locations. Ultimately, six regiments were raised, and more than 8,700 Maryland blacks served.

On October 21, 1863, Lieutenant Eben White was shot in the chest as he tried to recruit slaves belonging to Colonel John Sothoron, whose plantation, "The Plains," overlooked the Patuxent River in St. Mary's County. White had steamed down from Baltimore with two companies of the Seventh U.S. Colored Troops and had been recruiting in the area. He was greeted at the Sothoron estate by the colonel and his son Webster, a Confederate soldier on leave, standing defiant with pistols drawn. Webster was wounded, as was one of the lieutenant's men. The lieutenant was killed, and his two men hurried back to the steamer *Cecil* to report. The captain took a force of sailors and soldiers to "The Plains." They found Lieutenant White with his head stoved in and a couple of new and superfluous bullet wounds. Soldiers from Point Lookout subsequently confiscated the plantation. The Sothorons had fled to Richmond.

CHAPTER 9

"They will be held . . . as pirates"

PURSUING REPORTS OF suspicious goings-on, the gunboat *General Putnam* anchored off Wilton Creek, a Piankatank offshoot, on August 17. Acting Master Commanding William Hotchkiss led sixty men in five boats up the creek. Rounding a bend they spotted a lurker in the bushes. The shout went up and the sailors fired. "Shoot him! Kill him! Don't let the damned rebel get away!" The creek bank erupted with heavy gunfire. The boats had run into an ambush. The head boat ran aground. The crew dropped to the deck. Hotchkiss stayed standing and urged the men to action. He was shot in the neck.

The sailors were pushing the boat free when Hotchkiss fell. More were wounded. The flag was shot down. They raised it again and rowed back to the gunboat, their commanding officer dying as they brought him aboard. They headed downriver full-steam, shelling the Piankatank shoreline all the way to the Bay.

Up on Wilton Creek, John Taylor Wood realized it was high time to break camp.

He had rolled out of Richmond on August 12 with eleven officers, seventy-one men, and four of his wheel-mounted raiding boats. On this expedition—as Uncle Jefferson Davis had agreed after private planning meetings with Wood—the raiders' prey wouldn't be commercial shipping, but a Federal gunboat. The goal was akin to the French Lady's goal back in 1861: commandeer a U.S. Navy vessel and wreak havoc with it. On the night of August 16, Wood's raiders had rowed down the Piankatank to the Chesapeake. The two gunboats they spied were under way and thus unboardable. The rebels retired upriver, bivouacked at Wilton

John Taylor Wood.
His notoriety grew
after his capture of
U.S. Navy vessels on
Chesapeake Bay in
August 1863.

Chesapeake Bay
Maritime Museum

Creek, and had their run-in with the Federal boat patrol in the morning. Now that their location was known they started moving.

Wood's men took the boats up the Piankatank, braced them to the wagons, and overlanded it to the Rappahannock by August 19. They put in at Meachums Creek, ten miles up from the Bay. The new location meant new quarry, namely *Currituck*, *Reliance*, and *Satellite*, the Potomac Flotilla vessels known to anchor off the mouth of the Rappahannock. "One or all of these we were determined to have," wrote the correspondent for the *Richmond Dispatch*, along for the raid and filing his reports under the pen name "Bohemian."

The sun was setting as the boarding cutters entered the Rappahannock on August 19, "and at dark we were running down the dim shadow of the wooded shore," reported Bohemian. "It was a beautiful night. The land loomed up in the dark, the river ran calm and placid to the bay, the stars shone in the sky, and in the East brighter than all hung the crescent moon. Added to the picture was a line of black boats, filled with armed men, creeping snakelike over the water, prepared to spring upon the foe whenever he came in sight." At the mouth of the river the cutters came together as Lieutenant Wood gave the attack instructions; "then, after a fervent prayer, we pushed out into the bay."

The prayer was unanswered that night and the next. Their third foray was on August 22, and with a change in the weather came a change in their luck.

> The crescent moon, blood red and clouded, stood upon the tops of the trees, the stars shone dimly, the dark pines threw a solemn shadow upon the water, and from the shore came the thousand night sounds of bird and insect. Presently the sky became obscured, and a northerly storm rose

rapidly. Behind us a black cloud towered into the sky, from which came frequent flashes of lightning, and short gusts of wind began to agitate the waters. Before reaching the bay the storm had come, and we were tossing upon the waves like children's boats, while the wind whistled with fury around our ears.

Lightning cracked, and two black hulls came visible in the flashing light, gunboats pitching and rolling at anchor in the Bay off Windmill Point—"so close to each other," noted Lieutenant Wood, "that it was necessary to board both at the same time."

The raiders wore white armbands to avoid killing one another in the coming fight. They split into two parties, two boarding cutters for each gunboat. "There was no retreat now—death lay in the silent guns ahead and in the mad waters around," wrote Bohemian. "The waves had increased, and the sea was fast lashing itself into fury. Long black lines started from the horizon, ran towards us like some huge leviathan, for a moment raised us in the air, then rolled away in the dusky distance."

Former slave Nelson Frazier stood watch on the hurricane deck of USS *Satellite* and shouted above the roaring weather, "Boat ahoy!"

Fifty yards off the port bow and coming in, Wood replied, "Second cutters!"

"Come alongside," said the lookout. The boarding cutter collided against the looming hull. Wood leaped up, cutlass in hand, over the side, hacking through the deck netting, twenty men rising up behind him. Rifle shots popped. The alarm went up. "Boarders!" The men of the other cutter were swarming up the starboard side. A gunboat officer charged down the gangway, rousing the sleeping crew from their hammocks. The master-at-arms tried to grab a boarding pike and fell back as the cutlass blade slashed his head. Acting Ensign Rudolph Sommers was shot in the neck on his way to the quarterdeck. The raiders circled in close, and Sommers swung his pistol as the cutlasses sliced into his arm. The boatswain's mate came to his aid, and a shot from the upper deck drilled his shoulder. Ensign Sommers was down now, severely wounded but still not surrendering. They hauled him to his quarters and locked him in. Meanwhile, the ship's captain, Acting Master John Robinson, had locked *himself* in his quarters. When alerted to the attack he had curtly said, "Drive them off," and then shut the door. Now the rebels burst into the captain's cabin and hauled him to the quarterdeck. They threatened to blow his brains out, and he stood in his underwear on the gun carriage and surrendered at the top of his lungs.

Lieutenant Wood looked through the squally darkness toward the other vessel now. Through the windy storm noise, he could make out the sound of lively gunfire.

John Hand, forward lookout on the USS *Reliance*, warned the two boats that he'd fire if they came any closer. They kept coming. Anthony Spisenger, in charge of the watch, hurried forward toting his rifle. The boats were ten yards off now. Spisenger aimed down and shot. Hand ran aft, crying, "Rebel boarders!" The raiders rushed the deck as the gunboat crewmen spilled up through the hatch, grabbing swords and pistols on the way. Lieutenant Frank Hoge, the rebel leader, was first to gain the deck; he took a bullet in the neck and dropped by the water tank. The ship's captain, Acting Ensign Henry Walters, stormed into the thick of the fight, bellowing for someone to slip the anchor cable. The rebel-deserter crewman who tried to hammer free the pin was shot before he succeeded. The captain's hand was laid open by a cutlass. A pistol ball ripped through his abdomen, but he managed to make it to the pilothouse steps and blow the whistle before collapsing. It was a moot gesture; *Satellite* was already captured. The *Reliance* deck battle continued, both sides' commanders now down with wounds. Midshipman H. S. Cooke, rebel second-in-command, took charge of the attack. He was shot twice in the side; he staunched the bloodflow and kept fighting. A boatload of reinforcements arrived from *Satellite*, and the capture was complete.

The Confederate crews took their stations. Wood commanded *Satellite*, the larger prize. Lieutenant William Hudgins followed in *Reliance*. They went up the Rappahannock, and the U.S. Navy was minus two vessels that morning.

Beds for the wounded and a cavalry escort for the prisoners were waiting when the captures anchored off Urbanna after sunrise. Bohemian, a surgeon when he wasn't raiding and writing, cared for the wounded, friend and foe alike, with the help of the local women, at "Roseguild," Mrs. Bailey's residence. "The ladies were assiduous in their endeavors to make all comfortable," said Bohemian, "and I am sure the wounded will ever cherish kindly recollections of their care." The other prisoners were marched off to Richmond by Colonel T. L. Rosser of the Fifth Virginia Cavalry, who had rendezvoused earlier with Wood down along the Piankatank. Rebel deserters and runaway slaves among the captured crews were shackled in irons.

As Wood's raiders prepared to return to the Bay, this time hoping to catch the third gunboat, *Currituck*, they were joined by three officers and a company of sharpshooters from Rosser's cavalry regiment. The captured vessels were low on coal; the hunt would have to be a brief one. Heading downriver *Reliance* was losing steam. She could barely get up to two knots; maybe her Yankee engineer had sabotaged the engines during capture. Wood sent her back. She'd slowed them down enough already. It was 11 P.M. before *Satellite* reached the Bay.

"The sea was quite high, with a strong southeasterly wind, and every prospect of an approaching storm," reported Bohemian. "Having so little coal, it was impossible to go far; but Lt. Wood started boldly up the bay to see what there was afloat. The waves were every moment getting higher, and the *Satellite* creaked and groaned in every seam, and ran her head heavily against the sea, as if trying to commit suicide at the chagrin of capture."

The raiders prowled along the Eastern Shore. "Some few sails were seen looming up through the dark, but they were small and hardly worth the time when larger game was expected." The rough, rolling water made the cavalrymen seasick. *Currituck* was not to be seen and would have been tough taking in the high swells, anyway. The raiders returned to the Rappahannock, ran a few miles upriver and anchored off Grays Point in the dark morning. As the anchor hit the water, the long-awake crew hit the deck and slept hard. The wind rose and the waves raged through the day. In the twilight Wood saw three sails out on the Bay. The rebels got up steam, hoisted the U. S. flag, and ran down after them.

Wood made for the largest sail in a chase lasting nearly two hours. They finally caught her off Gwynns Island. The prize was timely: the schooner *Golden Rod*, out of Baltimore, bound for Maine with a load of precious coal. Bohemian described the coal schooner's captain and crew as "the most surprised men I ever saw."

The rebels hauled their coal-plump capture up the Chesapeake and caught the other two boats off the Rappahannock's mouth. U.S. flag flying, Wood came alongside and hailed them. They were Philadelphia anchor-sweepers, *Two Brothers* and *Coquette* by name, laden with anchors and chains. "You are my prisoners," Wood said, "and the vessels a prize to the Southern Confederacy."

The raiders towed the three vessels upriver as morning came on. The cavalrymen and prisoners were landed. *Satellite* coaled up alongside the prize schooner and headed back down toward the Bay to wait and watch for *Currituck* or any other unsuspecting victim. "The sea seemed to be higher than before," wrote Bohemian, "and we could see the white foam-caps flash in the light, and the heavy breakers dash upon the beach with their continuous, saddening roar." Crewmen rowed in, talked to pickets, and learned that *Currituck*, after contacting shore, had sped off full-steam for Fort Monroe. The surprise element was gone; the third gunboat had raced down for reinforcements. Night fell, and three large smokestacks loomed on the dark horizon. Wood wanted to clear the river's mouth and dash to open water before the gunboats got any closer. But the pilot said the engines couldn't stand the roughening seas. Federal vessels were approaching, the weather was worsening, and Wood reckoned it was time to head upriver. They made some distance, Bohemian on deck watching as the elements became angry. "The storm now burst upon us in all its fury, and the wind shrieked around us as if all the sea-demons had been turned loose."

The air was frigid and the river choppy at daybreak when they stripped the coal schooner and burned her. She drew too much to get her upriver without trouble. The rebels on *Reliance*, which by now had rejoined *Satellite*, had also had a chance to load up on coal. With the anchor-sweepers in tow, the captured gunboats fought headwind and ebb tide and made for Port Royal. On *Satellite*, Wood unfurled a Confederate flag. Behind him on *Reliance*, Lieutenant Hudgins and his men hoisted a makeshift rebel banner fashioned from old bunting. They proceeded upriver, a mini-flotilla of U.S. boats flying Confederate colors. Some people along the riverbank just stared, curious. Others cheered outright.

"The sun went down just as we entered Port Tobacco bay, its soft light lingering for a time upon the hazy hillsides," Bohemian wrote. "The picture that was then presented us was beautiful beyond description, and will linger long in some niche of the mind where memory shall hang it."

They continued upriver as night came on; when they approached Port Royal their greeting was a warning not to come any closer. The warning turned to a welcome when Wood sent a boat ahead. The raiders anchored off the town, where the Forty-seventh and Forty-eighth Alabama regiments were stationed, giving protection to a wagon train on a forage run. In the morning Wood reported to the commanding officer on shore. Soldiers and citizens were excited by the raiders' exploits, and some went out to tour the prizes. "During the day several parties of ladies came off to visit us," noted Bohemian, "some of whom recognized the gunboats, and had before seen them upon the river during the negro and chicken stealing expeditions of the Yankees." The moment to bask was brief; there was fast work to be done. Federal forces were just fifteen miles away at King George Courthouse. The prize ships were scuttled after being stripped clean—cannon, engines, more than twenty-six thousand dollars' worth of anchors and chains, and "everything of value except the boilers," as Wood put it.

One of the flotilla boats' guns, a thirty-two-pounder, was lost overboard during the stripping, but the other three guns were on shore and in place in time to fire back at the two-thousand-man Federal cavalry division and two artillery batteries that showed up across the river and shelled the rebels for four hours, to no great effect. The boats were sinking, the plunder was taken to the railroad station at Milford Landing, and John Taylor Wood, still uncaught and again triumphant, returned to Richmond. The Chesapeake was too hot for him now; opportunities for mischief beckoned in Carolina waters. He was soon promoted to commander, and on February 15, 1864, the Congress of the Confederate States of America gave him and his men a joint resolution of thanks for their "daring and brilliantly executed plans. . . ."

It was as if the man who had become the curse of the Potomac Flotilla had never left. Respectfully cautious gunboats continued to search for him among the creeks and coves of the lower Bay shore. Flotilla officers continued to imagine the hand of Wood behind disparate acts of sabotage and plundering in the Chesapeake as 1863 became 1864. As Bohemian's articles were picked up and run by newspapers North and South, Wood's fame, or infamy, grew, and the steamers patrolling the Chesapeake were at a heightened state of alertness. Wood had reminded people anew of the potential the Bay held for predation, for vandal warfare and symbolic acts of dash. Wood was gone, but like-minded troublemakers were roving in his wake.

The black boat and white boat were called *Raven* and *Swan*. They put out from Horn Harbor on the night of September 17 and sailed across the Chesapeake, making Devils Ditch by sunup. They headed for Cape Charles. When they passed within six-hundred yards of Smiths Island Lighthouse, it was a familiar sight to the expedition's captain. A month and a half earlier he had come here with some armed men and smashed up the lighthouse, stripped it of lamps and reflectors, and brought off twenty-five barrels of prime sperm oil much needed and much appreciated in Richmond.

It was a good thing that he avoided Smiths Island Lighthouse this go-round: A new three-gun battery had been erected to receive just the likes of him. But the captain had floating targets in mind now.

He was twenty-eight, religious, a Shenandoah Valley gentleman farmer, a University of Virginia law graduate. He had been shot in the chest while leading a cavalry charge in an upper Potomac skirmish in late 1861. The medical board said the war was over for him and discharged him, but he wasn't ready to retire yet. He wandered the country while recuperating, roaming across the Confederacy to the U.S. West and into Canada before working his way homeward. He secured passage down the Chesapeake on a blockade-running pungy out of Baltimore and showed up in Richmond in early 1863. He had a newfound determination and a new pair of plans. The one involving Great Lakes guerrilla warfare was deemed too risky from a British-diplomacy standpoint. The other plan, to strike hard and often in the Chesapeake, was just the thing, and in March 1863 John Yates Beall received his naval commission.

He was named an acting master, one not in line for promotion, a special designation shielding quasi-privateering with the official naval imprimatur. It was up to Beall to muster his own crew and secure his own boats, but the navy would supply him equipment. Beall and company would be paid by their own success; Yankee prize ships would be their pay.

Soon Beall had signed on ten men, and they set out for Mathews Courthouse. Like Wood in 1862 and a host of smugglers throughout, Beall saw the advantages of a Mobjack Bay base of operations. In April, the first month afield, Beall's party went foraging and broke up a camp of contrabands on Black River near Fort Monroe. The former slaves were armed. Beall's men attacked, killing one, capturing another, and sending the rest running. The raiders now had more weapons. In July they crossed the Bay and cut the telegraph cable linking Fort Monroe to Washington. In August they destroyed the Smiths Island Lighthouse. In September John Yates Beall had two boats and a crew that had grown to eighteen men, and at last was ready to hit the shipping lanes.

He commanded *Swan*; Acting Master Edward McGuire commanded *Raven*. Recent additions to the crew included young W. W. Baker, an apprentice with the *Richmond Enquirer*, who had joined with his boss, editor George C. Stedman. The boats continued past the lighthouse, up the Atlantic coast between the Eastern Shore of Virginia and the offshore islands. In Magothy Bay, *Swan* and *Raven* swooped down on their first prey: the sloop *Mary Anne*.

The quick capture also netted a couple of fishing scows, and the raiding crew saw an angling opportunity. "Being a little 'fish hungry,' Captain Beall allowed us to take as much fishing tackle as we wanted," recorded W. W. Baker, "and all of us spent the day fishing in the sand shoals, near Cobb's Island. After catching as many as we could manage, we returned to the *Mary Anne* and enjoyed one of the most elaborate fish suppers that I ever remember."

Well fed and with their first prizes in tow, Beall's raiders continued up the coast. Amid high winds and a fierce downpour, they sighted a large schooner anchored in Wachapreague Inlet on the night of September 19. Beall gave orders: *Swan* would take the vessel on the port side, *Raven* on starboard. The boats approached the schooner. McGuire was standing in *Raven*'s bow. The wild equinoctial wind and sea hurled *Raven* against the schooner. McGuire was pitched overboard. *Raven*'s tiller was smashed. McGuire struggled back aboard, while the irresistible current shoved *Raven* around the schooner's bow and sent her crashing into *Swan*. The raiders lashed their boats together, and both parties boarded from the port side after all.

Guns drawn, they overran the schooner. McGuire's men took the forecastle, Beall's men rushed aft. "The night was so dark and stormy that not a soul was found on deck," noted Baker. Captain David Ireland and the mate were playing dominoes when Beall threw open the cabin door. Captain Ireland tried to break and run. Beall threatened to shoot. The captain stared at the cocked revolver and surrendered the ship.

She was *Alliance*, out of Philadelphia and bound for Port Royal, South Carolina, with a valuable cargo of sutlers' stores for the Union troops. The rebels had her and they hadn't fired a shot. "After taking charge of the ship Captain Beall went below and directed that samples of everything be brought on deck," Baker recalled, "and we then had a veritable feast of good things, as there appeared to be everything to eat, drink, smoke and wear aboard."

The cargo was worth a fortune on the Richmond market, and after his crewmen were sated and freshly clothed, Beall ordered them to keep their hands off the remaining stores. If they needed something, they were to ask him. "He had always been so kind and gentle in his manner to each of us, frequently taking our places at the oars and cooking when we appeared tired, that none of us realized how stern he could be when his orders were disobeyed," stated Baker. But he and some of his mates tempted fate, learned what their captain's temper looked like, and almost got killed for the sake of a good smoke.

About six of them had gone below and started rifling through boxes of cigars, looking for better ones than those they had just been given. Beall found out, lined them up on deck, and ordered them searched. He told them that if he found cigars or any other pinched items on any of them, he would shoot them dead.

"I unfortunately had my pockets filled with the best Havanas," said Baker,

> as did several of the others. Realizing that we were in a tight place, we crowded back to the rail and as close together as we could get, and with our hands behind us emptied every pocket into the sea. I have thought that

Captain Beall knew what we were doing, although he could not see our hands at work. At any rate when the search was made we all were found to be innocent, and Captain Beall dismissed us with a fatherly caution not to again disobey him, and I can say that I am sure that in all the months after he never found real cause to complain.

The raiders double-anchored their latest capture, left a guard on board, headed back out into the storminess on *Raven* and *Swan*, and captured the schooner *J. J. Houseman* on the morning of September 20. The following night they added two more schooners, *Samuel Pearsall* and *Alexandria*, to their prize-train. With just two little boats and fewer than twenty men, in four days and in foul weather, John Yates Beall had succeeded in capturing seven vessels. He stripped them of valuables, set their sails, and cast them adrift—all of them, that is, except the grand prize, *Alliance*. He was going to take her into the Bay.

Beall had Captain Ireland brought on deck and asked him how well he knew the channel passage from the inlet into the Atlantic. Captain Ireland professed intimate knowledge of the coastline. Beall told him, "Your crew will be placed under your command, and you will please run us as soon as possible out into the Atlantic. I shall stand by you, and if you should allow us to run aground I shall be under the disagreeable necessity of shooting you."

Captain Ireland and crew navigated them through the sea-island gauntlet and into the Atlantic proper, where they scooted along under full sail. At Cobb Island Beall took on a Chesapeake pilot and set free those prisoners who took an oath of three-day silence. Those who would not, Captain Ireland among them, were put on *Raven* and *Swan*. The two raiding boats sailed up the Bay alongside the prize schooner as far as Cherrystone Light and then parted ways. Under command of McGuire, *Raven* and *Swan* made for Horn Harbor. Beall on *Alliance* made for the Piankatank; he intended to run her up there and unload her abundant cargo. The wind on the Bay was picking up and waves were running high.

They were running so high that *Raven* and *Swan* almost didn't make it across. They stayed close together as the waves crashed and filled them with water. Captain Ireland and the other prisoners bailed like madmen, and the boats limped into Horn Harbor at dawn on the twenty-third. "Captain Ireland remarked afterwards that he had been on the sea for a number of years, but that trip was about the closest call he had ever had," noted Bates, who also had been on *Raven*, "and that a little more wind and none of us would have ever seen the land again."

Alliance, meanwhile, ran aground near the mouth of the Piankatank. Beall and crew tried to unload the prize cargo. The Potomac Flotilla's *Thomas Freeborn* spotted them and fired. The raiders got off as much of the stores as they could and burned the schooner before fleeing the gunboat. The cargo was estimated to have been worth about $200,000 at Richmond prices; what Beall managed to salvage was worth about $10,000—a not unrespectable sum for less than a week's work.

"Increased vigilance has been enjoined on the officers of the blockade in Chesapeake Bay," Rear Admiral S. P. Lee assured Secretary Welles on September 30. On the same day, Lee instructed Lieutenant Commander J. H. Gillis that Chesapeake blockade-maintenance efforts, "as recent circumstances indicate, require an increase of strength and vigilance, not only to prevent illegal trade, but to protect the public interests from the naval expeditions of the enemy."

Word spread about the band of marauders responsible for the most recent deviltry. They were known to be based in Mathews County and to be led by Beall. They were being called the Marine Coast Guard, or the Confederate Volunteer Coast Guard. The U.S. Navy and Army combined forces to crush them.

After taking prisoners and prize cargo to Richmond, Beall's raiders had it in mind to try capturing a Federal gunboat as their next exploit. They returned to Mathews County, where Sands Smith, Thomas Smith, Colonel Tabb, and others treated them like family. "In fact," said Baker, "all the citizens in the neighborhood of Horn Harbor and Winter Harbor were as hospitable as was possible to be, and we were always cordially welcomed to their homes. Nor did we fully realize the vengeance that would be visited upon them by the Federals as soon as it became known that they were friendly to the 'notorious Beall and his party of pirates,' as Captain Beall was known and named by the Yankees. . . ."

Six North Atlantic Blockading Squadron gunboats and five army gunboats set out for Mobjack Bay on the morning of October 5. The naval force was commanded by Lieutenant Commander Gillis, the land force by Brigadier General I. J. Wistar. While the naval vessels blocked off every aquatic avenue of egress from Mobjack Bay to the mouth of the Piankatank, the infantry and artillery secured the Mathews County neck. The cavalry meanwhile cut a reconnoitering swath through the interior. Both the cavalry regiments and artillery regiments were New Yorkers and Pennsylvanians. The foot soldiers were one of the new Maryland outfits, the Fourth Regiment U.S. Colored Troops. The general spoke highly of their élan.

The joint expedition quickly yielded a harvest of prisoners, boats, and beef cattle. But most of the main culprits, including Beall, were still not found, nor were the raiders' boarding cutters, that distinctive black and white pair.

As the Federal forces approached, Beall ordered *Raven* and *Swan* run up Horn Harbor as far as possible. The raiders shoveled the boats full of sand and sank them. As word came that the Federals were getting ever closer, Beall reacted by calmly accepting Miss Lizzie Smith's invitation to have the whole crew over for supper. The Federal picket line had reached her father, Thomas Smith's, gate, less than a quarter-mile away. "I remember that a part of the supper consisted of sweet potatoes," said Baker, "and shall never forget how hard they were to swallow, as I thought of those Yankees at the gate."

They ate well—if too slowly for Baker's liking—and afterward Beall directed crewman McFarland, "who had seen service as an Indian scout, and who had a tread as soft as a kitten," to lead them out of there. The raiders followed single file behind McFarland, who would go ahead, scout the pickets, come back, and lead the rest of the crew forward.

Crewman Edmondson, a Marylander, had left his coat where the Federals would find it. He slinked off to retrieve it, and the rest of them had to wait. Said Baker, "We all laid down about five feet from the road, by the side of a ditch, and in a minute or two a Yankee relief guard came tramping by. I thought that my heart would punch a hole in the ground, it beat so fiercely as the Yankees moved up so quietly that it was impossible for us to move without being seen by them. We had to stay there and quietly hope that they would not see us. I am very glad to record they apparently did not." Edmondson returned with his coat, and the noiseless exit continued. Light-footed McFarland led the party safely past three picket lines. By morning the raiders had reached Dragon Swamp, where they hid for the next several days.

Not all were so fortunate. Second-in-command McGuire, for one, was caught, as were three other naval officers over the course of the three-day expedition. But the bulk of Beall's force was still at large, and the citizenry was being uncooperative. Sands Smith, whose waterfront was where the raiders' boats were submerged, perceived an insult in the words or actions of the cavalry squad that descended on his yard. He grabbed his double-barreled shotgun, killed one Yankee and was pulling another down from the saddle when hacking sabres finally put a stop to him. A drumhead court-martial rendered an instant sentence. The Federals loaded Sands Smith onto his own buggy, took him out, and hanged him from a roadside tree. His daughters, crying back at the house, weren't allowed to say good-bye. Bullet holes soon dotted his dangling body.

"After this tragedy Captain Beall was more anxious than ever to do all the injury that was possible to the Federals," recalled Baker, "and at once began preparations to capture the gunboats, on which he hoped to make the Yankees feel the force of his anger at the murder of Sands Smith."

Raven and *Swan* were raised. Beall's raiders set out across Chesapeake Bay again on November 10, in hopes of capturing a Federal navy vessel reportedly anchored off Chesconnessex Creek in Accomac. A schooner came their way first, though, and the quick and easy capture should have been a good omen, but it wasn't.

Beall remained on the schooner and sent a boat party off to hide with *Raven* and *Swan* on shore until the following night. The landing party found a fine, snug hiding place on a small island.

In the morning brightness on November 14, it turned out to be a terrible hiding place, terribly exposed. Most of the landing party had

gone off to sleep on the island. Only Baker and crewman Fitzgerald, a
Norfolk man, remained by the boats. A fisherman spied the boats and
approached, asking the two their business. They said they were from
Baltimore, down on a hunting trip. They couldn't tell if he believed them.
He was keeping his distance. "We were afraid to shoot the fellow, as any
firing would have attracted many of the hundreds of fishing smacks that
appeared to be near the mouth of the inlet," commented Baker. The wary
fisherman wished them happy hunting and departed.

Within a few hours the raiders were face to face with two barges
brimming with Federal soldiers, guns cocked and aimed. Fitzgerald
turned to Baker and said, "Baker, this is a hot thing, ain't it?"

"Surrender!" the Union officer yelled. He asked them to whose
command they belonged. One or the other of them made the mistake of
answering. Hearing Beall's name, the soldiers stormed onto the island
and fired at will. The roundup of raiders was swift and thorough. They
were taken to the nearby Federal gunboat, just the sort of boat the raiders
had intended to make their own.

An oystering vessel was alongside. Baker pleaded with his captor,
"Lieutenant, I am nearly starved; I wish you would let me get over into
that boat and get some oysters."

The officer appeared on the verge of ferocity, then he just said, "All
right, get over there, you little rascal, and help yourself."

Beall, meanwhile, had a chance to escape; he remained nearby out
of curiosity and concern. Next day, the prize schooner was surrounded
and the raiders overpowered. Two detachments of Company B, First
Eastern Shore Maryland Volunteers, led by Lieutenant John Conner and
Sergeant Robert Christopher, had succeeded in curtailing the Chesapeake
career of John Yates Beall, overnight legend.

Beall and his men were briefly held in Drummondtown Jail, then
sent to Fort McHenry. As the gunboat transported them up the Bay, Beall
saw an escape chance. Beyond the door to the cabin where they were
being held were only two guards—and a stack of muskets for the relief
guard. Beall whispered the plan: When he gave the signal, they would
jump the guards and grab those muskets. Only two agreed to take part.
According to Baker, "Captain Beall was terribly enraged when a majority of the party refused to join him, and did not hesitate to tell us, his

teeth gritting, that we were a set of dastardly cowards." Beall apologized once he learned that the whole thing was a trap, that there was an entire infantry company up on deck "whose men were waiting for us to rush out that they might shoot down every man and thereby have done with Captain Beall and his party without any trouble of trial."

To Brigadier General Henry H. Lockwood, whose troops had made the capture, Beall and company were neither fish nor fowl, but he preferred to err on the side of harsh-as-possible punishment. Lockwood wrote the authorities at Fort McHenry that the raiders were "unable to show anything which, in my judgment, would entitle them to be considered or treated as prisoners of war. They are without orders and many of them without uniform. . . . I would respectfully suggest that they be tried either by military commission or that they be sent back here for trial by the civil authorities of Accomac and Northampton Counties, where the depredations have been committed. . . . I am rather inclined to think the latter course would be the preferable one, inasmuch as some of the citizens seem to be considerably incensed against these raiders, and I think twelve men at least in the county of Accomac can be procured who will be disposed to deal with these fellows as their outrages deserve."

On November 21, 1863, Lieutenant Colonel W. H. Cheseborough, assistant adjutant general at Fort McHenry, wrote back to Lockwood, letting him know the status of Beall's raiders, now arrived in Baltimore: "They will be held for the present, not as prisoners of war, but as pirates or marauding robbers. . . ."

CHAPTER 10

Ship of salvation

THE GUERRILLAS, SOME forty or fifty of them, had been lying low for a
few days. They had crossed the Bay in open boats and waited for the
right moment to strike. At four in the morning on Saturday, March 5,
1864, they attacked and overpowered the guard at the Cherrystone Inlet
telegraph office on the Eastern Shore of Virginia. Telegraph operator
William H. Dunn threw his instruments into the Bay and made a run for
it. The rebels fired at, chased, and captured him. They cut the telegraph
wires and killed all the horses. Two Federal vessels lay at anchor two
miles offshore, and they made the mistake of heading in for the Cherrystone wharf. The first was the steamer *Aeolus*. The rebels pounced; the
capture was quick. The U.S. Army dispatch tug *Titan* soon followed, and
the rebels had her. They wrecked the telegraph office, set fire to the
guardhouse, burned the commissary stores, disabled *Aeolus*, took three
thousand dollars from her captain, and escaped in *Titan* across the Bay.

The chase was on by that afternoon. North Atlantic Blockading
Squadron vessels ran up the Atlantic and Chesapeake coasts of the
Virginia Eastern Shore. Potomac Flotilla vessels hurried to Cherrystone.
But the gunboats search-cruising on the western shore had a better
chance of recapturing *Titan*. Telegraph operator Dunn had overheard
the guerrillas talk about running their prize vessel up the Piankatank.
Indeed, a tug slipped past in the Bay fog, and the Potomac Flotilla's *Tulip*
chased her into the Piankatank. The pursuit stopped at the mouth
because *Tulip*'s pilot did not know the river. At least they had the tug
cornered now, and on the morning of the seventh a five-boat force made

the Piankatank ascension. The Potomac Flotilla's latest, and last, commander, Foxhall Parker, chose to lead the expedition himself.

His appointment to the flotilla command, which had taken effect on December 31, 1863, was the culmination of three active years of war service in the Chesapeake and tributaries. Early on, Parker had been attached to the Washington Navy Yard and had been lauded for his valor in rallying the demoralized Union troops to defend Alexandria in the wake of First Bull Run. More recently, while patrolling the York River and environs for S. P. Lee, Parker had earned the praise of Major General Erasmus D. Keyes, who commented, "That officer certainly combines in his character caution and enterprise in a remarkable degree." A career navy man, Parker was a veteran of the West India, East India, and Pacific squadrons. He had been reassigned to Washington Navy Yard duty when the Potomac Flotilla command was handed to him. His brother William, meanwhile, was down on the James River running the Confederate States Naval Academy, an institution founded in October 1863 and whose campus was the deck of the CSS *Patrick Henry*. While his rebel brother was thus engaged, Foxhall Parker had been handed charge of a Chesapeake that had been too rebelliously volatile for Northern comfort of late.

Parker had an enthusiastic subordinate officer in Acting Volunteer Lieutenant Edward Hooker, now commanding the First Division of the Potomac Flotilla. The Connecticut-born Hooker had been promoted for gallantry in action during the 1862 Burnside expedition and was ordered to the Potomac Flotilla in 1863. His recent successes included forays with the Point Lookout troops under Brigadier General Marston—the November 22 combined army-navy sweep of the blockade-runners' lair on St. George Island, netting thirty-one new prisoners for Point Lookout, and a similar raid on the Northern Neck in January. Perhaps more than any other flotilla officer, Hooker was ever watchful for the reappearance of John Taylor Wood. It was Hooker who had just dispatched *Tulip* in pursuit of *Titan* and first reported the sighting of the captured army steamer.

As Foxhall Parker headed up the Piankatank with five gunboats, Hooker remained off the river's mouth, and when a vessel of the North Atlantic Blockading Squadron arrived to join the chase, Hooker did not

FOXHALL A. PARKER, COMMANDER OF THE
POTOMAC FLOTILLA, 1864-65.
Special Collections, Nimitz Library, U.S. Naval Academy

let her pass. There were enough flotilla vessels there to take care of the situation, said Hooker.

Commander Parker took the boats all the way up to the head of navigation at Freeport. There they found *Titan*—what was left of her. She was burned to the waterline.

The gunboats shelled the wooded shoreline. Parker sent in armed boat crews to break up the burned tug's boilers, not leaving anything for

Before assuming command of the Potomac Flotilla, Foxhall Parker
saw service patrolling the York River and Mobjack Bay areas.
Here, crewmen of the gunboat *Mahaska* under Parker's
command destroy a rebel battery along the York.
Frank Leslie's Illustrated Newspaper

the rebels to salvage. The guerrillas had eluded capture. Hooker's first reports and the Northern press saw the Cherrystone raid as John Taylor Wood's doing. Captain Thaddeus Fitzhugh had actually led the party. Fitzhugh was in the Fifth Virginia Cavalry, the same regiment that had provided land support for Wood's 1863 raids. But Wood was now by all accounts in New Berne, North Carolina. Wood's reputation robbed Fitzhugh of the initial credit for Cherrystone, but by April, Hooker's dispatches were crediting Fitzhugh with the deed. Fitzhugh would become known because he would act again in the spirit of Zarvona, Wood, and Beall.

John Yates Beall and crew were shuffled all up and down the Chesapeake that winter and spring. Union deserters imprisoned at Fort McHenry crowded the yard for a look at the raiders as they were filed past after their November capture. One of the Yankees slapped W. W. Baker on the back and greeted him like an old friend. "I then noticed that each one of us had received a slap, and that the hand had been chalked."

Other rituals greeted them that first day. A Federal sergeant, telling Baker that he would have to be "initiated into the mysteries of the prison," warned him not to resist the upcoming game. In the yard were about twenty-five men with a blanket; they told Baker to jump into it. He obeyed. The men gave a hip-hurrah and blanket-tossed him three times. Some of Baker's cohorts refused the blanket treatment; they were beaten and robbed.

Beall and his crew had been at the fort a few days when the sergeant entered their garret quarters and yelled, "Here, you pirates, all of you are wanted down in the provost marshal's office."

They were lined up, roll-called, and told they were to be placed in irons. Beall protested; the provost marshal said he was just following orders. All the raiders were put in ankle shackles except Baker and two others, who had the good fortune to be wearing boots too thick for shackles to fit over. "I was congratulating myself that we would be permitted to go without any irons," recounted Baker, "when the officer in charge said: 'Sergeant, take these three men up to the blacksmith shop and have a ball and chain riveted upon each.'"

The prisoners were placed in a stable with guards barring the one entrance. It was a holding station for Federal soldiers whose behavior had warranted shackles. They were brought here to mull over their sins between being arrested and being returned to their regiments. Edmondson made friends with one of the Yankees, who taught him how to make a wooden key that would unlock the shackles. Soon, all the raiders were removing their shackles at night and putting them back on in time for the sergeant's morning inspection. But Baker and the other two ball-and-chain boys didn't benefit from the wooden key; their chains were secured with rivets, not locks.

Edmondson escaped. Yankees from elsewhere in the prison were allowed in to visit their shackled friends in the stable. At the end of the day the visitors were shuffled out. Edmondson loosed his shackles, merged with the departing visitor herd, and was taken with them to another, less stringently guarded building on the fort grounds. The prisoners were whooping it up; the guards were enjoying the spectacle. Edmondson jumped out a window and proceeded on hands and knees. A sentinel hailed him. He stayed low and made hog noises. He sneaked to the wall, studied the clockwork walking patterns of the wall guards, saw his moment, scrambled up and over, and scampered into Baltimore.

From there he made it to Frederick, where he ate and rested before crossing the Potomac and heading on to Richmond. He went to the Navy Department and reported on the plight of his mates.

Back at Fort McHenry, hell followed morning roll call. After being interrogated about the escape, the raiders were transferred into a cramped, dark cell built into the wall of the inner fort. "The room was so small that we were packed in like sardines in a box," said Baker. Baltimore, in the meantime, had recently seen the end of the Schenck-Fish era. In January 1864 William Fish was arrested on corruption and fraud charges related to his activities as provost marshal; he was found guilty and jailed at Albany. Major General Schenck had departed to pursue politics in his native Ohio, and in late November 1863 General Lockwood began his brief tenure as military commander at Baltimore. In essence, he had followed Beall from the Virginia Eastern Shore to Baltimore. Lockwood visited the raiders whose capture he had overseen down the Bay. Coming to the tiny cell, he told Beall that he would "soon have a court convened and try you and your band of pirates." Lockwood and his staff may have been less than congenial, but the Fort McHenry officers were decent toward the raiders. "We were treated with the utmost courtesy by the officers of the fort," said Baker, "who often spoke regretfully of our being shot or hung."

Deliverance came in the form of a retaliatory threat on December 15, 1863. The Confederate War Department's commissioner of exchange issued a statement to his Federal counterpart. The statement pointed out that Beall and his crew were rightfully part of the navy, "were engaged in open warfare and are entitled in every respect to the treatment of prisoners of war." To assure that treatment, the Confederate government was holding two U.S. Navy officers and fifteen seamen in irons as hostages for the proper treatment of Beall and company. When the news reached the Fort McHenry prison cell by way of a *Richmond Whig* article reprinted in the Baltimore *Sun*, the raiders rejoiced. Baker turned to the fort officer who had brought them the article and said, "Now Lieutenant, you all fellows can hang us, but those Yankees will surely swing in Charleston."

Liberated from their irons, the prisoners were marched into Baltimore and up the gangway of a Norfolk steamer, which transported them to Fort Monroe. Ben Butler was back. After earning the undying detestation of the South during his New Orleans military overlordship, General Butler was back in command at Fort Monroe as of November 1863. The command, of course, now included Norfolk, which it hadn't during Butler's 1861 stint. It was to Norfolk that Beall's raiders were shipped after a few days. They signed certificates stating that their irons had been removed and that they were being treated as proper prisoners of war. Then they were jailed at Fort Norfolk for two months. Toward the end of their stay, a man named Coffin was thrown in with them. He was guilty of being loudly pro-Southern. He had a lot of escape ideas which he liked discussing.

The prisoners were told they would be moved to Point Lookout in the morning. Beall devised an elaborate escape plan in which everyone would have his own part. The signal to act would be a dropped handkerchief. They would seize the guards and commandeer the transport boat. "We were all in a high glee when we got aboard of the steamer, fully expecting to be free before night," recollected Baker, "but when we stopped at Fort Monroe we were all surprised to find that a company of regulars was marched aboard, in addition to the small guard under which we had left Fort Norfolk. We were then placed in the main cabin of the steamer and formed in a circle with a heavy guard all around us with fixed bayonets." Coffin was a spy. Butler knew their plans.

They reached the dread destination at night. At Point Lookout the raiders ceased to be as cohesive a group, dispersed among the crowded tent rows and larger prison-camp population. After two months of life at Point Lookout, Baker saw his chance to get out. Some five hundred sick prisoners were about to be exchanged, "and being very anxious to see a young lady in whom I was deeply interested, I made up my mind to try and get away with the sick."

All the time he'd had to wear the ball and chain at Fort McHenry, he hadn't been able to take off his boot. Months later his ankle was still one big, nasty sore. "This had not made any progress towards a cure, but had become worse and turned into a kind of scurvy. I rubbed up this sore a good deal and spread the blood up on my leg so as to make it appear much worse, rolled up my pants and rushed to the surgeon who was examining the men as they were brought out. . . ."

Two lines were forming: the sick, who got to go South and be exchanged, and the well, who had to stay. Baker's messy leg failed to sway the surgeon, who bluntly ordered him to get in the well men's line. Baker, trembling, got in the sick men's line, anyway. He crept toward the front. Nobody stopped him. Up ahead was his salvation, the flag-of-truce steamer *New York*. He made it aboard, and she carried him home.

That steamer was the salvation of many. Her white flag flying was a blessed sight, the angel of deliverance to broken-down, half-dead boys fortunate enough to be exchanged or paroled. *New York* and other vessels likewise employed took Southern prisoners down the Chesapeake and Northern prisoners up. First, Aikens Landing and then City Point on the James were where the actual exchanges took place. The Federal and Confederate exchange agents would meet here with their prisoner boatloads, compare rolls, and work out the systematic trading spelled out in the agreed-upon cartel of July 1862. Based on the old exchange system used between Britain and the United States in the War of 1812, trading followed the simple principle of "an officer for an officer, a private for a private." But there were intricate permutations: A navy

THE FLAG-OF-TRUCE STEAMER *NEW YORK* DOCKING AT ANNAPOLIS.
Special Collections, Nimitz Library, U.S. Naval Academy

captain or army colonel equaled fifteen common seamen or fifteen privates, for example.

When the riverside exchanges were all calculated, one side generally was left with a surplus of prisoners it was eager to release, and thus no longer have to feed. These prisoners were paroled under oath they would not take up arms again until an equal number of their enemy had been later released, thus making it a proper exchange. Ultimately, despite the detailed articulation of the 1862 cartel, the exchange protocol was malleable, complex, and constantly evolving.

In the Eastern theater, Annapolis was the main center for the receiving of released Federal prisoners, brought to the Naval Academy wharf in increasing numbers as the battles grew larger and the war grew longer. The academy grounds were striped with long, low rows of hospital buildings. This was USA General Hospital, Division Number 1. Behind the Naval Academy, the campus green of St. John's College was blanketed by a sea of tents and barracks; the school was USA General Hospital, Division Number 2. Three miles west of town, a camp had been established to process the paroled soldiers, recuperating from prison life and waiting for the back pay they had accrued. As the soldiers were disembarked at the wharf, those who were well enough were marched in line to Camp Parole. Often, of course, considering they were arriving from Libby Prison and other hells on earth, the hospital was their necessary destination.

Great numbers of freed prisoners were shipped here, sometimes as many as 6,000 at a time. The site evolved; St. John's had initially been a way station for parolees, but Camp Parole became the sole spot for them as St. John's was needed for additional hospital space by 1863. The flag-of-truce boat returned, departed, and returned, delivering her rescued cargo—the wounded, starved, maimed, and dying.

"Every case wore upon it the visage of hunger, the expression of despair, and exhibited the ravages of some preying disease within, or the wreck of a once athletic frame," reported U.S. Army Assistant Surgeon S. J. Radcliffe in November 1863. *New York* had just steamed into port with soldiers released from Virginia's Belle Island prison camp. "I only generalize them when I say their external appearance was wretched in the extreme."

THE U.S. NAVAL ACADEMY GROUNDS, TRANSFORMED BY WAR INTO
USA GENERAL HOSPITAL, DIVISION NO. 1.
Special Collections, Nimitz Library, U.S. Naval Academy

When she left the exchange site at City Point, *New York* was carrying 189 sick and wounded soldiers. "Their hair was disheveled, their beards long and matted with dirt, their skin blackened and caked with the most loathsome filth, and their bodies and clothing covered with vermin."

Four died before *New York* reached Fort Monroe. "Their frames were in the most cases all that was left of them. A majority had scarcely vitality sufficient to enable them to stand. Their dangling, long, attenuated arms and legs, sharp, pinched features, ghastly cadaveric countenances, deep sepulchral eyes and voices that could hardly be distinguished (some could not articulate) presented a picture which could not be looked upon without its drawing out the strongest emotion of pity."

Four more died on the trip up the Bay, leaving 181 new admissions for Annapolis. "Upon those who had no wounds, as well as on the wounded, were large foul ulcers and sores, principally on their shoulders and hips, produced by lying on the hard ground, and those that were wounded had received no attention, their wounds being in a filthy, offensive condition, with dirty rags, such as they could procure, incrusted hard to them."

The officers of the army hospital at Annapolis.
Special Collections, Nimitz Library, U.S. Naval Academy

New York docked at the Annapolis wharf, and the patients were brought off. There was the stench of ragged clothes filled with "involuntary evacuations" and men too weak to care. Pneumonia ran rampant, several of its victims near death. "Delirious with fever, many knew not their destination or were not conscious of their arrival nearer home; or, racked with pain, many cared not whither they went or considered whether life was dear or not. In some, life was slowly ebbing from mere exhaustion and the gradual wasting of the senses."

The hospital had thirty-eight wards, grouped into five sections with a surgeon to each section. The head surgeon was Dr. B. A. Vanderkieft; the head nurse, Miss Maria Hall. The head chaplain, the Reverend H. C. Henries, held Sabbath services at two and seven o'clock. Every Wednesday evening there was a prayer meeting; every Thursday, a Bible class.

NURSES COMFORT THE WOUNDED AT AN ANNAPOLIS HOSPITAL TENT.
Special Collections, Nimitz Library, U.S. Naval Academy

Assistant Surgeon Radcliffe observed, "Every man who could rejoiced over his escape, deplored the scenes through which he had passed,
and mourned the lot of those he left behind."

The Confederate prison population at Point Lookout had swollen to
more than twelve thousand by May 1864, with thousands more on the
way. Since January, the Thirty-sixth U.S. Colored Infantry had been on
duty at the prison camp.

Troops from New Hampshire, Rhode Island, and Wisconsin rounded
out the Federal force. On March 20 Sergeant Edwin Young of the Second
New Hampshire Volunteers shot a newly arrived prisoner at point-
blank range. It was the culmination of a fight that started when the rebel
pointed to a black sentinel and said that "the negro is superior to the
Yankee." The board of officers investigating the killing ruled that the
New Hampshire sergeant had been "grossly insulted," that he was
"compelled to vindicate himself," and that "the circumstances . . . fully

U.S. Army privates, wasted away by Confederate prison life, are treated at the Annapolis hospital.

Special Collections, Nimitz Library, U.S. Naval Academy

justify the act. . . ." The prisoner had been drinking liquor on the boat from Baltimore, and he stood there baring his chest, daring Sergeant Young to shoot. The slug hit the rebel's aorta, and he died instantly.

Colonel Alonzo G. Draper, the white officer at the head of the Thirty-sixth U.S. Colored, assumed command of the entire garrison in April. Three times that spring, he operated in concert with the Potomac Flotilla, which in early 1864 established its new coaling station and operational base at nearby St. Inigoes Creek off the St. Marys River. On April 15, five days before his elevation to the Point Lookout command, Colonel Draper took black infantry and white cavalry and joined three Potomac Flotilla vessels in a raid on the Lower Machodoc River. They burned buildings, arrested the notorious smuggler Joseph Maddox, brought off forty thousand dollars' worth of tobacco and fifty contrabands. A Popes Creek raid in mid-June yielded a huge harvest of horses, cattle, mules, wagons, farm implements, and some six hundred contrabands, including sixty or seventy new army recruits. But the May expedition stood out as the one that had a purpose beyond nabbing blockade runners and confiscating provisions.

On the night of May 11 Lieutenant Hooker left St. Inigoes on the USS *Yankee*, docked at Point Lookout, and began boarding troops. A fifteen-man cavalry detachment and three hundred soldiers of the Thirty-sixth U.S. Colored Infantry headed down the Chesapeake to help the Potomac Flotilla stifle a growing tributary threat: rebel torpedoes.

Some mines were floated with barrel-buoys, others were sunken with a triggering line running to shore. The Confederates had been experimenting with the mines—they called them torpedoes—all along, but it was the waning phase of the war that saw the torpedo presence escalate in the rivers of the Chesapeake. When a double explosion rocked the starboard bow of the gunboat *Commodore Barney* on August 4, 1863, sending twenty of her crewmen flying into the James, it signaled the start of torpedoing in earnest. In October the rebels were reported to be planting torpedoes in the York and Pamunkey. In November one of the devices was discovered bobbing in the James near Newport News. Water travel was acquiring a new dimension of perilousness. It had been risky from the start, with ambushers, hostile vessels, and shore batteries. But at least a sailor could shoot back at a shore battery.

THE INCREASING THREAT POSED BY CONFEDERATE
TORPEDOES WAS SIGNALED BY THE EXPLOSION UNDER
USS *COMMODORE BARNEY* ON AUGUST 4, 1863.
Frank Leslie's Illustrated Newspaper

Lieutenant Hunter Davidson, CSN, the man behind the thousand-pound electrically ignited powder blast that had lifted *Commodore Barney's* bow out of the water, headed the Submarine Battery Service and was a pioneer in the art and science of aquatic explosives. After the war he chased Chesapeake oyster pirates for a living, as the first commander of Maryland's oyster navy. For now, he was busy retarding the Federal water advance. His torpedo-methodology repertoire was an expanding one, and at 2 A.M. on April 9, 1864, he startled the North Atlantic Blockading Squadron by bringing the mountain to Mohammed.

The torpedo boat was called *Squib*, and Davidson himself had designed her: She was thirty-five feet long and five feet wide, with a three-foot draft, an iron-encased engine, and (her most salient feature) a long spar with a torpedo on the end of it. With his six-man crew Davidson ran past the Federal fleet at Newport News and plowed the spar torpedo's fifty-three-pound powder charge into the port quarter of the flagship *Minnesota*. Water shot up into the sky, the frigate rolled to starboard, and as her deck officer cried, "Torpedo! Torpedo!" *Squib* escaped amid heavy gunfire. *Minnesota*'s damage was slight, but Davidson's audacity was not. He was praised for his "cool daring" and promoted to commander for "gallant and meritorious conduct." On the other side, the incident prompted Rear Admiral Lee to cancel all oystering from Newport News to Pig Point for the short remainder of the season. The congestion of oyster boats had provided *Squib*'s cover on approaching.

The toll mounted. USS *Commodore Jones* was blown to sticks while searching for torpedoes in the James on May 6. The torpedo found her first. Two days later, torpedoes indirectly led to the fate of *Shawsheen*. She, too, was on a James River torpedo sweep when she was destroyed by the rebel battery near Turkey Point. Her commanding officer was killed and most of her crew captured. Rear Admiral Lee ordered the formation of a special "torpedo and picket division" to drag the James. Foxhall Parker, meanwhile, gained evidence of a torpedo-planting gang at work on the Rappahannock and Piankatank. "I determined to attack them without delay," he declared, and the combined operation of May 12 ensued.

While the Potomac Flotilla vessels *Yankee*, *Currituck*, and *Fuchsia* torpedo-hunted on the waterways, Colonel Draper's Point Lookout soldiers combed the countryside from the Rappahannock to the Piankatank to Mobjack Bay. The land force was augmented by thirty-five seamen and a howitzer courtesy of the Potomac Flotilla. The sailors ran into rebel cavalry and threw out a skirmish line. A shootout in thick woods followed. The rebels were routed, their leader killed. At the mouth of the Rappahannock, the gunboats were pulling torpedoes out of the water. By expedition's end they had gotten rid of ten of them, exploding four and taking up six. The land party, meanwhile, reaped its requisite harvest of cattle, horses, mules, and wagons, but also found the powder cache that was feeding torpedo production.

Draper and the Thirty-sixth Colored exploded three torpedoes and raised two more at Mill Creek, crossed the Rappahannock-Piankatank peninsula, found four more torpedoes in the woods, burned the mill of an accomplice to the torpedo manufacturers, and skirmished with a Confederate detachment. The black soldiers in the vanguard did all the fighting before the officers arrived. Price, the black sergeant, stopped those in his ranks who wanted to kill the rebel prisoners outright.

The Federals were moving up the rivers, and torpedoes were not going to stop them. Through the late winter and spring of 1864 the Federals advanced up the James and York and engaged in riverfront fights from the Rappahannock to Pagan Creek. These were tentative waterborne proddings; the big push was coming.

The U.S. Army gunboat *Smith Briggs* was captured by rebels on February 1. The Union expedition up Pagan Creek was intended to break up a Confederate camp near Smithfield and come off with prisoners and tobacco stores. Sharpshooters and a rebel battery soon had the Federal troops on the run. *Smith Briggs* came alongside a wharf to retrieve them, and the hill and nearby houses roared with rifle fire. The *Smith Briggs* gunners were driven from their stations. The rebels charged downhill and swarmed over the gunboat as the Union soldiers withdrew down the Pagan on naval transports. "I think it was well we retreated," Acting Ensign James Birtwhistle reported. "Could they have managed the steamer, and outflanked us on the beach, we could not have returned." An army detachment was captured and *Smith Briggs* blown up.

A joint expedition moved up the Nansemond River on April 13, chasing the torpedo boat *Squib* in the wake of her attack on *Minnesota*. Acting Lieutenant Charles Wilder, commanding two launches from *Minnesota*, was killed by sniper fire on the fourteenth. "True to the reputation he had won among his shipmates for promptness and gallantry," praised *Minnesota*'s Lieutenant Commander John Upshur, "he fell while in the act of firing a shot at the enemy." Hunter Davidson's torpedo boat, meanwhile, had already gone to Richmond.

Reacting to reports that rebels were gathering an ad hoc armada of flotilla-battling boats on the lower Rappahannock, Foxhall Parker led an expedition up to Circus Point on April 18. The Potomac Flotilla vessels probed every creek on both banks from Windmill Point to Circus Point.

A five-hundred-man cavalry force was waiting to deter a landing at Bowlers Rocks. USS *Eureka* and a howitzer launch threw down fire and kept the horsemen in check. On April 21 Parker sent *Eureka* in below Urbanna to capture two hauled-up boats. Thirty yards from shore it was clear that *Eureka* had glided into an ambush, as rebels cut loose from their concealment with rifle and artillery fire. Acting Ensign Isaac Hallock kept his composure and in seconds was responding with *Eureka*'s twelve-pounder, "being fired about as fast as a man would discharge a pocket pistol," Parker reported. "The rebels were well thrashed. . . . It was quite a gallant affair and reflects a great deal of credit upon both the officers and men of the *Eureka*. . . ."

The side-wheelers USS *Morse* and USS *General Putnam* ascended the York on May 1, convoying 2,500 troops to West Point. The steamers' guns covered the soldiers as they landed and reoccupied the town. Probes of the Pamunkey and Mattapony Rivers followed. The York River thrust was a feint. In two days the big push would begin on the Rapidan. Ulysses S. Grant had come east and was heading south.

The new commander of all the armies of the United States was wasting no time. On March 10, the day after receiving his lieutenant general's commission in Washington, Grant was in Virginia, conferring with General Meade and surveying the Army of the Potomac. Meade maintained his command, but there was no mistaking that it was Grant's show now. On May 4 the Army of the Potomac crossed the Rapidan, and the final drive for Richmond began.

Ben Butler and the Hampton Roads–area troops, now called the Army of the James, were part of the plan. As Grant pushed on toward Richmond, General Butler's force would head upriver to attack the Confederate capital from the south. On May 4 Butler's army boarded the troop transports assembled at Hampton Roads and ascended the James. On May 5 the force landed at City Point and Bermuda Hundred, aiming to hit Richmond by way of Petersburg. On May 6 some 30,000 Federals were perched between the two cities with fewer than 10,000 Confederates in the area to oppose them. Butler tripped over his golden opportunity. The Army of the James retired after skirmishing with Pickett's hastily assembled force defending Petersburg. On May 7 part of Butler's army

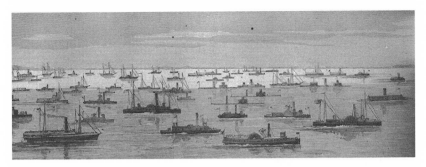

TROOP TRANSPORTS DEPART HAMPTON ROADS AND NEWPORT NEWS
WITH BUTLER'S ARMY OF THE JAMES, MAY 4, 1864.
Harper's Weekly

captured a section of the Richmond and Petersburg railroad and retired, failing to take the initiative again even though it was about 8,000 Federals versus fewer than 2,700 Confederates. By May 17 Butler was retreating to Bermuda Hundred after failing to stand up to Beauregard at Drewry's Bluff. If Richmond had been there for the taking, the chance had now passed. Beauregard pressed his advantage. Butler's army was trapped below the James.

General Grant, meanwhile, was fighting Robert E. Lee in successive massive battles—the Wilderness, May 5–6; Spotsylvania, May 8–21; the North Anna, May 23–26; Cold Harbor, June 1–3—big, confused, stubbornly fought affairs with death tolls galling even to people hardened by three years of tragedy. At the infamously ill-conceived charge Grant ordered at Cold Harbor on June 3, some seven thousand Union soldiers were killed in less than an hour. After the slaughter, the enemies remained entrenched, staring at one another, neither moving for days.

As Grant and Lee called a truce in order to gather the wounded and bury the slain, the National Union Convention assembled in Baltimore and nominated Abraham Lincoln for a second presidential term. The delegates, a mix of Republicans and War Democrats, gathered at the Front Street Theatre on June 7 for preliminaries and speeches. The party platform called for a continued war effort and a constitutional amendment to abolish slavery. The votes were cast, and the nominations handed down on the eighth. The vice presidential candidate was Andrew Johnson, the Tennessee War Democrat. Lincoln was the nearly unanimous presidential choice, and after the Missouri delegation switched its votes (twenty-two for Grant), that made it unanimous. The Front Street Theatre erupted with a great cacophony of exuberance, and the band added to the din by breaking into "Hail, Columbia." Delegates rushed from Baltimore to the White House the next day to congratulate the president.

Some worthies had made speeches at the Baltimore convention, including Senator Morgan from New York and Dr. Robert J. Breckinridge of Kentucky. At Fort McHenry, just a fortnight earlier, a different sort of individual had delivered a different kind of speech—one of the gallows variety. Andrew Laypole, alias Isadore Leopold, a convicted spy and guerrilla, was hanged on Monday, May 23, at 5:30 A.M., the military commission's death sentence having been approved by the president.

Major General Lew Wallace had replaced Brigadier General Lockwood in command at Maryland (now called the Middle Department) in March. Wallace, the future author of *Ben-Hur: A Tale of the Christ*, ordered Laypole's sentence be carried into execution. A scaffold was built on the Fort McHenry drill ground. On Sunday evening Laypole learned he was going to die. The Reverend A. A. Reese, the fort chaplain, spent several hours with the condemned man. Just after five o'clock in the morning Laypole was put in a cart and seated atop his coffin and taken to the scaffold. To the sound of muffled drums, he waved as he was carted past. He asked a fellow prisoner to "tell his friends that he died for his country," according to the *Sun* reporter. The 144th Ohio stood in hollow square formation around the gallows pole as the prisoner stepped up and the charges were read. Then Andrew Laypole addressed the crowd. "He said he freely forgave all having to do with his death," and asked the fort officers "to hand over to his friends his body, for their disposal. He then offered an extempore prayer to the Most High, on the conclusion of which the rope was placed around his neck, and everything being in readiness, the word was given and he was suspended in the air."

Eugene Lamar and William Compton, Confederate prisoners also sentenced to dangle at McHenry, had fared better. On Sunday night, May 15, the convicted spies had escaped with three other prisoners. "All the above parties were in the inner fort," reported the *Sun*, "and the mystery is how they escaped from there, and whether they swam across the harbor or walked to town."

Point Lookout, too, recorded the occasional escapee—six that May, one that June, two in July, and two in August. The death rate was a bit higher. July and August with their two escapes a month, posted deaths exceeding two hundred a month. The prison camp's population had shot up to around fifteen thousand in time for the stagnant swelter. "I have the honor to most respectfully call the attention of the commanding officer to the already crowded condition of the prisoners of war camp at this post, and as sanitary

MAJOR GENERAL LEW WALLACE, COMMANDER OF THE MIDDLE DEPARTMENT, HEADQUARTERED AT BALTIMORE.

Frank Leslie's Illustrated Newspaper

officer of the camp to most respectfully protest against the reception of additional numbers of prisoners," Surgeon James H. Thompson entreated in late June. He cited the need for water condensers, for less salt pork and more vegetables, and above all, for no more overcrowding. Writing after hearing a rumor that even greater numbers of prisoners were slated to be crammed into the camp, Surgeon Thompson warned, "We may see ere the summer is past an epidemic that will decimate not only the ranks of prisoners, but affect alike all the inhabitants of the Point."

Private Irving Williams of the Thirty-sixth U.S. Colored Regiment shot and killed prisoner Mark Lisk on April 21. The prisoner was answering the call of nature at the time. Camp rules dictated that prisoners use the receptacles—they called them sinks—set up for this purpose. In the diuretically inflamed environment of the prison pen, the men didn't always head for the sinks. They made for the nearest patch of ground when the exigency suddenly arose. When enforcing the sink rule, the sentinels' orders were clear: Give three warnings, then shoot.

Private Williams testified, "The prisoner went to the side of the kitchen to do his business. I told him to get up. He said he would do his business first. Then he went between his tent and the officers' tents to do his business. I told him to get up. He again remarked that he would do his business first. I then told him to get up or I would help him up. I told him to get up three times, then fired."

The in-camp Board of Investigation concluded that Private Williams had "acted in strict conformity to the orders he received," and no charges were brought. But the impression nagged of a man being shot dead for having trouble containing himself. More black soldier/white prisoner violence occurred in May, and Commissary General Hoffman sent Colonel Draper a warning from Washington: "The shooting of a prisoner, except when compelled by a grave necessity, cannot be excused, and such an act for a slight offense for which it would be sufficient punishment to take the prisoner in custody and turn him over to the guard can be considered little less than wanton murder."

Point Lookout's lengthening roster meant more than higher mortality rates, higher risk of scorbutic diseases, greater shortage of fresh water, and rising friction between former slaves on the fence and Southerners in the yard. Oddly, it also meant hope, a longshot chance, to a beleaguered Richmond wanting for a miracle. Grant's army crossed the James in mid-June, Petersburg was under siege, Richmond was threatened, and Point Lookout was positioned to play a part in a brash plan conceived by Robert E. Lee. What was at Point Lookout? In essence, a fifteen-thousand-man rebel army in marching distance of Washington.

All they needed were muskets and a means of escape. That's where John Taylor Wood came in.

On the night of July 2 Commander Wood visited General Lee's headquarters near Petersburg, and they mulled over the plan: Jubal Early was coming down the Shenandoah. He would cross the Potomac, attack Washington, and send cavalry around Baltimore to cut communications and burn bridges. Then the cavalry would gallop down to Point Lookout and liberate the prisoners. Wood, meanwhile, would run the Federal blockade off North Carolina, then head up the Chesapeake with gunboats and enough arms to turn the freed men into an attacking force, adding their significant numbers to Early's push on the capital. Wood's amphibious assault on Point Lookout would occur in concert with the cavalry attack. The Jubal Early Washington threat, it was also hoped, would divert the Potomac Flotilla's attention upriver, clearing the waterway for Wood's gunboats. "If successful in thus liberating and arming our imprisoned soldiers, Washington will be assaulted and no doubt carried," wrote Major John Tyler, Confederate assistant adjutant general. "This I regard as decidedly the most brilliant idea of the war."

Wood set out for Wilmington on July 5 to round up several thousand firearms and make ready his move. Lee sent a special messenger to Jubal Early on the sixth. Early's invasion was well under way. His Confeder-ates began crossing the Potomac on the fifth, and captured Hagerstown on the sixth and Frederick by the ninth. Washington was in a healthy panic. Troop transports hied up the Chesapeake with the Sixth Army Corps' Third Division, which arrived in Baltimore on the sixth, where Baltimore & Ohio Railroad President John Garrett had train cars ready and waiting at Locust Point to move the troops. Lew Wallace was rounding up a force to defend the capital; he had six thousand men between Early, advancing from Frederick, and Washington.

Lee's messenger reached Early on the eighth; Early read the message and learned the added Point Lookout dynamic. He summoned Brigadier General Bradley Tyler Johnson, the Frederick-born, Princeton-educated cavalryman who had been instrumental in forming the First Maryland Regiment in 1861 and the Maryland Line in 1863, and who in late winter of 1864 had saved Richmond from the Dahlgren-Kilpatrick cavalry raids. Commanding the First Maryland Cavalry and the Baltimore Light Ar-tillery, Johnson had crossed the Potomac ahead of Early's main force on this current invasion. On July 8 he came down from his mountain encampment in the drizzling rain and met with Early. Johnson had new orders. On the morning of July 9, as Early's army made ready to attack Lew Wallace's defending force at the Monocacy, Johnson kicked spur and set off on his wild circuitous raid.

His cavalry had to sweep north of Baltimore, circle down, and reach Point Lookout by the twelfth, when John Taylor Wood was set to steam in. "I told General Early that the march laid out for me was utterly impossible for man or horse to accomplish; it gave me four days, not *ninety-six hours*, to compass near three hundred miles, not counting for time lost in destroying bridges and railroads, but that I would do what was possible for men to do." They rode out from the Catoctins and took the Old Liberty Road, dashing through Westminster, Reisterstown, and Cockeysville by the tenth. At Cockeysville they burned the bridges of the Northern Central Railroad. Johnson sent a colonel into Baltimore to scout around.

The bad news had reached the city Saturday night. By six o'clock in the morning on Sunday the tenth, the general alarm had sounded over Baltimore and citizens grabbed their guns. The wounded troops started arriving by train and were taken to the Patterson Park hospitals. Stragglers and ambulances stumbled in from the Frederick Turnpike. Government stores were speedily emptied from dockside warehouses and loaded onto steamers, ready to clear port to dodge rebel seizure if necessary. Thousands gathered at Camden Station to watch as a thirty-car two-locomotive train pulled in at 7 P.M. from Ellicott's Mills with Lew Wallace's beaten soldiers. They had been outnumbered and overwhelmed at the Monocacy and had retreated in disorder. "The invading enemy is by the last accounts approaching the city," warned the joint proclamation of the mayor and governor. "Men, all the men that can be raised, are wanted to occupy the fortifications. . . . It is not important how you should come, but most important that you should come at once; come in your Leagues, or come in your militia companies, but come in crowds, and come quickly." Supervised by Generals Kenly and Lockwood, the civilian units manned the city's defenses, buttressed on the eleventh by black men who were quickly formed into companies and armed.

A hundred convalescents and veteran reservists were sent from Wilmington, Delaware, to Havre de Grace to guard the ferry and railroad. The Potomac Flotilla's *Currituck* also sped to the head of the Bay. Other Potomac Flotilla boats were sent to defend the Bush River and Gunpowder River bridges. The frigate *Minnesota* was ordered to Point Lookout, and four other Hampton Roads vessels to Washington's river to shore up the Potomac Flotilla's presence. On the thirteenth, gunboats arrived to protect Annapolis. Going ashore, Lieutenant Commander D. L. Braine found a defense force of three hundred hospital invalids who had taken up arms to defend against the rebel invaders.

After destroying the Cockeysville railroad bridges on the tenth, Johnson split his cavalry. Part of it would continue making the circle with him. The other part would veer upward, severing Baltimore's connections to all points north. What better officer to lead the detour than a Baltimore County bridge-burner of 1861? Followed by a 130-man detachment, Major Harry Gilmor rode off on a black mare to cut a swath of destruction—but he stopped by to visit his parents first.

His last visit to Baltimore's environs, on the eve of Antietam, had led to five months' imprisonment. Since then he'd been promoted and had seen action at Brandy Station, at Gettysburg, and up and down the Shenandoah. Right now, he was very close to Loch Raven and the home where he was born and raised. He and a few of his men rode there. His mother, father, sisters, and brothers were on the front porch of Glen Ellen when he arrived. Thrilled to see their Harry, they hugged him, and he stayed until night. He rejoined his men and they rode across Dulaney Valley, many of them, Gilmor included, falling asleep in their saddles. In the early morning of the eleventh they cut the telegraph wires at Harford Road and Bel Air Road. Up ahead, the major heard a gunshot.

Ishmael Day, a man well past sixty, had hung a U.S. flag over his gate. One of Gilmor's advance guard, Ordnance Sergeant Eugene Fields, ordered Day to take the flag down. The old man reportedly said, "Gentlemen, you may take my horses and my cattle or burn my house to the ground, but I will shoot any man who touches that flag."

Sergeant Fields climbed down off his horse and made for the flag. When Major Gilmor rode up, the sergeant lay on his back, his face and chest freckled with rude purple welts, his body peppered with buckshot from an old fowling piece. He died four days later. Ishmael Day had fled into the forest. Gilmor's men torched the house.

A mile or so from the Gunpowder River bridge, they galloped alongside the track and captured a train chugging out of Baltimore. The passengers and luggage were taken off. The engineer had bailed out, scotching Gilmor's hopes of rail-riding all the way to Havre de Grace on a destruction run. The rebels set the train on fire and waited for the next

MAJOR HARRY GILMOR, WHO VISITED HIS FAMILY WHILE LEADING
A RAID AROUND BALTIMORE IN JULY 1864.
Four Years in the Saddle

one. It came on schedule: twelve passenger cars, another fast capture. Gilmor's sharpshooters took to the riverbank and popped off shots at the Ohio National Guardsmen and Havre de Grace volunteers defending the bridge. Gilmor's men burned the second train and ran it out onto the bridge. The bridge guards pitched themselves into the water as the fire-spewing train came at them. The Potomac Flotilla's *Teaser* hove to off the mouth of the river too late. The steamer *Juniata*, the volunteers' transport, had been unable to do anything but watch. As the train's flames grew higher, it burned through the bridge and crashed blazing into the Gunpowder.

Bradley Johnson enjoyed lunch at "Hayfields," home of famed 1861 arrestee John Merryman, on the tenth, then headed off across Green Spring Valley. He wrote something on a piece of paper, handed it to Lieutenant Henry Blackistone, and sent him on a mission.

Blackistone and a twelve-man First Maryland Cavalry squad arrived at the Charles Street mansion of Governor Augustus Bradford early on the morning of the eleventh. The splendid place was just four miles north of the city. The governor was downtown. The rebel horsemen courteously forced Mrs. Bradford and the children to evacuate the house. Blackistone showed Mrs. Bradford the piece of paper: "This house is burned in retaliation for the burning of Governor Letcher's of Virginia, burned by the Union soldiers. Signed by order B. T. Johnson, General Commanding." As the mother and children screamed on the lawn, the rebels set fire to the governor's library and all the beds in the house. Mrs. Bradford begged them to let her rescue her husband's private papers. They wouldn't listen. Governor Bradford's mansion, described by the press as "one of the most extensive and elegant establishments in the vicinity of the city," went up in flames at 8 A.M. The people in the area tried to salvage as much furniture and other valuables as they could after the rebels rode off, but most of the property was destroyed.

The same fate had befallen the Virginia governor's Lexington home about three weeks earlier, at the hands of General David Hunter's Federal troops during their mid-June advance on Lynchburg.

Johnson's cavalry reached Owings Mills early on July 12. Workers for Painter's famous traveling ice-cream saloon were loading up a boxcar with chests full of the frozen dessert to be sold in Baltimore. Johnson confiscated the ice cream. Low on rations, his riders glutted on the Painter's Mill ice cream with orgiastic fervor. Some of the Virginia mountain boys had never seen ice cream before. They liked it, but found it too chilly, and crammed it into their canteens to get it nice and melted and drinkable.

During the previous night's bivouac, Johnson had received the information he'd been waiting for from the colonel sent to scout Baltimore. The Nineteenth Corps and two more divisions of the Sixth Corps had come up the Chesapeake and were waiting in their transports to board the B&O cars at Locust Point. Jubal Early, about to attack Washington, needed to know. Johnson sent a courier. Early got the message just in time.

After Monocacy, Early had marched unopposed to the outskirts of the capital. On the eleventh, while some of his troops burned down the Silver Spring home of Postmaster General Montgomery Blair, Early took stock of Washington's defenses. His troops were tired after fighting and marching in the dry heat. He met with his major generals and decided to attack at daybreak. That night, Johnson's message arrived: Ulysses S. Grant's reinforcements were pouring into Washington. "This caused me to delay the attack until I could examine the works again," stated Early, "and as soon as it was light enough to see, I rode to the front and found the parapets lined with troops." The picture had changed overnight, and Johnson's message had spared Early's finding out the hard way. Washington's skeletal defenses had turned into a force of more than twenty-thousand. "I had, therefore, reluctantly to give up all hopes of capturing Washington after I had arrived in sight of the dome of the capital and given the Federal authorities a terrible fright."

MANNING THE EARTHWORKS OUTSIDE ANNAPOLIS IN ANTICIPATION OF THE JOHNSON-GILMOR RAID, JULY 1864.
Special Collections, Nimitz Library, U.S. Naval Academy

Harry Gilmor was in Towson, drinking ale in the bar at Ady's Hotel. Old friends pressed around him, urging him to get a move on. By all accounts, a large cavalry force was on its way from Baltimore, and Gilmor was the reason.

So he sent his train prisoners ahead under a ten-man guard detail and then went out to pick a fight with the coming cavalry. He ordered Lieutenant William Kemp to take fifteen men and charge, spiking the approaching enemy's anger and enticing him to charge back. As Kemp retreated, his men would split to the sides of the road, and Gilmor would surge forward with the main column, hitting the advancing foe head-on. It was the night of the eleventh, pitch-black. Kemp's detachment drew pistols and sped down the turnpike. There was the sound of shots; then the detachment was riding back and clearing out of the road. Gilmor and the rest were waiting, sabres drawn, hats pulled down low.

"When I ordered the charge the men set up a most deafening yell, enough to convince any one that we were a full regiment," recounted the major, "and so must the enemy have thought, for we never got within sabre reach of them. They were finely mounted on fresh horses, and easily outran us. Seeing this, we drew pistols, gave chase, and let them have a volley from the top of every hill, with a fresh yell each time." The expected large cavalry force proved to be about seventy-five green volunteers. Some of the rebel riders kept chasing them all the way to Govanstown, just four miles from the city.

Gilmor's cavalry regrouped in Towson and rode on, spent. The major heard some of the men snoring in their saddles and started nodding off himself. They made it to Green Spring Valley, where the prisoners had been taken. The guards had fallen asleep. The prize prisoner—Major General William B. Franklin, a passenger on the first train they'd torched—had slipped off. Said Gilmor, "Being greatly provoked when I found that he had ceased to honor us with his presence, I swore with unusual energy."

Bradley Johnson's riders ripped up the railroad track, severed the telegraph lines, and burned train cars at Beltsville, along the B&O's Washington route. Then they tangled with five hundred to a thousand Federal cavalry and sent them packing toward Bladensburg. It was the morning of the twelfth, with little time left for the long, hard ride to Point Lookout. Johnson sent ahead a detachment to rouse the countryside, let the people know he was coming, and arrange for fresh horses all the way down to the tip of St. Mary's County. The general put his column on the road to Upper Marlboro. Then the courier came.

He was from General Early. There was a change of plans. Johnson was to scrap the whole Point Lookout effort and get his cavalry to Silver Spring.

They rode all day and into the night, skirting the Federal picket line, hooking up with Early past midnight. The rebel army was in retreat, and Johnson took charge of the rear guard. They fought their way through Rockville on the thirteenth, and after another all-night march, reached Poolesville. Throughout the fourteenth, Johnson's men fought back the Federals as Confederate infantry and artillery escaped across the Potomac. Major Gilmor's detachment, given up for dead or captured, arrived after an arduous ride down the center of the state. All the wagons were across, Yankee minié balls were flying, the blue line was closing in, and the sun was going down. Johnson, Gilmor, and all the worn horsemen crossed the river.

"We had been marching, fighting and working, from daylight July 9th, until sundown July 14th, four days and a half, or about one hundred and eight hours," Johnson noted. "We had unsaddled only twice during that time, with a halt of from four to five hours each time, making nearly one hundred hours of marching. We had isolated Baltimore from the North, and cut off Washington from the United States. . . ." And while it was true when he stated, "We had failed in the main object of our expedition, which was to release the prisoners at Point Lookout, convert them into a new army, capture Washington, . . ." he could take comfort in the rebel navy's not making it to Point Lookout, either.

By July 9 John Taylor Wood was ready to steam out of Wilmington, North Carolina, with twenty thousand firearms and a Confederate marine detachment led by General G. W. Custis Lee. But details of the supposedly secret plan had been leaked. The surprise element did not exist. Point Lookout had naval support and was expecting the attack. Wood received a telegram from Uncle Jefferson Davis on the tenth: "The object and destination of the expedition have somehow become so generally known that I fear your operations will meet unexpected obstacles. . . . I suggest calm consideration. . . ."

A disappointed Wood went raiding on the Atlantic coast instead. Well after the prison plan was abandoned, a wary U.S. Navy still harbored apprehensions that the notorious raider was returning to the Bay, and that Point Lookout was his target. In reference—and deference—to Wood, Secretary Welles on July 18 wired Rear Admiral Lee that "the mouth of the Chesapeake should be guarded night and day. . . ."

Early's attempt on Washington—the South's last major attempt to strike at the North—was killed by Grant's ability to peel off a few army divisions from the James River theater and have them at Washington with speed. It was the Chesapeake, the great fluid link between Richmond and Washington, that diluted Early's threat and provided Grant's deployment mobility. "Sharpsburg is four marches from Washington. It might be made in three forced marches," Bradley Johnson analyzed. ". . . On the other hand, transports from City Point could reach Baltimore on the Patapsco, or Washington on the Potomac, in twelve hours. They could have transported General Grant's whole army from the James to the Federal capital before General Early could possibly have marched from where he was forced to cross the Potomac."

The Point Lookout operation, had it unfolded on the twelfth as planned, would have augmented Early's numbers such that he could have still contemplated the attack, even in the face of the newly arrived troops in Washington's defenses. It was moot conjecture, the whole scenario consigned to "what if?" eternity. An outlandish idea, it would have been hailed as brilliant had it succeeded, bold even if it hadn't. It would always be just another Southern pipe dream.

A new commandant, Brigadier General James Barnes, took over at the Point Lookout prison camp on July 2, just in time for the invasion scare. The scare inspired new fortifications—stockade walls and ditch-surrounded gun emplacements—to protect the point from any overland approach (not to mention curtail any mass prisoner exodus); the new barrier was completed by late July. During the invasion scare, there was much flurry, with officer-prisoners transferred to Fort Delaware, a heightened naval presence, and the arrival on the twelfth of Commissary

General Hoffman to oversee matters. If the rumors of a pending attack sifted down to the prison pen, then the cramped and dirty prisoners themselves surely were the most disappointed people of all when the whole plan fizzled.

The prison population settled into the range of roughly 9,000 to 13,000, until war's end when it shot up to more than 20,000 men—twice the number originally intended for the facility. In May 1865, a month after the fall of Richmond and the surrender at Appomattox, Point Lookout had its highest monthly death toll ever, 324 men who died prisoners after the war was ended. Another 256 died in June 1865, when the final 18,580 prisoners were released. In that last year, camp life continued to be defined by its miseries: overcrowding, excessive heat, excessive cold, brackish water, rancid salt pork, rampant filth, rampant sickness, and cruel guards. The black soldiers "took particular delight in showing their former masters that 'the bottom rail was on top,'" said Charles T. Loehr, a prisoner at war's end. The white sergeants were just as sadistic. "Prisoners were sometimes punished by them too horribly to relate."

One of Point Lookout's denizens in the winter of 1864–65 was twenty-two-year-old Sidney Lanier, private of the Second Georgia Battalion, lately a signal officer on a blockade runner, the duty that ended in his capture. The future Johns Hopkins University professor, Baltimore boulevardier, and major American poet was a natural musician, accomplished on piano, organ, banjo, and guitar. But his chief instrument was the flute, on which he would become a celebrated virtuoso of his generation. He concealed his flute up his sleeve when he was taken to Point Lookout. He played sad and beautiful tunes that floated over the bleak and filth-caked prison pen, where he caught the tuberculosis that eventually killed him at the age of thirty-nine.

Charles T. Loehr kept a small copy of the New Testament with him at Point Lookout. On the flyleaf he drew a picture of an anchor and a cross, and he wrote, "If it were not for Hope, how could we live in a place like this?"

The action continued on the James, increasing the importance of the other tributaries as supply lines. The Rappahannock had been open for transports since May 19, when the Potomac Flotilla's *Yankee*, *Fuchsia*, and

"LES MISERABLES DE POINT LOOKOUT." THUS READS THE HANDWRITTEN
CAPTION ON THIS PHOTOGRAPH OF CONFEDERATE PRISONERS OF WAR AT
POINT LOOKOUT IN 1865. INCLUDED AMONG THEM ARE J.F. STONE OF THE
FIRST MARYLAND CAVALRY (1), MARYLAND CITIZEN WILLIAM BYRNE (4),
MARYLAND CITIZEN D.W. SLYE (5), C.E. INLOES OF THE FIRST MARYLAND
CAVALRY (10), AND G.R. COOKE OF THE FIRST MARYLAND CAVALRY (14).
Review of Reviews Co.

Jacob Bell reached Fredericksburg after the May 12 combined operation on the lower reaches. "As the gunboats were compelled to ascend the river . . . with their torpedo fenders down and to send flanking parties ashore and boats ahead (to sweep for torpedoes) in the narrow and shallow parts of it, their progress was necessarily slow, but they had the satisfaction of reaching Fredericksburg without the loss of a man," Foxhall Parker reported.

On the James, threading through the movement of armies, the river fighting was continuous, the naval aspect a constant of the campaign. The North Atlantic Blockading Squadron probed upriver and tangled and fought in a host of little-told engagements. Marines on picket duty from USS *Mackinaw* were surprised and captured by rebel infantry near Dutch Gap on May 22. On May 24 a rebel cavalry squad, driving in Yankee pickets near Fort Powhatan, was convinced to retreat by gunboat fire. It was the same day that rebels attacked General A. E. Wild's nine hundred black troops holding Wilsons Wharf, in an action lasting over five hours; the rebel charge was repulsed by the guns of USS *Dawn*. On June 20 and 21, as Federal gunboats covered the landing of supplies at

White House on the Pamunkey, rebel batteries opened up on the wagon trains and a three-hour firefight followed. On the twenty-first the Federal fleet clashed with Confederate ironclads and shore batteries near Dutch Gap at Howlett's. There would be other run-ins with the Howlett's guns.

On June 29 the fight was with the battery at Four Mile Creek. On July 14 and again on the sixteenth, vessels traded shots with the Malvern Hill battery. Also on the sixteenth, USS *Mendota* resumed the navy's dispute with the Four Mile Creek battery. Confederate sharpshooters and shore guns engaged Federal pickets and gunboats at Turkey Bend from July 26 to 27. On the twenty-eighth, gunboats gave fire during the two-hour fight that raged as Federal troops pontoon-crossed at Four Mile Creek. The shore guns were captured and prisoners taken. Federal vessels fought the batteries that were shelling Butler's troop transports near Wilcox's Wharf on August 3 and near Harrisons Landing on August 4. *Agawam* and *Hunchback* engaged Confederate batteries at three upper James River points on August 13 and 14. Gunboats provided shelling support to the advance of Butler's troops at Dutch Gap and Deep Bend on August 17. Four days earlier the Federals at Dutch Gap had been fired on, not only by shore batteries, but by vessels of the Confederate States Navy. As the U.S. forces worked closer to Richmond, the Confederacy's river squadron, held back to defend the city approach, began to make noise.

From his City Point headquarters, General Grant on August 9 wrote Rear Admiral Lee about the importance of Federal ironclads to counter the Confederate ironclads that lay in waiting upriver. "At least two such vessels, in my judgment, should be kept in the upper James. They stand a constant threat to the enemy and prevent him taking the offensive. There is no disguising the fact that if the enemy should take the offensive on the water, although we probably would destroy his whole James River navy, such damage would be done our shipping and stores, all accumulated on the waters near where the conflict would begin, that our victory would be dearly bought."

The Bay and tributaries were open for transports to fuel the fighting on the James, but the way was as dangerous as it had been all along. En route from Fort Monroe to Washington, the steamer *Kingston*—a two-

GUNNER ABOARD USS *HUNCHBACK* IN THE JAMES, 1864.
National Archives

hundred-ton side-wheeler, Philadelphia-owned and government-chartered—ran aground in the Chesapeake between Smiths Point and Windmill Point at 3 A.M. on Saturday, July 23. Captain John Smithers labored all day to get off Diamond Marshes. Log canoes circled and watched. On Sunday morning four men with a flag of truce appeared on the beach. They hollered to Smithers that he had fifteen minutes. The captain noticed about forty men coming through the marsh. They were in two squads, one dragging a caisson, the other a cannon. Smithers and crew abandoned ship. As they boated off, log canoe crews chased them and fired, but lost interest and made for the steamer. The fleeing crew watched as *Kingston* burned.

The Northern Neck, ever the hotbed, remained so until the last. A large force was said to be massing there, not just to defend the home peninsula, but to strike on the Bay as well. Reports varied, all of them indicating a buildup. In July Lieutenant Hooker told Commander Parker of "the gathering of cavalry on the neck between the Rappahannock and Potomac rivers. One company of the Second C.S. Cavalry is there under

Captain Eubank, and it is reported that five more companies are organizing near Heathsville and Whitestone. To-day there is a rumor of quite a body of them at Carter's Creek preparing ambuscades, etc., hoping to catch some of our boats."

No sooner had Washington-bound troop transports departed the Eastern Shore of Virginia, thereby leaving it less guarded, than the Eastville provost marshal on August 5 was wiring worriedly about a report that three hundred Northumberland County guerrillas were set to come raiding across the Chesapeake. The North Atlantic Blockading Squadron and Potomac Flotilla each sent a vessel. "My own idea of the reported movement is that they will leave this coast and cross in small boats and canoes to the eastern shore, where they hope to be out of the track of the gunboats, and there capture vessels for transportation to eastern Virginia and lower counties of Maryland, from which points most of our forces have been removed," Hooker wrote Parker. "From there, if not checked they may reach the lighthouse on the seacoast."

The people of Tangier Island and Smith Island joined the Virginia Eastern Shore in bracing for the August raid. It never transpired. By early September the word was that another one was brewing. "I have just received information . . . that the enemy are preparing for some sort of movement in the vicinity," reported Hooker from the mouth of the Rappahannock. "Three boats have arrived from Richmond with their crews, and are quartered at the house of Henry Barlock, in Mill Creek, and reports say that three more are expected. I shall of course be on the lookout. . . ."

According to Hooker, "the north side of the Rappahannock is full of guerrillas. . . ." His informant claimed that "in the four counties there are 1,500. A raid through that region would probably give us many prisoners."

"Between the Rappahannock and Potomac, from the bay to a line drawn from Carter's Wharf, on the Rappahannock, to Coan River, on the Potomac, there is a force of about 400 (home guards)," reported Acting Master Street on September 15. "In addition to the above, there is a guerrilla party of 12 men lurking on the bay shore. . . ."

The picket boat *No. 2*, a torpedo tug of the North Atlantic Blockading Squadron, experienced firsthand the Northern Neck's home-guard hospitality, when on October 8 her captain took her into the Great Wicomico

River, mistaking it for the Patuxent. They hadn't been long at anchor when riverbank musketfire began pelting them. They got under way, fled, and ran aground on an oyster bank. The tide dropped, the torpedo tug was trapped, and Captain Covington's home guard captured, stripped, and burned her. The guard acquired more muskets, a twelve-pound howitzer, and twelve prisoners, who were hauled off to Heathsville, and then across the Rappahannock and on to Richmond.

The army gunboat *General Foster*, subsequently searching the Great Wicomico and putting out landing parties on October 16, was attacked and shelled by a home-guard force numbering around three hundred. *General Foster* returned fire, and seven home guards were dead. Bullets smacked flat against the gunboat's iron plating, from behind which her crew poured out a withering fire. The gunboat anchored that night at the mouth of the river. A south-bank force resumed the attack. Acting Ensign Thomas Nelson, cruising in the Bay on the Potomac Flotilla's *Mercury*, heard the noise, saw the flashes, and stood in toward the fight. He beat to general quarters, cleared for action, got in range and blasted the shore party with a couple of well-placed shells. They disappeared into the darkness and trees.

On the Coan River, boats were being gathered for a Chesapeake raid. Two Potomac Flotilla vessels hit the lair on December 15, destroying thirty-one boats and two scows massed for mischief. "The home guards, in large force, made a show of resistance, but were quickly driven off," stated Parker.

Their land flanked by the rivers, jutting into the Bay, and pocketed between Northern and Southern capitals, the folk were resistant, armed, and still full of fight. They weren't about to go quietly. Acting Ensign Nelson noted, "The home guard in Northumberland County is said to number not less than 500 men, and may be collected in a body ready for service in a few hours. Westmoreland County is capable of furnishing as many more, and a force of 1,000 men well acquainted with all the roads and byways, giving them immense advantage over a force of equal numbers, can in case of emergency be raised in a very short time. . . ."

In Maryland, slavery was dead. Its official time of death was listed as November 1, 1864. The official cause of death was the new state constitution the legislature in Annapolis had been working on since April. There was much opposition, as expected, on the Eastern Shore and in Southern Maryland. On October 12 and 13 ratification went to a state-wide vote, which was close: 30,174 to 29,799. The new constitution had won by 375 votes. Many who would have voted against it were somewhere South wearing gray. Maryland Union soldiers cast absentee ballots. On November 9 Lew Wallace issued his General Order Number 12, creating a Maryland Freedmen's Bureau. He ordered that the Maryland Club, that symbol, that bastion of Baltimore secessionist society, be converted into the Freedmen's Bureau facility, a station to provide assistance to sick and homeless former slaves. Four years earlier the scenario would have been unimaginable.

The same could be said of the 1864 presidential election results. In the 1860 race Lincoln had done terribly in Maryland, coming in fourth out of a choice of four. This go-round, running against his former general, McClellan, Lincoln carried Maryland healthily, 40,171 to 32,739. Four years and an eternity ago, Lincoln had only received 2,294 votes in Maryland. The border state was coming around.

The 225-foot, two-thousand-ton iron double-ender USS *Monocacy* was launched from the Denmead & Son shipyard at Canton on December 14. She was all iron, a side-wheeler, with one-thousand-horsepower engines and rudders at each end. She was the largest fighting ship built or repaired in Baltimore during the war and only the second vessel of her class to be built in the United States. The ship, "it is confidently expected, will be one of the swiftest steamers in the navy," reported the *Sun*. Major General Wallace, the Baltimore naval station's Commodore Thomas Dornin, and other dignitaries both civic and martial were among the 250 people on hand for the launching ceremonies. At 3 P.M. the shipyard gang knocked away the props and stays, "but when all were removed the noble ship still stood on the stocks." They tried everything, but the iron craft would not budge.

They finally had to order a steam-tug with a long hawser to come over and make the ship move. Once she hit the water, the christening and the festivities went fine.

The Union ship was afloat in a city where the Union voice was now the strongest.

CHAPTER 11

"We have holed the rat but can't get at him"

SHE WAS THE MOST beautiful bride they had ever seen. The wedding was lavish—the highlight of the social season that lean Richmond winter. Those fortunate enough to be invited gathered at St. Paul's Church on Thursday, January 19, 1865, to witness the nuptials of Hetty Cary, the beauty of Baltimore and reigning belle of Richmond, to the dashing and gallant Major General John Pegram.

The bride's mother had made it from Baltimore, crossing enemy lines to attend the ceremony. Hetty's trousseau had been delivered by none other than Mrs. Lincoln's sister, back in Dixie after a visit north.

President and Mrs. Jefferson Davis lent the bride their carriage to deliver her in stately fashion to the church. But the horses wouldn't move. They just refused to move, and the party had to hastily hire alternate transportation. Some might consider it an omen, certainly no more so than the mirror Hetty had broken two days earlier.

As she started up the aisle, her veil ripped. She continued on, the assembly too in awe of her rare perfection to care much about a torn veil. Up ahead waited her Confederate general, dazzling to behold, her ideal match. After they had become engaged, Hetty had returned to Baltimore. When she learned that her handsome soldier had been severely wounded, she successfully ran the Chesapeake blockade yet again, arriving back in Richmond to find that John Pegram's wounds weren't as life-threatening as initially thought. The episode, the separation, had been scary, and they made their wedding plans.

The Reverend Dr. Minnigerode performed the ceremony. Then the couple marched down the aisle, and the Richmond press dubbed them the finest-looking pair ever to be wed at St. Paul's. The honeymoon was short. General Pegram reported to the Petersburg defenses.

She would ride out to visit him when she could. Major Randolph Barton, who took a bullet outside Petersburg, reminisced, "I have frequently recalled the superb picture of Mrs. Pegram, formerly the lovely Hetty Cary, of Baltimore, and a bride of about two weeks, handsomely mounted, and General Lee, on foot, with his hand resting on her horse's neck, engaged in conversation while awaiting the coming of the division to be reviewed by General Lee. You can imagine the splendor of the group: a beautiful woman, a noble man in appearance and every other respect, and a handsome horse."

Grant tested Lee's right flank, and a fight broke out along a plank road running out of Petersburg. The Battle of Hatchers Run began on February 5 and lasted until the seventh. On the morning of February 6 General Pegram rode away from his bride's side. He was shot that afternoon. Hetty managed to procure an ambulance, and as it bounced through the night from the Petersburg entrenchments to Richmond, she sat on the floor of the ambulance with his head in her arms. He was dead when they reached Richmond. That Thursday, Hetty Cary Pegram wore black. John Pegram's funeral service was held in the same church, with the same pastor, and the same people who had gathered for a wedding, exactly three weeks earlier.

The fleet left the Chesapeake on January 4—fifty-nine vessels with 627 guns, the mightiest array of firepower in the history of naval warfare—to make another attempt at conquering the last open Confederate port. The December expedition to Fort Fisher, North Carolina, had failed badly—Major General Butler, in charge of the land force, had bungled militarily for the last time. Lincoln put an end to Butler's nothing-if-not-colorful army career on January 7. Major General Edward O. C. Ord took over the Army of the James, while Major General Alfred H. Terry had command of the troops taking part in this second Fort Fisher foray. Rear Admiral David Dixon Porter, no Butler advocate he, had greater confidence of their chances this time.

Rear Admiral Porter, who succeeded S. P. Lee in command of the North Atlantic Blockading Squadron in October 1864, was the son of a

PORTER'S FLEET LEAVES FORT MONROE IN SQUALLY SEAS, DECEMBER 1864.
Harper's Weekly

War of 1812 naval hero and was himself an important figure on the Mississippi during the Civil War. He was ordered East for the final decisive engagements from Hampton Roads. He was in position and began the epic bombardment of Fort Fisher on Friday, January 13. The bombardment lasted two days, followed by the army's assault and capture of the fort at the mouth of the Cape Fear on January 15. The Twenty-third Army Corps was embarking from Alexandria and Annapolis by early February, to advance on Wilmington, North Carolina, from the newly gained ground. It was early March before Porter's fleet began returning to Hampton Roads. Meanwhile, only one Federal ironclad, the double-turreted monitor *Onondaga*, had been left on the James (with gunboats). To the bottled-up Confederate James River Squadron, the Fort Fisher expedition meant a chance to break out from behind Chaffins Bluff, to finally move downriver, and hopefully even to take City Point, the crucial Federal supply depot. With four of the five Federal monitors gone along with many of the gunboats, Flag Officer John K.

Mitchell of the James River Squadron saw his opportunity and made his move.

He had three ironclads, seven gunboats, and two torpedo boats, and a target—City Point—that would change everything. The waterborne supplies reached City Point, then went by rail to the Union soldiers in front of Petersburg. If Mitchell could force a Federal withdrawal from City Point, Grant's supply line would be choked, and a springtime move against Richmond might be called off. Secretary Mallory urged Mitchell to do it. "I regard an attack upon the enemy and obstructions of the river at City Point, to cut off Grant's supplies, as a movement of the first importance to the country. . . ."

To get at City Point, the Confederate vessels had to make it past the Federals' sunken-hulk obstruction barrier at Trents Reach. Success would spell a strangled supply route and Federal forces split by a Confederate-dominated James River. On January 23, after a heavy-fog delay, Flag Officer Mitchell attacked downriver. Foremost in his eleven-vessel squadron were the heaviest ironclads in the Confederate States Navy, *Richmond*, *Virginia No. 2*, and *Fredericksburg*. As they surged downstream, the monitor *Onondaga* and her gunboat consorts moved off to stay clear of them. The rebel boats arrived at Trents Reach and tried running past the obstructions. *Virginia No. 2* and *Richmond* ran aground and met with thick fire from the Federal shore batteries. The Confederate gunboat *Drewry* also ran aground, and exploded when a mortar shell hit her magazine. The Confederate torpedo boat *Scorpion* also grounded. Her crew abandoned ship, and she was captured soon after. Next morning, *Onondaga* returned and, with her fifteen-inch Dahlgrens, pounded the stranded rebel ironclads, which hastened upriver once they floated free. The Confederate vessels withdrew behind Chaffins Bluff. The war's last battle between ironclads had ended. Grant was in front of Petersburg and within twenty miles of Richmond. Richmond was still choked, while Grant's supply line was unbroken, and the supply boats kept coming up the river.

"The rebels are up to some deviltry on the Rappahanock," Foxhall Parker warned on January 4. The commander, who had just broken up a budding torpedo-manufacturing operation, had information that a major mine-dumping expedition was being planned on the river. He urged the Washington Navy Yard to work night and day to repair the Potomac Flotilla vessels there, as he was going to be needing them in a hurry. The Rappahannock wasn't alone. There was last-ditch deviltry brewing in various forms from the Potomac to the York.

The U.S. consular agent in Toronto wrote Secretary of State Seward in early January to apprise him of a spy network that used Port Tobacco as its crossing point. The spies' techniques were artful. "These messengers wear metal buttons, upon the inside of which dispatches are most minutely photographed, not perceptible to the naked eye, but are easily read by the aid of a powerful lens. Letters are written but are closely interlined with imperceptible ink (as they term it) to which when a certain chemical is applied, is easily deciphered." The spies made nocturnal Potomac crossings in India rubber boats. The secretary of state told the secretary of the navy, who told Foxhall Parker to keep an eye on Port Tobacco.

From the York came troubling news in mid-January that Captain Fitzhugh was back in business. The cavalry-captain-turned-Bay-raider, who had sacked Cherrystone the previous March, now evidently was bringing up boats and gathering a crew to attack and destroy the Wolf Trap light-boat in Chesapeake Bay and then set upon any luckless shipping that happened their way. "If successful, they contemplate a raid upon the oyster fleet in this river," reported Acting Volunteer Lieutenant Peter Hayes of the North Atlantic Blockading Squadron. He sent warning to the Wolf Trap light-boat and the York River oyster fleet, and ordered a boat to cruise off the mouth of the Severn in Mobjack Bay, where Fitzhugh was expected to emerge.

The naval presence at Mobjack Bay was beefed up even more after January 31, when Secretary Welles again extended the Potomac Flotilla's jurisdiction. Foxhall Parker stationed a vessel permanently at Mobjack Bay, which had lately been limited to once-a-month patrols. And Parker soon found himself inspecting his old patrolling grounds, the York River. His early-March investigation there disturbed him. "I found that oyster schooners were allowed to proceed nearly to West Point, and to have free intercourse with the shore, while at Yorktown, persons from Gloucester County, Va., upon merely taking the oath of allegiance, were permitted to cross the river and trade with a sutler named Gallagher, so that by this strange regulation the very rascal who to-day in the uniform of a rebel soldier fires upon the Potomac Flotilla from the banks of the Piankatank, to-morrow, in the dress of a citizen, trades peacefully and in full security at an army post." The commander put the oyster fleet under gunboat supervision and restricted the watermen's upriver access.

Smuggling, and the war against it, meanwhile continued in earnest. The Potomac Flotilla's *Primrose* captured three blockade runners in one week in February. Sabotage, smuggling's cousin, likewise continued thriving on the Bay. The steamer *Knickerbocker*, her health and well-being having been threatened before, failed to avoid destruction a second time when she grounded near Smiths Point on February 15. Rebels boarded her, burned her, and vanished. There were bigger raids pending. Talk of Captain Fitzhugh increased, with more detail. Informants had him on the Northern Neck now, with four hundred men, fifteen large boats, and a number of canoes, ready to rage out from Indian Creek and Dymer Creek to commit Chesapeake depredations. Other sources were warning that Rice Airs—a known plunderer whose exploits were said to include the 1863 *Reliance* raid with Wood—was about to strike again.

On February 25 Acting Ensign Thomas Nelson of the Potomac Flotilla's *Mercury* was told that Rice Airs had set out with 154 guerrillas in several boats, including *Reliance*'s cutter, from Little Wicomico River, bound across the Bay to Smith Island. "The whole party is a most desperate set of thieves, robbers, and murderers, who use the cloth of the rebel flag to cover their crimes," stated Ensign Nelson. "Their design on the island is to rob the stores, capture and bring back the numerous refugees and deserters who have gone there from Virginia, and probably capture some steamer, with which they intend to attack and destroy the light vessel, and even surprise the blockading vessels." After the Eastern Shore raid didn't transpire, at least one report had it that the rebels crossed the Bay and turned around without landing because it was clear they were expected.

Along with sea raiders, there were land raiders to contend with, Mosby's raiders, in fact. Part of the "Gray Ghost's" legendary guerrilla force was finishing out the war on the Northern Neck, as the Potomac

Flotilla discovered firsthand on a couple of occasions. Acting on information from the Charles County provost marshal, Foxhall Parker sent a seventy-five-man force across the Potomac to seek and destroy a large boat the rebels had stashed for an upcoming Maryland raid. The flotilla force probed Chotank Creek on March 3 and Passapatanzy Creek on the fifth. Both days saw skirmishes with Colonel Mosby's men. The sailors pushed the guerrillas back to the interior and found the boat up the Passapatanzy. It was "a remarkably fine one," reported Parker, "painted lead color, and capable of holding fifty men. It had been recently brought from Fredericksburg, and its rowlocks carefully muffled for night service." The sailors destroyed the boat. The five boxes of tobacco found nearby were distributed among the men.

By the war's last season, the Potomac Flotilla had grown to include thirty-one vessels, and there still were cavalry bands, shore batteries, and blockade runners threatening the Chesapeake water routes up until the final weeks of warfare. March was spring-cleaning time, as the Potomac Flotilla joined with the army in a series of sweeping operations aimed at keeping Grant's Fredericksburg supply base secure and erasing the mounting threat from the Rappahannock to the Potomac once and for all. On March 7 Lieutenant Hooker took *Commodore Read*, *Yankee*, *Delaware*, and *Heliotrope* up the Rappahannock to back up an army raid at Hamiltons Crossing, six miles below Fredericksburg. "You will be particularly careful in looking out for torpedoes," admonished Parker, "having all narrow channels and shoal places carefully swept by the small boats kept in advance of the flotilla. At points where torpedoes may be exploded from the shore, you will land flanking parties, and you are to shell as usual all heights. . . ." The army-navy force cut the telegraph lines and destroyed the depot, the railroad bridge, twenty-eight cars, an army wagon train, and several miles of railroad track. They brought off huge amounts of tobacco and cotton cloth, not to mention nearly forty mules and forty prisoners.

On March 12 Hooker was back on the Rappahannock, working the lower part of the river and acting again in concert with the army by routing out rebels still rowdy from Tappahannock down to the Bay. USS *Morse* found trouble first, at Paradise Landing, by the supposedly abandoned rebel battery. Two rifled fieldpieces opened fire at 5 A.M. on March

THE POTOMAC FLOTILLA'S USS *COMMODORE READ*, COMMANDED BY
ACTING VOLUNTEER LIEUTENANT-COMMANDER EDWARD HOOKER.
THE VESSEL WHICH EMPTIED SOUTHERN SADDLES ON THE NORTHERN
NECK HAD 18 OFFICERS AND 140 MEN. SHE WAS ARMED WITH FOUR
9-INCH GUNS AND TWO 100-POUND RIFLES.
Special Collections, Nimitz Library, U.S. Naval Academy

13, dispelling any delusions of battery abandonment. The army gunboat
Mosswood had her galley pipe shot off, and *Morse* was shelling the woods
when Hooker, aboard *Commodore Read*, arrived from upriver at 7:30 A.M.
He sounded general quarters and joined in on the shore bombardment.
The constant shelling was stirring up Confederate horsemen. Squads of
cavalry were riding up the river road, and Hooker "emptied some of
their saddles."

It was hard to tell if the guns were in the old battery or in the woods
nearby. Hooker sent in a landing party to glean the whereabouts. The
sailors talked to blacks on the beach. The guns had gone up the road,
and there were some one hundred cavalry in the woods. The guns were
possibly being dragged north to Tappahannock, to a ferry big enough
to haul both artillery and cavalry across the river. If they got across, it
could mean trouble for the Federal army detachment on the Neck. USS
Delaware was already at Tappahannock destroying boats. Hooker sent
Morse to reinforce her. A landing party hit the Tappahannock shore and
destroyed nine vessels, including a large ferryboat. In addition to boat

eradication, *Morse* and *Delaware* bombarded the bridge linking evacuated Fort Lowry to Tappahannock. The first shot spanked the bridge just as a cavalry squad was crossing.

Hooker and company had emptied some Southern saddles, shut down a revived shore battery, and kept rebels from crossing to the Rappahannock-Potomac peninsula. Another expedition followed in their wake on March 15. Lieutenant Commander Thomas H. Eastman took USS *Don*, *Heliotrope*, *Resolute*, and *Stepping Stones* up the Rappahannock to Mattox Creek. They were out to destroy a rebel supply base nurturing the peninsular guerrillas. On the sixteenth a forty-man search party ransacked area houses, uncovering and destroying rebel ammunition stores. Some fifty cavalry came down. Eight or ten of them charged the sailors' left flank. When the sailors drove them off, the rest of the riders retreated, too. On the seventeenth Eastman commanded a landing force that took the creek's right fork. Acting Ensign William H. Summers led the party up the left fork. Eastman's seventy sailors and marines torched four rebel boats. Summers's men in the howitzer launch destroyed three schooners while under heavy musketfire from three hundred to four hundred rebels. In minutes, the musketry had cut away the oars, riddled the launch, and blown off Summers's musket barrel.

"The crew of the boat were all black but two," reported Eastman, "and P. Mullen, boatswain's mate of the U.S.S. *Don*, and Aaron Anderson, landsman (colored), of the *Wyandank*, are reported to me by Acting Ensign Summers as having assisted him gallantly—Mullen lying on his back while loading the howitzer and then firing so carefully as to kill and wound many rebels, besides driving them all away. . . ."

President Lincoln headed down the Chesapeake aboard the steamer *River Queen* on March 23. It wasn't the president's first visit to Grant's army; he had ventured down in the summer of 1864. It also wasn't his first time aboard *River Queen*. On February 3 he had sat in the salon of the spacious Bay passenger steamer now in government service, anchored in Hampton Roads beneath the guns of Fort Monroe, with Secretary of State Seward and three delegates of the government of the Confederate States of America, including Vice President Alexander H.

Stephens. Lincoln and Seward had insisted on unconditional restoration of Federal authority, the Confederates had insisted on an armistice between two nations, and the Hampton Roads conference had gone nowhere. This time, Lincoln was not en route to a conference with Confederates, but was traveling to meet with his own top military and naval commanders. Accompanying the president down the Bay were Mrs. Lincoln and their son Tad. In convoy with the swift USS *Bat*, *River Queen* arrived at Fort Monroe on the twenty-fourth and proceeded up the James. Later that night they reached City Point, a floating forest of supply ships along a riverside military boom town, piled high with vast stores and a huge arsenal.

On the twenty-fifth, as Lee made a last fierce attempt to break through the Union lines, capture City Point, and wreck Grant's spring plans, Lincoln visited with Grant, took the specially built army railroad to the Petersburg front, and rode a horse across part of the battlefield at Fort Stedman, where the Confederates had just launched their futile attack that day. On the twenty-sixth, as Lee thought about having to abandon Petersburg and Richmond and heading out to link up with Johnston's army in North Carolina, Lincoln reviewed the troops and watched with pleasure as General Philip Sheridan's cavalry crossed the James, adding to Grant's numbers. On the twenty-seventh, as evening settled in on the river, President Lincoln, General Grant, General William Tecumseh Sherman, and Rear Admiral David Dixon Porter gathered on board *River Queen* to discuss the future of the United States.

Sherman's army had swept through the Deep South and up the coast and was at present encamped near Goldsboro, North Carolina. The general had come up from Morehead City on the steamer *Russia*. Sherman and Admiral Porter, comrades from the Mississippi campaign, greeted each other with pleasure at Grant's headquarters. Then the three commanders went to meet with the president. The conference continued the next morning. They sat in the after-cabin of the steamer, the commanders fleshing out what remained to be done to win, the president explaining his hopes for how the aftermath would unfold and what tenor the victory would take.

Grant and Sherman described the coming final phase. Grant had Lee overwhelmed; Sherman had Johnston on the run. Ideally, each could force a surrender before the two rebel armies united. Both generals and the admiral concurred that one big fight remained.

Lincoln wanted mercy for the vanquished, to guarantee the defeated troops' rights as citizens, and to let them go home with amnesty and get back to their lives. So argued Sherman when, in the near future, he came under heat for the lenient surrender terms he offered Johnston. Sherman claimed—and Porter backed him up—that the liberal terms were based on Lincoln's wishes, as expressed in the after-cabin of a Bay steamer in the waning days of war.

Sherman headed back to his army on the twenty-eighth. Porter dispatched *Bat*, much faster than the lumbering *Russia*, to deliver the general in haste. On March 29, in a driving rain, Grant's army swung to the southwest of Petersburg and launched the end campaign. Porter and Lincoln kept each other company. As telegrams arrived hourly from the front, the admiral and the president went to the City Point telegraph hut together to get Grant's dispatches. They discussed them and pored over maps.

"To me he was one of the most interesting men I ever met," Admiral Porter said. "He had an originality about him which was peculiarly his own, and one felt when with him as if he could confide his dearest secret to him with absolute secrecy against its betrayal. There, it might be said, was 'God's noblest work—an honest man,' and such he was all through. I have not a particle of the bump of veneration on my head, but I saw more to admire in this man, more to reverence, than I had believed possible."

The Confederates pretended they were sinking. There were twenty of them, armed, aboard a yawl in Chesapeake Bay off the mouth of the Patuxent on March 31. They came alongside *St. Mary's*, a 115-ton schooner out of the town she was named after and laden with an assorted cargo worth twenty thousand dollars. The rebels claimed their yawl was sinking long enough to come alongside the schooner, board her, and make her their own. She was bigger, better, and more suited to their intentions. They took her to sea.

Their leader was Master John C. Braine, CSN, who since 1863 had been privateering from Cape Cod to Havana. *St. Mary's* passed Cape

Charles and headed up the coast. They were off Hog Island when they captured another schooner, *J. B. Spafford*, which was out of Wicomico and New York–bound. The rebels placed both schooner crews aboard *Spafford* and set them free, after having robbed them all of their personal effects. The released crews headed for the Delaware Breakwater. The rebels headed south. The master of *Spafford* told the inspector of customs at Lewes, Delaware, of a southeasterly light on the ocean horizon after *St. Mary's* was out of sight, like the light of a vessel captured and burned. Braine had said he was taking the prize schooner to St. Marks, Florida. But *St. Mary's* next showed up in Nassau, where the U.S. consul tried to have the vessel seized and the rebels dealt with as pirates. The governor of the Bahamas ruled that the schooner was a legitimate prize, and Braine's raiders set sail again. In June, they appeared in Kingston, Jamaica, where the U.S. consul tried in vain to have Braine extradited. The privateer dumped the schooner and booked passage to Liverpool. The U.S. consul in Liverpool was wired to be on the lookout. But John Braine managed to fade and was never heard from again.

His kindred spirit, John Yates Beall, hadn't exited so successfully. After being paroled in 1864, the Chesapeake raider had fulfilled his dream of performing Canadian-border exploits. He disrupted shipping on Lake Erie, was arrested while trying to free prisoners en route to Fort Lafayette, and was hanged on February 24, 1865.

The most prolific rebel raider of them all had been a Southern Maryland man. When Raphael Semmes of Charles County assumed the captaincy of the CSS *Alabama* in 1862, it was the beginning of nearly two years at sea, with eighty-two U.S. vessels as victims. The raider's wild run ended when *Alabama* was sunk by the USS *Kearsarge* off Cherbourg in 1864. Semmes returned to Richmond in time for the collapse of the Confederacy. He was made rear admiral on February 10, 1865, and assigned to command the James River Squadron, which he took over from his old friend John K. Mitchell with reluctance.

The Federals had further built up the Trents Reach obstructions, and there was nothing for the James River Squadron to do but continue serving as a defensive presence, along with the shore batteries, on the Richmond river approach. On April 2, as Lee retreated from Petersburg, Secretary Mallory gave Rear Admiral Semmes his new orders.

Semmes destroyed the James River Squadron. Near Drewry's Bluff, he scuttled and burned the ironclads *Fredericksburg, Richmond*, and *Virginia No. 2*. It was 3 A.M. on April 3. Semmes's four hundred men boarded the remaining squadron vessels and made for Richmond. "My little squadron of wooden boats now moved off up the river, by the glare of the burning ironclads," Semmes recounted. When *Virginia No. 2*, the squadron's flagship, exploded, "the spectacle was grand beyond description. Her shell-rooms had been full of loaded shells. The explosion of the magazine threw all these shells, with their fuses lighted, into the air. The fuses were of different lengths, and as the shells exploded by twos and threes, and by the dozen, the pyrotechnic effect was very fine. The explosion shook the houses in Richmond, and must have waked the echoes of the night for forty miles around."

Semmes's men, armed and equipped for the field, were directed to join Lee's troops in clearing out of Richmond. Semmes torched all the gunboats. The now-boatless squadron fired up a train and took it to Danville, where they manned the defenses until the surrender at Appomattox. Fifty midshipmen of the Confederate States Naval Academy, in the meantime, carried the Confederate government's archives and the Confederate treasury's specie and bullion out of Richmond. Ten midshipmen stayed behind and set fire to their school-ship, the CSS *Patrick Henry*. The smoke of the burning ship rose up and became part of the larger cloud, as the warehouses, magazines, downtown dwellings, and business district of Richmond burned. By 8:15 A.M. on April 3 the Federal troops were entering the city.

That day, President Lincoln, his son Tad, and Rear Admiral Porter traveled to Petersburg and met with Grant. Returning to City Point, they found a telegram waiting for the president. It was from Secretary Stanton, advising Lincoln to be cautious and avoid going to the front. "I will take care of myself," Lincoln said, pointing out that he'd already been to the front and returned.

The steamer *River Queen* had returned to Washington with Mrs. Lincoln on April 1. President Lincoln and Tad joined Rear Admiral Porter aboard his flagship, USS *Malvern*. Lincoln's bunk was too short, and he had to keep his legs bent to fit. The admiral's carpenters secretly fixed the bunk's dimensions. The next morning at breakfast the president joshed that he'd shrunk "six inches in length and about a foot sideways." In the evening he sat on the upper deck of the flagship with the admiral as they listened to the distant gunfire.

On April 4 they steamed up the James. Obstructions eventually blocked *Malvern's* way. They boarded her barge and continued upriver, birds chirping in orchards, the sky black up ahead. And in a boat rowed by twelve sailors, Abraham Lincoln arrived in Richmond.

The rumors about Thaddeus Fitzhugh came true at two in the morning on April 5, 1865, when he led the raiding party that committed the last piratical act on the Chesapeake Bay in the Civil War. The steamer *Harriet De Ford* was boarded and captured in the Bay about thirty miles south of Annapolis by Captain Fitzhugh's band. The twenty-seven guerrillas released the steamer's captain, mate, and white passengers, and then took off in the commandeered vessel in pursuit of two government barges being towed down the Bay.

When the district commander at Annapolis found out, he telegraphed the commanding officers at Fort Monroe, Point Lookout, and Baltimore. Commander Foxhall Parker sent ten Potomac Flotilla vessels in pursuit, with orders to "be prepared to sink the *De Ford* should you fall in with her." On April 6 Lieutenant Hooker telegraphed Parker: "We have holed the rat but can't get at him. . . ."

Hooker had been cruising off the mouths of the Rappahannock and Piankatank in *Commodore Read*, overhauling everything that passed in the Bay. At daylight on the sixth the flotilla's *Jacob Bell* came out of the Rappahannock with a pair of informative passengers. Simon Brown and James Hudson had been captured crewmen on *Harriet De Ford*. They said the steamer had been taken into Indian Creek, on the Bay shore above the Rappahannock. Accompanied by *Heliotrope* and *Coeur de Lion*, Hooker pursued. A woman pilot led them up the creek. After about five miles, *Commodore Read* could go no farther. They continued on in the light drafts, shelling the woods. Contrabands were emerging, and the boats let them aboard. Among them was a crewman from *Harriet De Ford*. From the black men Hooker learned that the captured steamer was actually at Dymer Creek, just below.

They rushed to Dymer Creek and found the wreck of *Harriet De Ford*, a final sacrifice to wartime depredation, burned to the waterline. She was still blazing brightly when they boarded her. Before lighting the fire, the rebels had unloaded the steamer's cargo with the help of neighborhood farmers, according to the black witnesses.

"Contrabands which I have report that the negroes captured in the steamer were taken to Kilmarnock and sold at auction yesterday afternoon," reported Hooker. "I would respectfully suggest that there are many rank rebels, male and female, within our reach who might be seized as hostages for these negroes."

"Our gunboats are keeping a bright outlook for the enemy on the bay," Foxhall Parker informed the navy secreatary on April 9, the day the rebellion died. For four years, men along the rebel shore had harassed Federal boats, had smuggled, sabotaged, and fought. Now they disappeared into their marshy land, elusive and uncaught to the end.

On April 6, seamen of the USS *Ada* had chased a large yawl into Hooper Strait on the Maryland Eastern Shore. The sailors captured the landed yawl, but the armed men who had manned her quickly vanished. And as the war wound down, the navy party on the Chesapeake shore carried out a final futile duty: "searching for the rebels in vain."

Exuberant festivity took over the streets of Annapolis when the news came that Lee had surrendered on April 9. On the night of Wednesday the twelfth the sky danced with the soaring, popping lights of rockets shot from the balcony and steps of the Maryland Statehouse. Soldiers cheered and rejoiced and clogged the roadways down to the city dock. Buildings were illuminated like Christmas trees, the St. John's College hospital the crowning jewel in the light show. The brass bands from USA General Hospital Divisions 1 and 2 took turns blaring forth with celebratory airs. The patients, the survivors, would all be going home that summer. By October the army's long occupation would end, students would return to St. John's, and cadets would return to the U.S. Naval Academy. It was ending.

The man who would be the first postwar head of the Naval Academy was currently on the James, making ready to travel up the Bay. Rear

The USA General Hospital, Division No. 1 brass band, Annapolis.
Special Collections, Nimitz Library, U.S. Naval Academy

Admiral David Dixon Porter had said good-bye to a beaming President Lincoln on April 8. On April 10, in the wake of the news from Appomattox, Porter had listened to the proud echo over the river as the ships of his fleet fired a thirty-five-gun national salute. And on April 14 he raised his colors on the USS *Tristram Shandy* and steamed up the Chesapeake. It was time for a short vacation.

Tristram Shandy put in at Baltimore on the morning of the fifteenth. Porter came ashore and learned that his president had been shot. The admiral sped to Washington by rail. When he got there, he learned that the president was dead. Admiral Porter lowered his head and cried.

"To prevent the escape of the assassin who killed the President and attempted the life of the Secretary of State, search every vessel that arrives down the bay," read the secretary of the navy's directive of April 16. "Permit no vessel to go to sea without such search, and arrest and send to Washington any suspicious persons."

Five assassination suspects were arrested on April 17. More were at large. To Foxhall Parker on the Potomac, Welles wired, "Search all vessels going out of the river for the assassins. Detain all suspicious persons. Guard against all crossing of the river and touching of vessels or boats on the Virginia shore."

On April 17 Acting Master J. H. Eldridge of the USS *Delaware* reported that the killer had been spotted near Point Lookout. "In consequence of information having been received that the murderer of the President has been seen in this vicinity, I would request that you patrol the bay from Point Lookout to the mouth [of] Patuxent River, keeping a strict watch on the movements of all vessels and on any small boats that may attempt to leave the west shore of the bay," said Eldridge in his message to Acting Master W. A. Arthur on *Thomas Freeborn*. "All steamers bound down the bay you will hail, and order them to proceed to Point Lookout and remain until further orders."

Acting on Eldridge's information, Welles telegraphed Hampton Roads: "Send any vessels that may be unemployed to blockade eastern shore of Virginia and Maryland coast from Point Lookout to Baltimore. . . ."

It was raining on April 21 when Abraham Lincoln passed through Baltimore for the last time. His funeral train pulled into Camden Station. Four years ago, it had been the last fearful stop before Washington and the presidency. Today, it was the first main stop on the long last ride home to Illinois and burial. Before proceeding, there was a parade beneath a nasty sky through Baltimore.

The crowd filled the streets early. The ceremonial guns began firing at dawn and continued through the day. Business was suspended. Schools were closed. The seven-car funeral train keened into Camden Station at 10 A.M. The third car from the rear contained Lincoln's remains. When the train stopped, the Lincoln car was under the depot shed at Lee Street. The depot sheds, the whole station, were bedraped in dark mourning decorations. Throughout the Camden yards, train engines tolled their bells in continuous tribute.

Politicians, dignitaries, and officers were permitted in the station. After ceremonies there, Lincoln's coffin was lowered into a dark rosewood hearse with French glass side plates and gilded empaneling. Six black plumes adorned the sides, with another plume rising from the top. Bands played solemnly and gun salutes popped as the coffin was placed in the hearse.

The hearse, said to be one of only two of its kind on the continent, was on loan from Elisha Cox's East Baltimore livery stable for the day's cortege. Cox himself was driver. Six jet-black horses pulled the hearse. The parade wound through downtown, along Camden, Eutaw, Pratt, Howard, Charles, Baltimore, and Gay Streets. Scores of military units and civic groups escorted the slain man's remains through packed streets. On they marched: marines, sailors, and officers from the U.S. Receiving Ship *Alleghany* at harbor; the Veteran Reserve Corps, stationed in Baltimore, swords drawn and very regimental; the Eleventh Maryland Infantry; the Eleventh Indiana, stationed at McHenry; five hundred men of the Seventh New York Artillery; Major General Lew Wallace, with Kenly and other mounted officers; the Second U.S. Artillery brass band marching and performing in red uniforms topped with long, red plumes.

Then came the hearse. The people who packed the roadways could glimpse the coffin through the hearse's glass.

Those accompanying the corpse on the funeral train to Springfield followed next. They were congressmen, relatives, judges, military men. Then, in carriages, came Governor Bradford, Governor-elect Swann, B&O President Garrett (who organized the funeral train's route to Springfield), and others. Civic organizations paraded past, as did union leagues, the fire department, protestant clergy, the Germania Society,

Jewish groups, the First Colored Christian Commission of Baltimore, the Grand Order of Nazarites, the First Colored Grand Lodge of Maryland, and many other black organizations.

The coffin was placed on an elaborate black-draped catafalque in the lobby of the Exchange Building. Thousands filed past to see the dead man. The crowd outside the Exchange jostled and pushed, and women and children were caught in the crush. The city police and the military guard had to use their bayonets to keep things under control.

Lincoln lay inside and people stared at him, his face arranged in a beatific half-smile, his beard trimmed neatly down to a chin tuft.

The *Sun* reported: "The long and bony body is now hard and stiff, so that beyond its present position it cannot be moved any more than the arms and legs of a statue. It has undergone many changes. The scalp has been removed, the brain scooped out, the chest opened and veins emptied. All that we see of Abraham Lincoln, so cunningly contemplated in this splendid coffin, is a mere shell, an effigy, a sculpture. He lies in sleep, but it is the sleep of marble. All that made his flesh vital, sentient and affectionate is gone forever."

The actor from Bel Air, Maryland, escaped from Washington with a friend and made it down to Charles County, where a country doctor, Samuel Mudd, set the actor's broken leg. The fugitives rode through swampland and reached "Rich Hill," the home of Samuel Cox, early on April 16. Cox fed them, hid them in the woods, and sent for Thomas Jones, head of the Confederate spy network in Southern Maryland. The two lay low in the woods while Jones watched for the right moment to get them across the Potomac. They made it over in a skiff on the night of the twenty-second, landing at Mathias Point. They crossed the Rappahannock to Port Royal and were holed up in a barn when Federal troops surrounded them on April 26. The friend, Davy Herold, surrendered. The actor played the scene with melodrama, just like he had when he murdered the president. The troopers torched the barn to smoke him out. Then a shot was fired, and John Wilkes Booth was dead. Herold and the other assassination conspirators were hanged that July. Most of them, like Booth, had been Marylanders.

The heavy cell door of Casemate Number Two slammed shut on May 22, 1865, sounding the start of Jefferson Davis's long imprisonment at Fort Monroe.

His flight from Richmond had ended near Irwinville, Georgia, on May 10. The escaping party during the long trek had dispersed along the way. Some, like Davis's nephew John Taylor Wood, had managed to find freedom.

With Secretary of War John C. Breckinridge and others, John Taylor Wood made it down to the wilds of Florida and in a rickety eighteen-foot sloop, battling lightning, towering waves, reefs, exposure, starvation, and thirst, they reached the coast of Cuba. They were serenaded in the streets of Cardenas, where a huge banquet was laid out for them by the Confederate expatriate colony.

Jefferson Davis was among those who had not fared so fortunately. The steamer *William P. Clyde* dropped anchor at Hampton Roads on May 19 with a cargo of Confederate prisoners. Along with President Davis and family, there was Vice President Stephens, Postmaster General John Reagan, Commissioner to Canada Clement Clay, Lieutenant General Joseph Wheeler, two colonels, aides, and various other officers. Crowds gathered on the waterfront, wondering whether there would be hangings.

The prisoners remained on the steamer under heavy guard. In Fort Monroe, bricklayers, carpenters, and blacksmiths were transforming Casemates Two and Four into prison cells. On May 21 most of the prisoners were shipped elsewhere—Stephens and Reagan to Fort Warren, Wheeler and the colonels to Fort Delaware, and most of the rest to Fort McHenry. Jefferson Davis and Clement Clay remained, until the next day.

The women cried as their husbands were led over the side into the boat for shore. Sentinels lined the path from Engineer Wharf to the casemate cells. A detachment of the Fourth Michigan Cavalry, which had captured Davis in Georgia, led the procession. Davis followed, wearing a suit of Confederate gray and a gray slouch hat. He appeared gaunt and unhealthy, but his face was composed, his posture straight. Major General Nelson Miles, the fort's new commander who had just arrived that day from Baltimore, had Davis by the arm. Behind them

JEFFERSON DAVIS AS HE APPEARED AT THE
TIME OF HIS CAPTURE AND SUBSEQUENT
IMPRISONMENT AT FORT MONROE.
Nimitz Library, U.S. Naval Academy

marched six soldiers, then Clay and Colonel Benjamin Pritchard of the Fourth Michigan. More soldiers brought up the rear. Major General Henry Halleck from Richmond and Assistant Secretary of War Charles Dana from Washington had come to oversee.

The converted casemate had an inner and outer cell. The inner was for the prisoner, the outer for his two sentinels. The prisoner's cell had an iron cot, a table, a chair, and a Bible. The embrasures in the thick wall offered a slim view. Davis asked the sentinels which direction the embrasures faced. They didn't answer.

On his second day in the cell, the former president was shackled in irons. His food lay on the table, untouched. He hadn't slept well, and he was lying on the cot when Captain James E. Titlow of the Third Pennsylvania Artillery entered with two blacksmiths. Titlow, the officer of the day, said he was just following orders. Davis rose up, shouting. When the blacksmith tried to slip on the fetter, Davis grabbed him and shoved him across the room. More guards were rushed in. Davis was thrown on the cot, and it took four of them to hold him down while the heavy irons were slapped in place. After they all left, he just lay there at first. Then he sat up and started sobbing, rocking back and forth.

The fort surgeon, Brevet Lieutenant Colonel John J. Craven, visited Davis on May 24. The prisoner appeared malnourished, feverish, his nerves rattled, his age-old neuralgic condition in an active state. Dr. Craven managed to get Davis better food, more reading material (a prayer book)—and tobacco. Davis had used tobacco his whole life. He hadn't been permitted it at the fort. When he smoked his first pipeful in a long time, a look of calm came over his face, the doctor said. On May 28 the shackles were removed. Davis's health continued to worsen, however. In July the doctor got permission to let the prisoner take a walk. For one hour each day, Jefferson Davis was allowed to walk along the ramparts at Fort Monroe—this crucial piece of Virginia that never left Federal hands, this water-dominating bastion that by virtue of location had contributed so greatly to Davis's inevitable defeat. Now he walked its ramparts as its prisoner, and he saw sky over water and tasted the air off the Bay.

On May 3, 1865, Secretary Welles ordered the Potomac Flotilla reduced to half-strength. The fighting was all but over, the reason for the flotilla was gone, and the reduction didn't stop at half. On July 31, 1865, Foxhall Parker issued a general order to the officers and men of his command:

> The war for the preservation of American liberty being at an end, the Potomac Flotilla, which took its rise with it and grew with its growth until it had become a fleet rather than a flotilla, this day happily ceases to exist.

In taking leave of those with whom I have been so long associated, my heart is filled with varied emotions—with sorrow at parting, gladness that our beloved country no longer has need of us, and pride, just pride, that when I reflect upon the past and remember the taking up of the torpedoes from the Rappahannock with the destruction or capture of the whole rebel force engaged in placing them there, thereby making Fredericksburg a secure base of supplies for General Grant's vast army, the burning of the schooners at Mattox Creek under the severe musketry fire of the enemy, and the almost daily expeditions up the rivers, in the creeks, and through the marshes of the northern neck of Virginia—all requiring skill and nerve— I can truly say "the Potomac Flotilla has not been unmindful of the traditional honor and glory of the Navy."

Your services, however eclipsed by the daring deeds of your more fortunate comrades in arms on other stations, have, equally with theirs, contributed to the suppression of the rebellion, and in discipline, in drill, in all the requirements in short of an organized force, I have not, in the course of a naval experience of twenty-eight years, served in a squadron which excelled the one which for the last nineteen months it has been my good fortune to command.

The future Chief of Staff to the North Atlantic Fleet concluded:

For those of you who are about to return to civil life I would say: Render the same cheerful obedience to the civil that you have rendered to naval law; cast your votes, as good citizens, regularly and quietly at the polls, so keeping your hearts "with malice toward none, with charity for all," so that after each Presidential election, whether it be with or against you, you may be enabled to respond heartily to our old navy toast: "The President of the United States, God bless him."

And now may God be with you all. Farewell.

When Admiral Franklin Buchanan returned to the Eastern Shore, his home was gone. It had burned down, under mysterious circumstances, in April 1863. The Confederacy's highest ranking naval officer was now in his sixties and limping, and he set about rebuilding his life.

He had been seriously wounded, again, during the Battle of Mobile Bay on August 6, 1864, when he commanded the Confederate squadron in a hard-fought battle that was lost. Buchanan was hospitalized for three months and finally was able to get around on crutches. He was then imprisoned at Fort Lafayette until March 1865. At one point, he was visited by his brother McKean, against whom he had fought, and whose ship he had burned, at the Battle of Hampton Roads.

Franklin Buchanan was exchanged just in time to have to surrender again when the war ended. He put his signature to a parole: "I, the undersigned, a prisoner of war and an admiral in the Confederate Navy, do hereby give my solemn parole of honor that I will not hereafter serve in the Navy of the Confederate States, or in any military capacity whatever, against the United States of America . . ." and was allowed to hobble home. From the flagship *Malvern* to Fort Monroe, he made his way back.

In December 1867 Buchanan was visited by Jefferson Davis, who was feted by Buchanan's in-laws, the Lloyds, at Wye House with a grand reception attended by hundreds. Davis had been released from Fort Monroe that May. His wife, Varina, had been allowed to join him there, and he had been moved out of his casemate cell into more comfortable quarters. Davis was out on bail, his trial for treason having been postponed until spring of 1868. The original charges against him, implicating him in the assassination of Lincoln, had long since been dropped. The charges still pending would eventually be dropped as well.

Not far from where the Jefferson Davises were honored in the old tidewater way, another prosperous Talbot County landowner, the U.S. Army veteran Colonel John Cowgill, parceled off part of his property for blacks who had fought in the war. The former slaves built a new community, which came to be called Unionville.

In the years after the Civil War, Franklin Buchanan worked to improve his estate and support his family. His family had been staying with friends and continued to do so until Buchanan finished building a new home. It was called "The Rest," like the grand house that stood there in the old days before the fire. The new house wasn't as fancy as the original had been, but they were glad to be in it.

Notes

The *Official Records* are referred to as *OR Navies* or *OR Armies*. All *OR* listings are Series 1 unless otherwise noted.

CWNC refers to *Civil War Naval Chronology*.

CHAPTER 1

The marine detachment's Fort McHenry orders are in *OR Navies* 4: 263–64. The arrival of the artillery companies from Fort Leavenworth is recorded in the *Baltimore Republican*, January 14, 1861.

Baltimore's political rowdyism is described in Beirne, pp. 142-51; and Brugger, pp. 263–64. Free blacks are discussed in Brugger, pp. 264–69; and Dozer, pp. 435–37. For other population statistics, abolitionism details, and ethnic political loyalties, see Dozer, pp. 424–39.

For the background on **Franklin Buchanan**, see Lewis, pp. 1–126; and Todorich, "Franklin Buchanan: Symbol for Two Navies," in Bradford, pp. 87–102. His order to defend the Washington Navy Yard to the death is quoted from *OR Navies* 4: 411.

For **Lincoln's train ride** through Baltimore, see Cuthbert, pp. 1–85; and Lamon, pp. 505–27. See also Potter, which does give an engaging day-by-day account, but seems too prone to accept Pinkerton's conspiracy theory lock, stock, and barrel. The arrival of a loud minority of Baltimore ruffians at Washington for inauguration festivities is mentioned in Leech, p. 42.

The history of **Fort Monroe** is found in Weinert and Arthur, pp. 23–87. For the number of vessels in commission in the U.S. Navy prior to war's outbreak, see *CWNC* I : 5–6. For a description of the Norfolk Navy Yard, see Guernsey and Alden, pp. 81, 84. For the preparations to defend the Norfolk Navy Yard, see *OR Navies* 4: 273–80; and Welles, pp. 41–46.

The harassment of the Pennsylvania troops passing through Baltimore is recorded in Scharf, *Baltimore*, p. 129; Scharf, *Maryland*, pp. 400–401; and Toomey, pp. 10-11. The incident was a precursor to the infamous **April 19 riot**, the account of which given here is culled from *OR Armies* 2:7–21; the Baltimore *Sun*, April 20, 1861; and Brown, pp. 42–59. The Richard Fisher quotes are from an addendum to MS. 1064, Wardwell Reminiscences, Maryland Historical Society Library Collection. See also Scharf, *Maryland*, pp. 403–11; and for the most thorough current scholarship, Towers, pp. 1–26.

The early history of the Naval Academy is found in Lewis, pp. 92–113; Todorich, "Franklin Buchanan: Symbol for Two Navies," in Bradford, pp. 94–100; and Norris, pp. 245–53. The account of the departing Southerners, and the incident by the commandant's doorway, are in Norris, pp. 257–61.

John Taylor Wood's quotes are from MS. 2381, John Taylor Wood Diary, Southern Historical Collection of the Library of the University of North Carolina at Chapel Hill, April 13 and 15 entries. For biographical background on Wood, see Shingleton, pp. 2–6.

Secretary Welles's unintentional double-entendre order to "defend the *Constitution* at all hazards" is quoted from *OR Navies* 4: 272. For the **arrival of Butler's troops**, see Holzman, pp. 28–31; and Norris, pp. 263–75.

The **burning of the Norfolk Navy Yard**, and the efforts to counteract the odd stalling of McCauley leading up to it, are logged in *OR Navies* 4: 281–313. See also Welles, pp. 46–54; Soley, *The Blockade and the Cruisers*, pp. 47–54; *CWNC* 1: 9–10; and Guernsey and Alden, pp. 81, 84–85.

The journey of the **New York Seventh** is described in Winthrop, "New York Seventh Regiment," pp. 744–48; and Roehrenbeck, pp. 48–105.

For Franklin **Buchanan's resignation**, see *OR Navies* 4: 418. See also Lewis, pp. 158–63; the anecdote about Lincoln at Nannie Buchanan's wedding is related on p. 163, footnote 1; the *National Intelligencer*, April 25, 1861, article is abstracted in Lewis, pp. 162–63. In the description of John Taylor **Wood's resignation**, the quotes are from MS. 2381, John Taylor Wood Diary, Southern Historical Collection of the University of North Carolina at Chapel Hill, April 19, 20, and 21 entries. See also Shingleton, pp. 15–17.

The **departure of USS** *Constitution* from Annapolis is recorded in *OR Navies* 4: 341; and *CWNC* 1:11. The sad farewells of Northern and Southern classmates are told of in Norris, pp. 261–62.

CHAPTER 2

The **march of the New York Seventh** and Massachusetts Eighth to the Capital is recounted in Winthrop, "New York Seventh Regiment," pp. 748–56. See also Roehrenbeck, pp. 106–27. For the subsequent influx of troops to Washington via the Chesapeake, see *OR Navies* 4:344–45, 362; and Gray, p. 11.

The beginning of the career of premier Baltimore smuggler **Levi White** is recounted in White, part I, December 15, 1907. White, at the time he serialized his memoirs, had left illicit trafficking behind and was an attache of the Criminal Court.

The description of the **birth of the Potomac Flotilla** is culled from *OR Navies* 4:342–43, 420, 430, 458, 467. Ward's quote describing the proposed flotilla is on p. 420. Ward's biographical background is from the Baltimore *Sun*, June 30, 1861.

The account of **Butler's entry into Baltimore** is based on *OR Armies*, 2:28–32.; Scharf, *Baltimore*, pp. 131–32; and Holzman, pp. 33–36.

The **Virginia Tidewater rebels** were encouraged to organize and resist. The Advisory Council quote is from *OR Armies* 51,pt.2:75. The *Richmond Dispatch*'s call for the formation of guerrilla groups is reprinted in *Rebellion Record*, 3:84.

Winthrop's quote on his decision to join Butler's staff is from Winthrop, "Washington as a Camp," p. 118. The **Fort Monroe** troop statistics, and the outline of expansions beyond the fort, are from Weinert and Arthur, pp. 99–102. For the naval participation in the Newport News landing, see *OR Navies* 5:675. The account of Butler's far-famed "contraband of war" decision is from Butler, pp. 256-59. See also Carr, "Early Operations of 1861 about Fort Monroe," *Battles and Leaders* 2: 144-47.

The first actions of the **Potomac Flotilla** are recorded in *OR Navies* 4:475, 477–82, 484–85, 490–501, 525–27. Ward's Mathias Point quote is on p. 475. See also the Baltimore *Sun*, June 5, 1861, for the *New York Herald* article reprint about the Aquia Creek engagement.

Werth's report on the **Virginia cavalry reconnaissance** to Newport News is in *OR Armies* 2:75–77. The account of the **fight at Big Bethel** is culled from the reports in 2:77–104; 51, pt.1: 3–5; the Baltimore *Sun*, June 12–16, 1861; and Carr, "Early Operations of 1861 about Fort Monroe," *Battles and Leaders* 2:148–51. See also Weinert and Arthur, pp. 103–6.

The burning of the schooner *Christiana Keen* and the retaliatory torching of the rebel house are incidents recounted in *OR Navies* 4:516-17, 533–35; the **engagement at Mathias Point** and the fall of Ward are reported on 536–45 and in the Baltimore *Sun*, June 30, 1861.

For the overview of the naval career of **George Hollins**, see Hartzler, p. 6. The account of his childhood meeting with Commodore Perry, and the later resignation quote, are found in MS. 2310, George N. Hollins notebook, Winder Family Papers, Maryland Historical Society Library Collection; the notebook also evidently includes the original rough text of Hollins's report in *OR Navies* 4:553–55.

CHAPTER 3

The colorful *St. Nicholas* **incident** is described here based on *OR Navies* 4:549–55, especially Hollins's account, pp. 553–55; the Baltimore *Sun*, July 6, 1861; and the Baltimore *Evening Sun*, August 27, 1910. See also Earp, pp. 333-38; Hartzler, pp. 29–30; Holly, pp. 70-71; Scharf, *Baltimore*, p. 135; and Robinson, pp. 179–85.

Hollins insisted he conceived the plan; both Zarvona and the First Tennessee's Lieutenant Henry Lewis also claimed to have originated the idea. Probably because he was the one who donned women's clothes, Zarvona seems to have gained the most fame from the exploit.

The account of the **arrest of Marshal Kane** and the Baltimore police commissioners is based on *OR Armies* 2:138–56. Banks's proclamation is on pp. 140–41; the Lincoln quote is on p. 156. See also Scharf, *Baltimore*, p. 133, 136; and Clark, "Suppression and Control," pp. 257–58. For the arrest of Ogle Tilghman, see the Baltimore *Sun*, July 4, 1861.

For the background on **Hetty Cary** and the Monument Street Girls, see Hetty Cary Martin obituary, Baltimore *Sun*, September 28, 1892; Moberly transcript, pp. 1-3; and Beirne, pp. 112-13. For the date of the Carys' Potomac River crossing, and other details, see Jane M. Cary, Application No. 186, United Daughters of the Confederacy, Maryland Chapter, June 25, 1895, on file at the Maryland Historical Society Library. See also Harrison, "Virginia Scenes in '61," *Battles and Leaders*, 1:165–66.

The presentation by Baltimore's pro-Union citizens of a silk flag to the soldiers of the Sixth Massachusetts is mentioned in Scharf, *Baltimore*, p. 136. The account of the **capture of Zarvona** is gleaned from reports in the Baltimore *Sun*, July 9, 1861; and *Baltimore American*, July 9, 1861. See also Earp, pp. 338–43; Scharf, *Baltimore*, pp. 135–36; and Robinson, pp. 185–86. The suspicion that the steamer *George Weems* would be Zarvona's next target is shown in *OR Navies* 4:569–70. Lowry's quote about the hostile reception given him by the passengers on *George Weems* is from 4:573. Secretary Welles's citing of the memorandum about would-be Zarvona imitator James Hurry is in 4:569.

Bay smuggling was on the rise and would last throughout the war. The letter describing the pungy boat and schooner's smuggling route from Baltimore to Virginia via the Eastern Shore is in *OR Navies* 5: 761–62. The quote about the use of punts for smuggling is from 4:663. The Potomac Flotilla's Nanticoke expeditions are recorded in 4:577–78.

The **Virginia Eastern Shore** was an inevitable trafficking conduit. The letter citing the Snow Hill port collector is found in *OR Navies* 6:19–20. General Dix's quote on the need for armed Eastern Shore companies due to the growing secessionist camp at Eastville is in *OR Armies* 2:770. Budd's detailed report on the Virginia Eastern Shore is in *OR Navies* 4: 586-87. The New York customhouse collector's letter about smugglers' routes and smugglers' flagrancy is in 6:76-77. Welles's anecdote about whiskey barrels filled with pistols is in 4:590.

For the post–Big Bethel movements around **Old Point Comfort**, see Weinert and Arthur, pp. 106-11. For the deployment of troops from the Fort Monroe area to the Washington area in the wake of Bull Run, see *OR Armies* 2:761, 763–65. The burning of Hampton is chronicled in the reports of Butler, Phelps, and Magruder in 4:567–73.

As for the **Potomac rebels**, Budd's report on the August 10 Machodoc Creek raid is from *OR Navies* 4: 604. Also from vol. 4 are the following: Craven's quote about Potomac-shore Marylanders' disloyalty, 603; the intercepted Jefferson Davis missive describing a proposed attack through rebel-friendly Southern Maryland, 612; Governor Hicks's warning of a possible attack, 617; *Resolute*'s run-in with snipers, 609–10; Ely's account of his undercover visit to Captain Code, 620–22.

In the **lower Chesapeake**: The Confederate steam tug *Harmony*'s attack on the U.S. frigate *Savannah* is described in *OR Navies* 6: 148, 150. For the replacement of Stringham by Goldsborough as North Atlantic Blockading Squadron flag officer, see 6:232; for the division of the Atlantic Blockading Squadron into North and South entities, 6:313. For the replacement of Butler by Wool, see Weinert and Arthur, pp. 112-15. Wool's quote about the importance of Fort Monroe is in *OR Navies* 6:168.

Franklin Buchanan's failed attempt to withdraw his resignation, and his subsequent decision to lend his services to the South, are depicted in Lewis, pp. 163–73. See also Swartz, pp. 65–68; and Todorich, "Franklin Buchanan: Symbol for Two Navies," in Bradford, pp. 103–4. **John Taylor Wood**'s decision to cast his lot with the Confederacy, and his journey across the Potomac, are chronicled in Shingleton, pp. 17–19.

The capture and escape of George Henry is reported in *OR Navies* 4: 649–50. The **arrest of Frank Key Howard** and the other Baltimore political prisoners is recounted here based on Howard, pp. 4–17; Sangston, pp. 7–21; and *OR Armies* 5: 193–97. Dix's quote on overcrowding at Fort McHenry is from series 2, 1:593. See also Matthews, pp. 150–57.

Among discussions of confrontations with the **Confederate shore batteries** along the Potomac, the fight between the Federal gunboats and the Freestone Point battery is reported in *OR Navies* 4:689. General Hooker's quote about the elusiveness of the enemy batteries is from *OR Armies* 5:407–8. For the role of the First Maryland Confederate Light Artillery, see Scharf, *Maryland*, p. 455, n. 1. The broadsheet-ballad verses about Marylanders taking up "arms for the gallant South, On Old Virginia's shore . . ." are from the Maryland Historical Society's collection of Civil War song sheets. The lines quoted here also are found in Semmes, p. 210.

The destruction of the privateering schooner outfitting at **Chincoteague** is reported in *OR Navies* 6:288; the oath of loyalty of the Chincoteague Islanders is on p. 337, and Goldsborough's plea on their behalf is on p. 336.

For background on the November 1861 **Maryland general election**, see Clark, *Politics*, pp. 65-83; and *OR Armies* 5:385-87. General Hooker's White Horse Tavern quote is from 5:640.

The Federal **Virginia Eastern Shore expedition** is recorded in *OR Armies* 4:424-37, 641-42; Dix's proclamation to the citizens is on pp. 431-32. Lincoln's quote is in series 3, 1:718–19. See also the Baltimore *Sun*, November 21-22, 1861, and Ames.

CHAPTER 4

The narrative of *Virginia* vs. the Hampton Roads fleet and subsequent battle with *Monitor* is based on the reports in *OR Navies* 6:776–77, 780-81; 7:8, 10–12, 18–19, 21, 23–27, 31, 34–36, and 43–59.

Other firsthand accounts quoted herein are Wood, "The First Fight of Iron-clads," *Battles and Leaders* 1:692-705; Greene, "In the Monitor Turret," *Battles and Leaders* 1:719–29; and the Ramsay article. For the Buchanan quote as he grabbed the carbine and ordered *Congress* burned, see Lewis, p. 189 n. 2.

The background on *Virginia*'s construction is in Brooke, "The Plan and Construction of the 'Merrimac,'" *Battles and Leaders* 1:715–17; *Monitor*'s construction is detailed in Ericsson, "The Building of the 'Monitor,'" *Battles and Leaders* 1:730–44.

The secretary of the navy's account of the White House meeting is in Welles, pp. 61–65.

See also Keeler, pp. 27–42; Colston, "Watching the 'Merrimac,'" *Battles and Leaders* 1:712–14; Soley, *The Blockade and the Cruisers*, pp. 54–75; and Lewis, pp. 174–99.

CHAPTER 5

The overview of the **Peninsula Campaign**, from its planning stages to the Battle of Williamsburg, is based on Webb, pp. 1–82; see also McClellan, "The Peninsular Campaign," *Battles and Leaders* 2:160-72. Details and figures pertaining to the embarkation are from *OR Armies* 5:24–25, 27–28; Cullen, p. 4; and Weinert and Arthur, p. 131. McClellan's quote on the unprecedented scale of the operation is in *OR Armies* 5:27. The quotes of Private Goss are from Goss, "Campaigning to No Purpose," *Battles and Leaders*, 2:159; and Goss, "Yorktown and Williamsburg," 2:189-99. The soldier's quote about fear during the assault on Fort Magruder also is from Goss, pp. 196–97.

The *Anacostia* crew's discovery that the Confederates had abandoned the Potomac shore batteries is reported in *OR Navies* 5: 23, 25. Lincoln's General War Order No. 3 is in *OR Armies* 5: 50. McClellan's quote on the decision to change the landing site from Urbanna to Fort Monroe is from McClellan, "The Peninsular Campaign," *Battles and Leaders* 2:167. The inspired use of upper Chesapeake canal boats to land troops and supplies at Old Point Comfort is explained in Catton, pp. 188–89.

For the **return of CSS *Virginia***, see *OR Navies*, 7: 219–22; and Wood, "The First Fight of Iron-clads," *Battles and Leaders* 1:707.

The **North Atlantic Blockading Squadron**'s participation on the York River is logged in *OR Navies* 7:201, 205–6, 209-10, 225, 240, 243, 253–54, 259, 261–63, 305, 310–12, and 319; Missroon's quote about the power of the Confederate works in the Yorktown vicinity is on p. 259. See also Soley, "The Navy in the Peninsular Campaign," *Battles and Leaders*, 2:264-70.

Abraham Lincoln's Chesapeake trip aboard the revenue cutter *Miami*, and the quotes of Viele, Chase, and Lincoln, are in the account by Viele, pp. 813–22; see also Kern, pp. 10-1 to 10-6, which includes the background on *Miami* and her crew, pp. 10-1 to 10-3. Lincoln's visit to the *Monitor* deck is based on the May 6 journal entry in Keeler, pp. 106–8. For the Lincoln-ordered gunboat expedition up the James, see *OR Navies* 7: 328–32. For the bombardment of Sewells point, see 7:332-33; see also Wood, "The First Fight of Iron-clads," *Battles and Leaders* 1:709, for the Tattnall quote calling off *Virginia*'s reappearance during the Sewells Point bombardment.

In addition to Viele, the account of the **capture of Norfolk**, is culled from *OR Navies* 7:342–43; *Rebellion Record* 5:40–46, doc. 11; and Keeler, pp. 115–22.

The account of the **destruction of CSS *Virginia*** is from Tattnall's report in *OR Navies* 7: 335–38; and Wood, "The First Fight of Iron-clads," *Battles and Leaders* 1:709–10.

For the background on the **Battle of Drewry's Bluff**, see Wood, "The First Fight of Iron-clads," *Battles and Leaders* 1:711; Soley, "The Navy in the Peninsular Campaign," *Battles and Leaders* 2:270; and Keeler, pp. 124–31. See also *OR Navies* 7: 356–71.

The anecdote about the safety valve from CSS *Virginia* being presented to Lincoln is in Kern, p. 10-6.

CHAPTER 6

The account of **Baltimore unrest** in late May 1862 is based on coverage in the Baltimore *Sun*, May 26–28, 1862; and the *Baltimore American*, May 26, 1862.

The arrest of **Judge Carmichael** is chronicled in the Baltimore *Sun*, May 29, 1862; Marshall, pp. 426–448; and Scharf, *Maryland*, pp. 490–91. The judge's charge to the grand jury, quoted here, is found in Marshall, pp. 430–36.

The brawl between police and the inmates of **Campbell's Slave Jail** is detailed in the Baltimore *Sun*, June 2, 1862.

The smuggling exploits of **Levi White** described here are recounted in White, part 1, December 15, 1907; part 2, December 22, 1907; and part 3, December 29, 1907.

Former Governor Hicks's quote about smugglers is in *OR Navies* 5:56. For the **expansion of the Potomac Flotilla**'s jurisdiction to include the Rappahannock, see 7:244–45. Wyman's report on the April 20 Rappahannock expedition is in 5:37. The capture of Eastern Shore smugglers on the western shore is recorded in 5:40. The engagement with the Piankatank shore batteries is described in 5:45-46; the Mobjack Bay reconnaissance in 5:44–45. Morse's quote on Union sentiment in Mathews County is from 7:636.

For **Hetty Cary**'s incognito visit to Baltimore and blockade-running return to Richmond, see Hetty Cary Martin obituary, Baltimore *Sun*, September 28, 1892; and Moberly transcript, p. 3.

The secret journey of **Henry Hollyday** from the Eastern Shore to Richmond is detailed in Henry Hollyday, pp. 93–96. For the biographical background on Henry Hollyday, see Frederic Hollyday, pp. 1–2.

The assignment of **Charles Wilkes** to the newly styled James River flotilla, including Secretary Welles's quote, is from *OR Navies*, 7:548. For details about Wilkes's James River duties, see Wilkes, pp. 867-90. Goldsborough's quote about Wilkes is found in *OR Navies* 7:573-74. McClellan's message to Wilkes is in 7:611.

Commander Smith's quote about gunboat assistance to McClellan's troops is from *OR Navies* 7:315-16. The **Peninsula Campaign** synopsis is gleaned from Cullen, pp. 6-24. McClellan's "banks of the James" quote summing up the campaign is from McClellan, "The Peninsular Campaign," *Battles and Leaders* 2:187.

CHAPTER 7

For **Gilmor's capture** on Baltimore's outskirts, see Gilmor, pp. 57-59. For Gilmor's biographical information, see Toomey's well-researched introduction to the Butternut & Blue reprint edition.

The **Baltimore invasion preparations** before the Battle of Antietam are described in Scharf, *Baltimore*, pp. 140–41; and Scharf, *Maryland*, pp. 498–500; for the deployment of the mortar boats, see *OR Navies* 5:72.

Orders for the assignment and rapid reassignment of **Wilkes** are in *OR Navies*, 5:72, 82. The assignment of **S. P. Lee** to the North Atlantic Blockading Squadron is in 7:695. For the expansion of the **Potomac Flotilla**'s range to include the Piankatank, and the splitting of the flotilla into two divisions, see 7:695; 5:99-100. Harwood's quotes on the elusive "Sable" are in 5:69–70. The depredations on civilians by Federal transport steamer crews are described in 5:70. Harwood's general orders about crews' alleged misconduct are quoted in 5:205. The report on *Jacob Bell*'s spy sent to St. Georges Island is in 5:90–91.

Magaw's capture of **oystermen/smugglers** is recorded in *OR Navies* 5:80-81. S. P. Lee's quote about oystering limits can be found in 8:114. For Parker's November interception of oyster smugglers, see 8:228–29; for his December burning of the oyster shack, see 8:310. The court-martial proceedings of would-be waterfowler **Private Gill** are in 8:222–26.

Reports pertaining to the late 1862 raids by **John Taylor Wood** on the Potomac and the Chesapeake are in *OR Navies* 5:118-19; 5:137–41; 8:163–69. Peter

Smith's quotes are from his deposition, found in 8:167–69. See also Shingleton, pp. 61–69.

For the November army-navy raid on **Mathews Courthouse**, see *OR Navies* 8: 227–28.

The gunboat engagements on the Rappahannock before, during, and after the **Battle of Fredericksburg** are chronicled in *OR Navies* 5:182-204. Magaw's December 11 quote is on p. 195. Burnside's December 18 message to Magaw is on p. 204.

The sinking of *Monitor* is described in *OR Navies* 8: 338–59.

CHAPTER   8

Smuggler Levi White's run-in with Federal cavalry below the Rappahannock is recounted in White, part 4, January 5, 1908.

Rear Admiral Lee's quote about the impossibility of an iron-tight **Chesapeake blockade** is from *OR Navies* 8: 450–51. The destruction of the Dividing Creek salt manufactory is recorded in 5:210. The canoe chase at the Rappahannock mouth is in 5:223, the Ware River grain raid and cavalry engagement in 8:643–46. For the Confederate advance toward Yorktown and the resulting requests for gunboat assistance, see 8:711–13.

The **fighting along the Nansemond** as the Confederates threatened Suffolk is covered in *OR Navies* 8:718–48, 771–94. Specific quotes (all vol. 8) are as follows: Harris February prediction, 495; S. P. Lee's "impolicy" quote, 717; Cushing's Chuckatuck report, 771–72; and Peck's summation, 793.

The accounts of the spring 1863 **newspaper arrests**: the Thomas Robson account is based on Mullikin, pp. 49–57 and the J. S. Downs account on Hammett, pp. 111–12.

Baltimore in the **Schenck-Fish** era is outlined in Clark, "Suppression and Control," pp. 265–69; and Scharf, *Baltimore*, pp. 141–42. Fanny James's treason charge is reported in the Baltimore *Sun*, May 12, 1863. Baltimore's invasion precautions are detailed in Scharf, *Baltimore*, pp. 143–44. The naval precautions as the Army of Northern Virginia moved north are mentioned in *OR Navies* 5:292–94; 9:97. Schenck's declaration of martial law is in *Rebellion Record*, 7:328–29, doc. 86.

Point Lookout's early history and development into a prison camp are outlined in Hammett, pp. 122–24; and Beitzell, no. 4, pp. 16–19. The orders to establish the prison camp, the creation of a separate St. Marys District, and the first reports of prisoner arrivals are in *OR Armies* series 2, 6: 132, 140–42, 243. Secretary Welles's Point Lookout quote is from *OR Navies* 5:313. The Swalm report, with its vivid picture of prison-pen life, is in *OR Armies*, series 2, 6: 575–81.

For background on the **recruitment of black troops**, see Birney's report, *Rebellion Record* 7:394–95, doc. 116. See also the *Easton Gazette*, September 19,

1863; the *Chestertown News* quoted in the Baltimore *Sun*, September 28, 1863; Blassingame, pp. 20–29; Scharf, *Baltimore*, p. 144; Toomey, p. 95; and Wennersten, pp. 139–40. The Marylanders' meeting with Lincoln is written about in the Baltimore *Sun*, October 5, 1863. The shooting of Lieutenant White while recruiting slaves is described in Toomey, pp. 94–95; and Hammett, p. 120.

CHAPTER 9

The **ambush of the gunboat** *General Putnam* is reported in *OR Navies* 9: 160–61; see also Shingleton, pp. 76, 78.

The account given here of John Taylor **Wood's Chesapeake raids** is woven from the various ships' reports found in *OR Navies* 5:323–345; Wood's quoted report is on 344–45. See also Bohemian, *Richmond Dispatch*, September 2, 1863. Bohemian was almost certainly William G. Shepardson (see Shingleton, p. 228), "Assistant Surgeon Sheppardson" in Wood's official report. Bohemian provided coverage for Wood's later North Carolina and Atlantic expeditions as well as the 1863 Chesapeake raids; his articles had much to do with the spread of Wood's fame. See also Shingleton, pp. 74–89.

Then came John Yates **Beall's Chesapeake raids**. His August assault on the Smith's Island Lighthouse is recorded in *OR Navies* 5:315. The capture of *Alliance* and other vessels is recounted by Baker, pp. 15–23. Baker, a newspaper apprentice before joining Beall's raiders, later enjoyed a long and distinguished career as a member of the Virginia General Assembly. He drafted the 1908 bill that created the State Department of Health. (See Baker, pp. 8–10.) His firsthand account of Chesapeake privateering with Beall ran in the *Richmond Times-Dispatch* before emerging in book form. See also *OR Navies* 9:203–6; Robinson, pp. 221–29; and Pelzer, pp. 39–43.

Rear Adm. S. P. Lee's calls for greater vigilance in light of increased Chesapeake depredations are found in *OR Navies* 9:206, 222–23.

For the joint army-navy expedition to Mobjack Bay, see Baker, pp. 24–28; and *OR Navies* 9:207–10. The capture of Beall's raiders is in Baker, pp. 29–32; and *OR Navies* 9:306–7. Cheseborough's message to Lockwood about the prisoners' status as pirates is in *OR Navies* 9:318.

CHAPTER 10

The **guerrilla raid on Cherrystone Inlet**, and the subsequent pursuit of *Titan*, are reported in *OR Navies* 5:399–402; 9:527–28. See also 5:414 for Hooker's first dispatch linking Fitzhugh with the raid. The biographies of Edward Hooker and Foxhall Parker are out of Hamersley, pp. 60–61 and 195, respectively.

The **imprisonment of Beall's raiders** is a Bay-spanning saga recounted in Baker, pp. 33–44. The ancillary mention of Major General Schenck's resignation is based on the Baltimore *Sun*, November 23, 1863; and Clark, "Suppression and Control," pp. 269-70. For the arrest and conviction of Colonel Fish, see the Baltimore *Sun*, January 26, 1864; and Scharf, *Baltimore*, p. 146.

For background on the **flag-of-truce steamer** *New York* and prisoner trades, see Thompson, "Exchange of Prisoners," in Miller, 7:98–122; and appendix A (Cartel of July 22, 1862), 345–46. Assistant Surgeon Radcliffe's quotes about the **military hospitals at Annapolis** are from *OR Armies* series 2, 6:475-76. For details on hospital layouts and personnel, see Bolander, pp. 1612–15, and Tilghman, pp. 80–92.

Point Lookout's spring 1864 population figures are from Beitzell, no. 5, appendix A (Point Lookout population chart). The information on regiments stationed at the camp is from *OR Armies* series 2, 7:153-54. The Sergeant Young shooting incident and subsequent inquiry are logged in *OR Armies* series 2, 6:1097-1104. For Draper's raids with the Potomac Flotilla, see *OR Navies* 5:450; and Beitzell, no. 4, pp. 20, 23.

In reference to **torpedoes** in the tributaries: The explosion of *Commodore Barney* and other late-1863 torpedo incidents are noted in *CWNC* 3:123, 157-58. Hunter Davidson's exploit on *Squib* is described in *OR Navies* 9: 603, 608; and *CWNC* 4:39. The destruction of *Commodore Jones*, *OR Navies*, 10:9–16; the destruction of *Shawsheen*, *OR Navies* 10: 26–31; the formation of a James River torpedo division, *CWNC* 4:59. Accounts of the combined army-navy torpedo sweep up the Rappahannock are in *OR Navies*, 5:421-24; and Beitzell, no. 4, p. 21.

The **capture of** *Smith Briggs* is in *OR Navies* 9:431–32. For the Nansemond expedition, see *OR Navies* 9: 615–16, 620–21. For the *Eureka* incident, see *OR Navies* 5:411-12. For the troop-deployment feints up the York and Pamunkey, see *OR Navies* 9:728. The movements of Grant with the Army of the Potomac and Butler with the Army of the James are synopsized in Long, pp. 492–517.

The **nomination of Lincoln** for a second term is described in Scharf, *Baltimore*, p. 147; and Long, pp. 517-18. The **execution of Andrew Laypole** was covered by the Baltimore *Sun* on May 24, 1864. For the escape of other condemned prisoners a week earlier, see the Baltimore *Sun*, May 17, 1864.

The **Point Lookout** escape statistics, death statistics, and rising population statistics are from Beitzell, no. 5, appendix A (Point Lookout population chart). Surgeon Thompson's missive about health hazards facing the overcrowded camp is printed in *OR Armies* series 2, 7:399-400. The shooting incident involving Private Williams is described on pp. 163-65. Hoffman's warning about continued shootings is on p. 177.

The **attempted Point Lookout raid** has inspired much hypothetical speculation. John Taylor Wood's meeting with Robert E. Lee to discuss the plan is depicted in Shingleton, pp. 116-17. Tyler's quote on the brilliance of the idea is in *OR Navies* 10: 721. The Johnson and Gilmor rides around Baltimore are described by Bradley Johnson, pp. 215-25; Gilmor, pp. 191-205; and Toomey, pp.

124-31. Gilmor's *Four Years in the Saddle*, collaborated on by Col. Francis H. Smith, has its detractors and defenders; in all, it is more reliable for "color" commentary than for "play by play," to employ a broadcasting metaphor. See Toomey's introduction to the Butternut & Blue reprint.

Baltimore's invasion preparation is detailed in Scharf, *Baltimore*, pp. 147-48. The governor's and mayor's proclamation was printed in the Baltimore *Sun* on July 11, 1864. For naval precautions in the upper Bay, see *OR Navies* 5:459, 462; 10:254. How Braine found Annapolis guarded by invalids is described in *OR Navies* 10:269-70. For Ishmael Day's quote, see the Baltimore *Sun*, July 12, 1864. For Gilmor's burning of the Gunpowder River bridge, in addition to *Four Years*, see also *OR Navies* 5:460, 470-71.

Johnson's written order to burn Governor Bradford's mansion is quoted from the Bradford Papers, Maryland Historical Society Library Collection, MS. 1215. See also the Baltimore *Sun*, July 12, 1864; and Bradley Johnson, p. 219. The Owings Mills ice-cream anecdote is found in Johnson, pp. 219–20; Scharf, *Baltimore*, p. 147; and Toomey, p. 125.

Early's quote about delaying the attack on Washington is from Bradley Johnson, p. 220. Jefferson Davis's quote canceling Wood's naval attack is from *OR Navies* 10:721. Welles's warning to keep a lookout for Wood at the mouth of the Bay is from *OR Navies* 10:281.

Point Lookout's added fortifications in the wake of the attack threat are described in Beitzell, no. 4, p. 25; and Hammett, p. 124. Prison-camp population statistics through the end of the war are from Beitzell, no. 5, appendix A (Point Lookout population chart). Loehr's quotes about guard cruelty are from Loehr, pp. 118–19; his Bible inscription is on p. 114. For background on Sidney Lanier at Point Lookout, see Short, p. 124–26.

The summation of the action on the **James River** is culled from *OR Navies* 10:80–92, 165–68, 176–93, 215–25, 268–78, 310–11, 318–19, 329–35, 348–57, and 366–68. Grant's quote about the Federal ironclad presence on the upper James is out of *OR Navies* 10:373.

The capture and **destruction of the steamer *Kingston*** is chronicled in *OR Navies* 5:469–70.

The Northern Neck's guerrillas kept the Potomac Flotilla busy. Hooker's rebel cavalry quote is from *OR Navies* 5:457-58. The potential raid from the Northern Neck to the Virginia Eastern Shore is mentioned in *OR Navies* 5:476-7; see also 10:403. Hooker's quote about a possible September raid is from *OR Navies* 5:480; Street's quote about the same is from *OR Navies* 5:482. The capture and destruction of picket boat *No. 2* is recounted in *OR Navies* 5:486-88. Parker's quote about repulsing the home guard at Coan River is from *OR Navies* 5:495. Nelson's quote about the home guard is from *OR Navies* 5:488.

Emancipation of Maryland slaves, the election of Lincoln, and the establishment of a Freedmen's Bureau are all found in Toomey, pp. 140-42. The launching of USS *Monocacy* was reported in the Baltimore *Sun*, December 15, 1864.

C H A P T E R   1 1

For the background on **Hetty Cary's wedding** and the death of General Pegram, see Moberly transcript, pp. 3–4; Hetty Cary Martin obituary, Baltimore *Sun*, September 28, 1892; and Beirne, p. 113. For Barton's quote, and his account of the Battle of Hatcher's Run, see Barton, p. 119.

The Confederate **James River Squadron's** attempt to move downriver is described in *OR Navies* 11:632–94, 12:189–90. See also *CWNC* 5:22–26, and Soley, "Closing Operations in the James River," *Battles and Leaders* 4:707.

The Potomac Flotilla's **final actions on the Rappahannock** and other tributaries are recorded in *OR Navies*, 5:497–536. The specific quotes used herein are as follows: Parker's "deviltry" quote, 497; spies wearing metal buttons, 499; Hayes quote about Fitzhugh, 599–600; Parker quote about oyster schooners, 524–25; Nelson on Rice Airs, 511; Parker on the Passapatanzy expedition, 520–21; Parker's instructions to Hooker, 522; Hooker's Rappahannock report, 527–28; and Eastman's Rappahannock report, 535–36.

For **Lincoln's trip on** *River Queen*, see *OR Navies* 12: 81-82; Soley, *Admiral Porter*, pp. 439-46; and *CWNC* 5:65–66, 69.

The **capture of the schooner** *St. Mary's* is described in *OR Navies* 5:540-41. See also Robinson, pp. 291-301. For the death of John Yates Beall, see Robinson, p. 228.

The account of Raphael Semmes and the **destruction of the Confederate James River Squadron** is based on *OR Navies* 12:184-85, and *CWNC* 5:76.

For the details of **Lincoln on Porter's flagship**, and the president's arrival by boat at conquered Richmond, see *OR Navies* 12:101, Soley; *Admiral Porter*, pp. 446-49; and *CWNC* 5:75, 78–79.

For the **capture of** *Harriet De Ford*, see *OR Navies* 5:542-47.

The account of the **Annapolis victory festivities** is based on Bolander, p. 1616.

For how Porter learned of **Lincoln's death**, see Soley, *Admiral Porter*, p. 451; West, p. 297, and *CWNC* 5:86.

The telegraphic correspondence pertaining to the **Chesapeake manhunt** for Lincoln's assassins is found in *OR Navies* 12:119, 123; 5:555–57.

For the background on **Lincoln's funeral train** in Baltimore, see the Baltimore *Sun*, April 22, 1865.

For a concise account of **the pursuit and death of Booth**, see Toomey, pp. 151–52.

The account of the imprisonment of **Jefferson Davis at Fort Monroe** is based on Craven, pp. 22–43, and Weinert and Arthur, pp. 147–158. For the flight to

Cuba of John Taylor Wood et al., see Davis, pp. 164–67. Dr. Craven's *Prison Life of Jefferson Davis*, ghostwritten by Charles G. Halpine, has its detractors and defenders. See Weinert and Arthur, p. 159, n. 14, and Davis, p. 301.

Foxhall Parker's farewell to the Potomac Flotilla is in *OR Navies* 5:578.

The account of **Franklin Buchanan's return home** is based on Lewis, pp. 246-53. For additional details about Jefferson Davis's latter days at Fort Monroe and release on parole, see Weinert and Arthur, pp. 156-58, and Davis, pp. 234–37. The Davises' visit to Talbot County apparently was a brief side trip from their December 1867 Baltimore sojourn, prior to departure for Havana and then a tour of the Deep South.

For more on Colonel John Cowgill and the establishment of **Unionville**, see the Easton *Star-Democrat*, August 21, 1974.

Bibliography

Ames, Susie M. "Federal Policy toward the Eastern Shore of Virginia." *Virginia Magazine*, October 1861.

Baker, W. W. *Memoirs of Service with John Yates Beall, C.S.N.* Richmond, Va.: The Richmond Press, 1910.

Barton, Maj. Randolph. "The Battle of Hatcher's Run." *Confederate Veteran*, 25, no. 3 (March 1917): 119.

Beirne, Francis F. *The Amiable Baltimoreans.* New York: Dutton, 1951.

Beitzell, Edwin W. "Point Lookout, Maryland." *Chronicles of St. Mary's* 2, no. 4 (April 1954): 16-26; 2, no. 5 (May 1954): 27–33.

Blassingame, John W. "The Recruitment of Negro Troops in Maryland." *Maryland Historical Magazine*, 58, no. 1 (March 1963): 20–29.

Bohemian [William G. Shepardson]. "The Capture of Gunboats on the Rappahannock." *Richmond Dispatch*, September 2, 1863.

Bolander, Louis H. "Civil War Annapolis." United States Naval Institute *Proceedings* 63, no. 11 (November 1937): 1612–16.

Bradford, James C., ed. *Captains of the Old Steam Navy: Makers of the American Naval Tradition, 1840–1880.* Annapolis, Md.: Naval Institute Press, 1986.

Brown, George William. *Baltimore and the Nineteenth of April, 1861: A Study of the War.* Baltimore, Md.: N. Murray, 1887.

Brugger, Robert J. *Maryland: A Middle Temperament, 1634–1980.* Baltimore, Md.: Johns Hopkins University Press, 1988.

Butler, Benjamin F. *The Autobiography and Personal Reminiscences of Major-General B. F. Butler: Butler's Book.* Boston: Thayer, 1892.

Catton, Bruce. *Reflections on the Civil War.* New York: Doubleday, 1981.

Clark, Charles B. *Politics in Maryland during the Civil War.* Chestertown, Md., 1952.

Clark, Charles B. "Suppression and Control of Maryland, 1861–1865; a Study of Federal-State Relations during the Civil Conflict." *Maryland Historical Magazine* 54, no. 3 (September 1959): 241–71.

Craven, Bvt. Lt. Col. John J., M.D. *Prison Life of Jefferson Davis.* New York: G. W. Dillingham, 1905.

Cullen, Joseph P. *Richmond Battlefields*. 2d ed. Washington, D.C.: Department of the Interior, 1992.

Cuthbert, Norma B., ed. *Lincoln and the Baltimore Plot, 1861: From Pinkerton Records and Related Papers*. San Marino, Calif.: The Huntington Library, 1949.

Davis, Burke. *The Long Surrender*. New York: Random House, 1985.

Dozer, Donald Marquand. *Portrait of the Free State: A History of Maryland*. Cambridge, Md.: Tidewater Publishers, 1976.

Early, Gen. J. A. The Advance on Washington in 1864." *Southern Historical Society Papers* 9, (July–August 1881): 297–312.

Earp, Charles A. "The Amazing Colonel Zarvona." *Maryland Historical Magazine* 34, no. 4 (December 1939): 334–43.

Gilmor, Col. Harry. *Four Years in the Saddle*. New York: Harper & Brothers, 1866. Reprint edition, including an introduction by Daniel Carroll Toomey, is Baltimore, Md.: Butternut & Blue, n.d.

Gray, Ralph D. "'The Key to the Whole Federal Situation'—The Chesapeake and Delaware Canal in the Civil War." *Maryland Historical Magazine* 60, no. 1 (March 1965): 1–14.

Guernsey, Alfred H., and Henry M. Alden. *Harper's Pictorial History of the Great Rebellion in the United States*. New York: Harper & Brothers, 1866.

Hamersley, Lewis P., ed. *The Records of Living Officers of the U.S. Navy and Marine Corps*. Philadelphia, Pa.: Lippincott, 1878.

Hammett, Regina Combs. *History of St. Mary's County, Maryland*. Ridge, Md.: Regina Combs Hammett, 1977.

Hartzler, David D. *Marylanders in the Confederacy*. Silver Spring, Md.: Family Line Publications, 1986.

Hayes, Rear Adm. John D., U.S.N. (Ret.). "Sea Power in the Civil War." United States Naval Institute *Proceedings* 87, no. 11 (November 1961): 60–69.

Holly, David C. *Tidewater by Steamboat: A Saga of the Chesapeake*. Baltimore, Md.: Johns Hopkins University Press, 1991.

Hollyday, Frederic B. M., ed. "Running the Blockade: Henry Hollyday Joins the Confederacy." *Maryland Historical Magazine* 41, no. 1 (March 1941): 1–10.

Hollyday, Henry. "Running the Blockade." *Confederate Veteran* 29, No. 3 (March 1921): 93–96.

Holzman, Robert S. *Stormy Ben Butler*. New York: Macmillan, 1954.

Howard, F. K. *Fourteen Months in American Bastiles*. Baltimore, Md.: Kelly, Hedian & Piet, 1863.

Johnson, Bradley T. "My Ride around Baltimore in Eighteen Hundred and Sixty-Four." *Southern Historical Society Papers* 30 (1902): 215–25.

Johnson, Robert Underwood, and Clarence Clough Buell, eds. *Battles and Leaders of the Civil War*. 4 vols. New York: Century Co., 1884–87.

Keeler, William Frederick. *Aboard the U.S.S. Monitor: 1862: The Letters of Acting Paymaster William Frederick Keeler, U.S. Navy, to His Wife, Anna*. Edited by Robert W. Daly. Annapolis, Md.: United States Naval Institute Press, 1964.

Kelley, William J. "Baltimore Steamboats in the Civil War." *Maryland Historical Magazine*, 37, no. 1 (March 1942): 42–52.

Kern, Florence. *The United States Revenue Cutters in the Civil War*. Bethesda, Md.: Alised Enterprises, n.d.

Lamon, Ward H. *The Life of Abraham Lincoln; From His Birth to His Inauguration as President*. Boston: James R. Osgood and Co., 1872.

Leech, Margaret. *Reveille in Washington: 1860–1865*. New York: Harper & Brothers, 1941.

Lewis, Charles Lee. *Admiral Franklin Buchanan: Fearless Man of Action*. Baltimore, Md.: Norman, Remington Co., 1929.

Loehr, Charles T. "Point Lookout." *Southern Historical Society Papers* 18 (1890): 113–20.

Long, E. B. *The Civil War Day by Day: An Almanac 1861–1865*. New York: Doubleday, 1971.

Marshall, John A. *American Bastile*. Philadelphia, Pa.: Thomas W. Hartley, 1883.

Matthews, Sidney T. "Control of the Baltimore Press during the Civil War." *Maryland Historical Magazine* 36, no. 2 (June 1941): 150–70.

Miller, Francis Trevelyan, et al., eds. *The Photographic History of the Civil War*. 10 vols. New York: Review of Reviews, 1912.

Moberly, Elizabeth H. "Baltimore's Barbara Fritchie." *Sun Magazine*, n.d. Typed transcript of article in the Maryland Historical Society Library's Hetty Cary file.

Moore, Frank, ed. *The Rebellion Record: A Diary of American Events*. 11 vols. New York: G. P. Putnam, 1861–83; Van Nostrand, 1864–68.

Mullikin, James C. *Story of the Easton Star-Democrat*. Easton, Md.: Easton Publishing Co., n.d.

Naval History Division, Department of the Navy. *Civil War Naval Chronology, 1861–1865*. Washington, D.C.: Government Printing Office, 1961.

Norris, Walter B. *Annapolis: Its Colonial and Naval Story*. New York: Thomas Y. Crowell, 1925.

Pelzer, John, and Linda Pelzer. "The Ghost of the Chesapeake." *Civil War Times Illustrated* 26, no. 1 (March 1987): 39–43.

Porter, John W. H. *A Record of Events in Norfolk County, Virginia, from April 19th, 1861, to May 10, 1862*. . . . Portsmouth, Va.: W. A. Fiske, 1892.

Potter, John Mason. *Thirteen Desperate Days*. New York: Ivan Obolensky, 1964.

Ramsay, Col. H. Ashton. "The True Story of the *Monitor* and *Merrimac*." *Easton Gazette*, January 8, 1898.

Robinson, William Morrison, Jr. *The Confederate Privateers*. New Haven, Conn.: Yale University Press, 1928.

Roehrenbeck, William J. *The Regiment That Saved the Capital*. New York: Thomas Yoseloff, 1961.

Rush, Lt. Comdr. Richard, U.S.N., et al., eds. *Official Records of the Union and Confederate Navies in the War of the Rebellion*. 31 vols. Washington, D.C.: Government Printing Office, 1894–1914.

Sangston, Lawrence. *The Bastiles of the North*. Baltimore, Md.: Kelly, Hedian & Piet, 1863.

Scharf, J. Thomas. *History of Baltimore City and County from the Earliest Period to the Present Day*. Philadelphia, Pa.: Louis H. Everts, 1881.

——— *History of Maryland from the Earliest Period to the Present Day*. 3 vols. Hatboro, Pa.: Tradition Press, 1967 (reprint).

Scott, R. N., et al., eds. *The War of the Rebellion: A Compilation of the Official Records of the Union and Confederate Armies*. 70 vols. Washington, D.C.: Government Printing Office, 1880–1901.

Semmes, Raphael. "Civil War Song Sheets." *Maryland Historical Magazine* 38, no. 3 (September 1943): 205-29.

Shingleton, Royce Gordon. *John Taylor Wood: Sea Ghost of the Confederacy*. Athens, Ga.: University of Georgia Press, 1979.

Short, John Saulsbury. "Sidney Lanier, 'Familiar Citizen of the Town.'" *Maryland Historical Magazine* 35, no. 2 (June 1940): 121–46.

Soley, James Russell. *Admiral Porter*. New York: D. Appleton and Co., 1903.

——— *The Navy in the Civil War: The Blockade and the Cruisers*. New York: Scribner's, 1883.

Swartz, Oretha D. "Franklin Buchanan: A Study in Divided Loyalties." United States Naval Institute *Proceedings* 88, no. 12 (December 1962): 61–69.

Tilghman, Tench Francis. "The College Green Barracks: St. John's during the Civil War." *Maryland Historical Magazine* 45, no. 2 (June 1950): 77–94.

Toomey, Daniel Carroll. *The Civil War in Maryland*. 7th ed. Baltimore, Md.: The Toomey Press, 1994.

Towers, Frank. "'A Vociferous Army of Howling Wolves': Baltimore's Civil War Riot of April 19, 1861." *Maryland Historian* 23, no. 2 (Fall/Winter 1992): 1–27.

Viele, Egbert L. "A Trip with Lincoln, Chase and Stanton." *Scribner's Monthly* 16, no. 6 (October 1878): 813–22.

Webb, Alexander S. *Campaigns of the Civil War: The Peninsula: McClellan's Campaign of 1862*. New York: Scribner's, 1881.

Weinert, Richard P., Jr., and Col. Robert Arthur. *Defender of the Chesapeake: The Story of Fort Monroe*. 3d rev. ed. Shippensburg, Pa.: White Mane Publishing Co., 1989.

Welles, Gideon. *Diary of Gideon Welles*. 3 vols. Boston and New York: Houghton Mifflin, 1911.

Wennersten, John R. *Maryland's Eastern Shore: A Journey in Time and Place.* Centreville, Md.: Tidewater Publishers, 1992.

West, Richard S., Jr. *The Second Admiral: A Life of David Dixon Porter 1813–1891.* New York: Coward-McCann, 1937.

White, Levi S. "Running the Blockade on the Chesapeake Bay." Baltimore *Sun,* December 15, 1907; December 22, 1907; December 29, 1907; January 5, 1908.

Wilkes, Charles. *Autobiography of Rear Admiral Charles Wilkes, U.S. Navy, 1798–1877.* Edited by William James Morgan et al. Washington, D.C.: Naval History Division, U.S. Navy, 1978.

Winthrop, Theodore. "New York Seventh Regiment: Our March to Washington." *Atlantic Monthly* 7, no. 44 (June 1861): 744–56.

——— "Washington as a Camp." *Atlantic Monthly* 8, no. 14 (July 1861): 106–18.

Index

Numbers in italic designate illustrations.